The Northun

Northumberland – the most remote, and least populated, of England's counties. Stage to more fortified buildings than any area of similar size in Europe as well as home to descendants of long established Border families, many of them former Reivers, the mounted thieves who incessantly raided Scotland.

These include Forsters – originally Anglo-Saxons who were among the invaders who landed near Bamburgh after sailing from Northern Germany sometime after the fifth century.

Kiap – Melanesian Pidgin English noun describing government officers who worked as bush administrators, or Patrol Officers, in pre-Independence Papua New Guinea (PNG).

Bamburgh Castle dominates Northumberland's northern coast. © Matt Forster

Typeset in Minion Pro

Design, typesetting and publishing by UK Book Publishing

www.ukbookpublishing.com

ISBN: 978-1-912183-36-4

Contents

An unusual bush training school – 1968-1970

A Kiap's life – 1971-1975

Kiaps took the government flag, and all it represented, to every corner of Papua New Guinea – no matter how remote. In late 1974 PNG's new colours were for the first time hoisted in the Pilitu section of the Goilala Sub-District and then saluted. The police constable is Apua.

For my grandchildren

Acknowledgements

Several individuals, patient and obliging, contributed to this account. Ian Douglas's advice was as invaluable as his library of pictures. Graham Forster's photographs taken during a visit to Tapini in 1974 were another mainstay and Paula Forster highlighted details that would otherwise have been overlooked.

Other information gaps were uncovered by Matt Forster; Anne Corbett maintained family life was just as interesting as bush activity; and Marge Rastall was adamant that if I described myself as a Kiap from Northumberland more information about the county, with links between it and contemporary developments in PNG, would have to be included. The final text was edited by UK Book Publishing.

Biography

Robert Forster was born near Hexham, Northumberland, in 1947, left its Queen Elizabeth Grammar School in 1965, trained as a journalist at Birmingham College of Commerce until 1968 and spent most of the next seven years doing bush work in Papua New Guinea – some of it for London-based Voluntary Service Overseas.

He returned to Northumberland in 1975 and began a career as an agricultural writer on the *Hexham Courant* in 1980. Other posts included North of England reporter for *Farmers Guardian* and a period as Livestock Correspondent for BBC Radio Four's *Farming Today.*

In 1998 he became founding chief executive of the UK's farmer funded National Beef Association which established its head office in Hexham. In 2017 was presented with the Royal Smithfield Club's Bicentenary Trophy for lifetime service to the British livestock industry.

Farmers Guardian

Introduction

I hope Papua New Guineans forgive the anglicisation that has infiltrated this text because many clans and communities are not identified by their traditional (*tok-ples*) name but by geographic location instead.

I can be specific about the Oganas near Munumul, the Mekeo of Kairuku, and the Kunimeipa at Guari. But British practice, in which groups of people are categorised by their location, not their established clan name, dominates elsewhere.

Therefore the Gene people of Bundi are Bundis, those who live beside the Ramu River are Ramus and villagers at Inika are described as Inikas. It is the British way.

Spelling of personal, clan, and village names may annoy PNG readers too. This cannot be avoided. In the 1960s and 70s it was phonetic with individual interpretation dictating selection of consonants and vowels.

Where possible I have tracked spelling adopted by census books and contemporary administrative records filed in government offices. However, village people could, even then, pronounce the same name in different ways and a time lapse of almost fifty years suggests new spelling and pronunciation templates may have emerged.

Aussies might also be baffled by my description of a ute (utility) as a pick-up and other Pommie linguistic misdemeanours.

Attempts to indicate the relative value of the Australian dollar and British sterling, but not PNG's kina which was introduced just weeks before Independence, may be puzzling too.

For the sake of simplicity it should be assumed that within this account a British pound (£) is worth roughly two Australian dollars ($) and in 1975 a Kina could be traded for roughly one Australian dollar.

I have stuck to pre-Independence administrative descriptions as well because, for example, in the context of this account to switch from Mid-Wahgi Sub-District to Jiwaka Sub-Province would be inaccurate as well as confusing.

Maps are always illustrative and seven have been included in this book. Unfortunately nothing contemporary could be found to cover some of the locations within PNG that are important to the text. These have been sketched in from memory – and may not be positioned as accurately as people from those villages would like. Each map highlights only places and features featured in The Northumbrian Kiap's text.

Apart from the obvious post-scripts detailed in its final pages this commentary expires in August 1975. The bulk of the information it contains was typed up, with the help of records, over February-May 1977. The temptation to indulge in hindsight has therefore been resisted.

Robert Forster, *Northumberland*, 2018

Great Britain

Scotland

Edinburgh

Jedburgh

Carter Bar

Hawick

Hexham   **Newcastle/Gateshead**

Blaydon

England

Birmingham

London

PAPUA NEW GUINEA

PACIFIC OCEAN

INDONESIA

Sepik River

Bismarck Sea

Ramu River

Rabaul ●

Mount Hagen

Simbai ●

Alexishafen ●

Mount Wilhelm. 4509m ▲

● **Madang**

Laiagam ●

● Bundi

Minj ●

Goroka

Lae ●

New Britain

Bouganville

Solomon Sea

● Wau

Bereina ● ● Tapini

Trobriand Islands

Gulf of Papua

☆

SOLOMON ISLANDS

Port Moresby

AUSTRALIA

Coral Sea

■ 100 km

CHAPTER ONE

A chance beginning

"And there the great island lies, with its archaic bird-reptile shape. The smoking mountains speak low thunder, the earth shakes lightly, the sun glares down on the impenetrable mantle of the forest, cloud shadows skip over its baroque folds, a white cockatoo rises off the tree tops like a torn scrap of paper ... like an unread message."

James McAuley's always evocative introduction to his book "My New Guinea".

There is a crossroads in Hexhamshire, a moorland girded basin in South West Northumberland, that in the 1960s was home only to a school, a community hall, football field, and a pub.

St Helen's church overlooks Whitley Chapel from its nearby mound. My parents were married there and buried as well. I expect to be planted – it's a Pidgin English term – in its graveyard too.

I did not attend the school. My family lived at Slaley, which stood four miles away on the other side of the Devils Water, but I had my first pint of beer in the Click'em Inn and danced in the hall, mainly to accordion music, on winter Friday nights.

Records confirm John Forster, a forebear from six generations back, was christened and buried at St Helens and since then its graveyard has been stuffed with other, progressively less far flung, blood relations too.

I grew up aware of this inheritance and also with an appreciation of the emotional entangelements generated by land ownership. Houtley, a modest mixed farm of sixty or so acres in the 'Shire's Low Quarter, had been my newly-wed parents' first home and a great-grandfather had owned a fourteen acre smallholding at Smelting Syke, which the family still talked about even though it had been sold to the Robson family, who ran the community's bus fleet, sometime after 1918.

The Forster family outside their smallholding home at Smelting Syke, Hexhamshire, in 1900. My great-grandparents, John and Margaret (Symm), are with their children who from rear left, are: Kate, Sally, Cud (my grandfather), Mary and Willie. From front left: Meggie, Robbie and Annie. #1–see notes at end of chapter.

This is important because when I became a Kiap in distant Papua New Guinea it helped me understand the strong, impossibly visceral, connection that bound its tribal people to village land where their ancestors, their *tumbunas,* had roamed in the past.

The road from the familiarity of Slaley and the 'Shire to a remote, and unbelievably strange, PNG was long in miles but not in time. I had been a difficult pupil at Hexham's Queen Elizabeth Grammar School and this cussedness was only inflicted on tutors at Birmingham's College of Commerce because my parents, knowing I was desperate to join Saturday night friends around pints of Scotch Ale at The Globe in Hexham, had locked the house doors one August evening and would not open them until a course application form had been signed.

My signature, which was all they wanted, had been a hurried scrawl because Robson's bus was already nosing its way up the village and I did not want to miss my night out.

My preference, after only a moderately successful Sixth Form, would have been to take a local job, perhaps swinging a chain saw, or an axe, in nearby pine woods because I enjoyed physical labour.

I'd had a place from fifteen onwards in Healey Mill's weekend thrashing team on the back of, even then, being able to heave bags of grain, regularly earned beer money pushing dairy cows and hay bales around at White House, and could turn up whenever I liked to hack out stone with Willie Jameson at Ladycross Quarry.

The work ethic, God smiles on honest toil, was, after all, a core feature of a Methodist upbringing. The Chapel entertained hopes, on the strength of my public comfort with dialect free English and words I was obliged to speak as the desperately fresh, and as it turned out final, chairman of Slaley's struggling Young Farmers' Club, that I might eventually become a Circuit Minister.

Others in the community, aware of my height and fondness for misbehaviour, thought it might be better for everyone if I joined the army and signed up with The Guards.

Hardly six years later the cultural sensitivities developed as result of this deeply rooted rural background made it easier for me to empathise with the Wahgi Valley's leaders when, after land ownership emerged as the hot, pre-Self-Government, issue in PNG's politically explosive Highlands, they spoke for an army of worried villagers by making it unbendingly clear they loved every inch of ground surrounding their home – even the parcels occupied by Europeans – because they had named each hill, swamp and stream and also knew where their ancestors were buried and their homes had stood.

But the prudishness and provinciality of a Chapel upbringing were no help when, during their post-fight trial after an assault on a Tangilka village, I watched Kauga Kua, the magistrate, round on a group of Kambilika warriors and, gesturing first at the row of plaintiff young women sitting at his feet, then hammering his index finger at the men in turn, bellow in robust Pidgin *"Yu goapimim! Yu goapimim! Yu goapimim!"* (*You raped her! You raped her! You raped her!*) before frowning even more fiercely and sentencing each of them to six months in jail. #2 –see notes at end of chapter

Only days later I would play a critical part in bringing this simmering inter-clan struggle under a degree of control but despite bi-lingual ability in Pidgin I was jolted by the depth of Kauga's anger and the stoic acceptance of that long line of expressionless Tangilka women that they had been violently molested.

Birmingham was not Northumberland. Curry with rice, not meat and two veg, was already one of its typical meals, a West Indian bus conductor was the first black skinned adult I had hand-to-hand contact with, and top rock performers like Cream and Alan Price whose music I danced to until my feet bled, not fiddle players, held the stage at Students' Union bops.

I was not good at attending lectures but, like many English students, my course was Communications, joined a clique which dominated the presentation and weekly publication of the Aston campus newspaper, the *Birmingham Sun. #3*

And I was in good company because Jim Crace was the editor before I took over in October 1967 and during both these periods a relentlessly eccentric Gordon Burn was a regular provider of unconventional arts reviews and features. Most of the remainder of my time was devoted to rugby, dancing, and drinking beer. #4

In March 1968 I should have been ready to hand over an impressive thesis but was not. The cares I did carry were shared between whether I could captain the Aston Cobras First XV to their next win and if it would be possible to persuade printers to produce yet another edition of the cash-strapped student paper. However, the Cobras went on to play several games without me, the *Sun* managed one more edition which I did not edit, and I was taken to hospital with glandular fever.

Two letters lay in ambush when I returned. Northumberland Education Authority, angry that I had not attended lectures over the Easter term, wanted its £80 grant to be refunded, and an equally furious course tutor was demanding my thesis. These incendiaries could only provoke a heavy shrug because not a sentence had been written and any hopes I might still have entertained of advancing a qualification-led career were in self-imposed freefall.

The *Birmingham Post's* education correspondent, Ian Fazey, had been a regular presence on the campus when it staged its share of demonstrations during 1967-68's Europe-wide surge in student unrest.

The *Sun's* coverage of lock-ins, walk-outs and other disruptive activity organised by Aston's Students' Union had been read carefully by its news desk and on Ian's advice I arranged an interview with the editor. A staff job would have been a shoe-in. It was mine as long as I did not dribble, pick my nose or fart.

Half-way through, the editor, who was of course observant, cocked his head and said: "You don't want the job, do you?" He was amused rather than critical and not in a special hurry to wind things up.

His office was on the top floor of the *Post & Mail* building, which in those days was the tallest in the city centre. I had been looking through the window at a distant thicket of red brick Victorian terraces and queue of double decker buses struggling to negotiate Gosta Green roundabout at the end of Steelhouse Lane.

We had already discussed my starting salary, which, because I worked each summer to top up my student grant, would deliver less each week than the cash still being withdrawn from my current account.

I had not been absorbing the city's formidable landscape but instead reflecting that this reduced income would have to fill a wardrobe with unusually clean shirts, fund regular haircuts, buy a jacket and tie, and provide food without having access to a subsidised Student Union canteen.

"No," I replied. Building a career from a poorly paid first stepping stone demanded painstaking levels of discipline that I knew I was not ready for. The world back then was wide and before I took my place on the treadmill I wanted to bank some excitement first. He smiled, still amused, and showed me the door.

Just days later I began work as a builder's labourer on an extension to

Birmingham's New Street Station. My job was down a huge hole, chipping out the brick and concrete foundations of a demolished building with a pneumatic drill then heaping the debris into piles which could by picked up by a bucket flung down from a hydraulic crane. The ganger-man was a teak hard Irishman, Big Jim Ford, and there were no concessions for slackers.

Just after my hands had hardened I travelled to London to be interviewed by Voluntary Service Overseas (VSO) – a government-sponsored organisation which recruited restless young people who wanted to exhaust their surplus energy while working in underdeveloped countries.

It offered two jobs. One was on an African game park supervising the building of a chain of rest houses. I liked the idea of driving a bucking Land Rover over grass savannah while being lazily scrutinised by squinting lions, but just six months' service was needed and I had volunteered for fifteen.

The other was in Papua New Guinea. There was a floundering pause while I tried to remember where in the world it was. Eventually I had it located, or thought I had, because when an atlas was dug out later I had confused it with Sumatra and not realised it lay immediately north of Australia.

"Would you like to work in a saw mill?" they asked. I had not done so before, but had spent part of a recent summer in Slaley Forest lopping branches off felled trees and stacking pit props for in-coming lorries.

There was silence as I contemplated a lumber camp submerged in rainforest where tropical downpours dripped daily off an endless palisade of leaves. "Do you know what a flitch is?" they prompted, looking for the answer "It's a slab of sawn wood." "Yes," I said, thinking of a leg of bacon being drawn through a grocer's slicer, and the job was mine.

Later that summer I was back in Northumberland visiting saw mills in a desperate effort to pick up something, anything, which would prevent me being a complete novice when I arrived in PNG. Books on the country were devoured too. They described an unusually exotic landscape of deep jungles, blue seas, tall mountains and long rivers, which was dotted with remote villages occupied by equally colourful people – many of them only recently introduced to steel tools.

Most narratives focussed on the recent discovery of these stone age cultures, surviving cannibal practice, the relentlessly rugged hinterland, determined explorers, their lines of local carriers, the hordes of eager missionaries that followed them in, the emergence of cargo cults, still undiscovered valleys, regular earthquakes, active volcanoes, dangerous airstrips and perhaps a paragraph or two on Birds of Paradise or the introduction of democracy.

I showed a selection to my best loved great aunt, born Annie Forster in 1890, who was cousin or half-cousin to almost everyone who then lived in the 'Shire and may only have travelled beyond her immediate stamping ground for a seaside holiday on Cumbria's west coast.

She turned their pages until she came to a picture of a man who had been ritually disembowelled. Her hands flew to her face. "Oh my," she said, shocked to her core. "Whatever do you want to go there for?"

Northumberland was difficult to leave because the reliably tranquil 'Shire was at its rustic best. Honeysuckle still lined its lanes, bees droned, the air was filled with the scent of cropped grass, cattle cudded contentedly and when I walked its fields I was able to see almost all the wild animals that usually take cover and hide.

Deep in its valley the Devil's Water tumbled and splashed, a sweep of pine was home to a chain saw's muted drone, higher still clouds floated over a heather coloured hill and where gorse spread beneath a nearby line of oak there were skylarks which hovered and sang.

The journey to PNG's distant lumber camp was a nightmare. The Boeing 707 left Heathrow for Sydney but stopped at Rome, Beirut, Bahrain, Karachi, Delhi, Singapore, Kuala Lumpur and Darwin to refuel. Each time it landed passengers were bussed to an isolated transit lounge where they twiddled their thumbs before again taking their seats. Progress eastwards was such a crawl it staggered through two sunrises.

The highlight was Mount Everest – its towering silhouette unmistakable to anyone who had been at primary school in Britain during the nationalistic surge that trailed Hillary and Tensing's triumph in 1953. At Delhi a distant Indira Ghandi was inspecting a parade of soldiers, some shouldering wooden staves instead of rifles, and Darwin's heat was like an oven. An Aussie pilot was proud of Sydney Harbour but I could not share his unashamed appreciation because at that stage I was out on my feet.

I waited just an hour before flying, again in a 707, for eight hours to Port Moresby – the capital of Australia's PNG protectorate. I should have been wide eyed and curious but instead sat slumped, completely dazed, in its shabby airport for two hours before yet another flight, this time in a Fokker Friendship, took me to Madang on the northern coast.

More than 14,000 miles were covered while scarcely leaving my seat. No wonder the overriding impression of what should have been an exciting journey was the persistent whine of cabin air conditioning and pain as my ankles continued to swell inside my tight new shoes.

First thoughts on PNG were entirely spoiled. Some, dominated by coconut palms, corrugated iron homes, and people who did not wear many clothes, were picked up through the window of an airport bus – but these were hazy. Jet lag was a condition that had still to acquire a slot in the English language and I was the victim of a supra-super dose.

The saw mill, a strange Camelot for a long haired college drop-out, had been built by the Divine Word (SVD) Catholic Mission whose PNG headquarters were at Alexishafen about a dozen miles west of Madang. VSO made no distinction between church and government when it posted volunteers as long as their work was secular and assisted the host country's development.

It was at Bundi, about eighty miles inland, on the second shoulder of the Bismark Highlands which ran parallel to much of PNG's north-western coast. The first Europeans to contact the Bundi people were SVD clerics who walked through in 1932 – and again in 1933 after which a mission station was established as a base for yet more evangelistic exploration into the Chimbu Valley and then the wider Highland region beyond.

This SVD diocese was powerfully funded, some of its money coming from the United States, and it had strong German roots too. The latter reflected its establishment at Alexishafen in 1905 when the northern half of a still scarcely explored PNG was administered from Berlin.

It was a huge organisation covering dozens of out-stations, overseeing the activities of hundreds of artisan lay-missionaries and school teachers as well as its clerics, and backed by a multi-million pound annual budget fed not just by overseas donations but copra, cattle, and timber assets scattered around its headquarters as well.

Bundi was home to a pioneering boarding school for primary children and oversaw an economic expansion project focussed on beef cattle, which was being established at Brahmin in the nearby Ramu Valley as well.

I waited three days for a plane, must have used a mosquito net for the first time, put on shorts for the first time since being breeched as a twelve year old, and found the heat oppressive. Beyond that I remember little except some foolishness.

Scattered throughout Alexishafen were many coconut palms. Careful study confirmed they were genuine although my only points of reference were holiday brochures and Caribbean song.

Sea breezes rustled their fronds, sunlight was reflected by their ribbed trunks and coconuts hung in clusters from their crown. Why were they smooth and green, not matt brown and hairy like those offered as fairground prizes on The Sele at Hexham, or Town Moor in Newcastle?

Some grew at the edge of the Coral Sea and in places leaned over it. I selected one with exceptional tilt, sat beneath it, commanded my mind to open, and waited to be soothed by tropical tranquillity. I waited patiently and then began to worry because according to all I had read about the South Seas I should have been immediately seized by all embracing euphoria in the type of hit more usually associated with heroin or crack cocaine.

Enlightenment arrived when a passing village boy warned against sitting under coconut palms when it was windy in case a nut was dislodged and shattered my skull like an egg.

The hop to Bundi was in a four seater, twin-engined, Baron Beechcraft. This was real flying. I climbed in off the wing, slid into the seat next to the pilot, then sucked in my stomach to avoid interfering with the duplicate joystick.

Like everyone who lived on a PNG outstation, I flew many times in many types of plane, most of them with a single engine, and always enjoyed it. It was exciting to glide between threatening peaks or level out above massed cloud then surf over its sunlit upper layer.

That morning jet lag had gone. The plane's shadow skipped over the endless forest below, white cockatoos lifted from the tree tops, brown rivers meandered crazily – often to lose themselves in a serpentine series of ox-bow lakes. We crossed the Ramu River at about 6,000 feet and ahead lay the endless blue-black ridges of PNG's Highlands.

In 1968 there were sections that had still to be mapped and in the most remote valleys there were, as I discovered hardly eighteen months later, village men and women who continued to have no contact with anyone but themselves and for whom knowledge of a rapidly changing world was passed on, like a rumour, through ridge hindered word of mouth.

Many young pilots had died out there, flying blindly through cloud into a tree clad mountain, and other dangers surrounding air travel in PNG were notorious too. But visibility that day was good. We slipped over the first range of the Bismarks, dropped a wing, and began to spiral down. The plane hugged the shoulder of a mountain and deep within the valley a frothing river flowed.

Beside it stood the saw mill I had crossed the world to work in. Sunlight winked off its corrugated iron roofs then the plane dropped its other wing so I could see thatched huts clinging to mountain sides, and cleared patches of land I later learned were local people's food gardens.

"Bundi," said the pilot, gesticulating above him at a nondescript profile of mainly wooden buildings topped by rusty tin punctuated by thin leaved casuarinas and banana trees. Then the airstrip loomed in front of us, its dramatic character exaggerated by the angle of the plane's approach.

Each side fell away steeply while at its head was a hill that was home to both the Catholic Mission and a government Patrol Post. It was like landing on an aircraft carrier with an earth wall at the end of the flight deck.

I bounced out and like everyone else who had flown from the coast into the Highlands immediately found the cooler air a pleasant surprise. It always was no matter how many times you travelled. Blue-green slopes stood above and behind. Below was a valley of impossible steepness. There was not a level section of land in sight. Everything had been torn and tortured by busy mountain streams.

It was an overpowering landscape. Later, a sawmill worker, Mori, who had left Bundi to complete a two year stint contract labouring on a coastal plantation, confided that when he returned he almost obeyed an impulse to jump back on the plane. The challenges raised by the improbable gradients surrounding his home had been almost too much for him to consider.

I was immediately given a motorbike and while out on this, not yet a week away from the UK, came across an elderly woman who had caked her face with yellow mud, was towing a piglet on a length of string, and was, to my Methodist Chapel shock, naked to the waist as well.

Never before had I seen anyone so strange and I could not prevent myself chasing her down, skidding to a stop, and pressuring her to stand in front of my shiny new camera.

She posed readily enough for the astonished young man fresh from Hexhamshire but I flinch at my reaction now. She had covered herself with mud because she was mourning a family death and was almost naked because she did not think it necessary to hide her body. I was an ignorant, although culturally dominant, intruder who was unaware of her bereavement and had overridden her simplicity.

My first PNG picture. What was this old lady thinking? She was walking home, minding her own business, when a lanky youth with a blindingly white skin roars up astride a stinking machine and demands she stands still while he excitedly, and shakily, points a camera at her.

By far the greatest shock during those hazy first days in PNG was an unstoppable plunge into apathy. I realised this while lying on my stomach, chewing on a stalk of grass, beside Bundi's football pitch.

Immediately in vision were carved posts which framed the entrance to a cane built house the players used as a social club. Beyond them the short, muscular men who staffed the station were sweating as they chased their ball under a brassy sun.

Blue mountains frowned around and above. I glared at them through a particularly pretty, red leaved shrub. They were hugely hostile and represented the visual limits of my self-chosen stage. More importantly everything on it, both players and props, were dauntingly strange.

"Hell," I said bitterly to the fellow VSO beside me. "Here a week and bored already." I later realised tedium was not the problem. I was fundamentally disorientated after being wrenched from my cultural comfort zone and profoundly disturbed because I could not find anything familiar to retreat to.

That evening I stood on the edge of the mountain and looked into the valley where the sawmill lay. I could hear the Imbrum River's muffled swell. It was a sound I liked. Both the Devil's Water and the Allen in Northumberland are the source of a simliar echo.

A tropical moon lit the landscape so well pink hibiscus could be seen in the ditch below. A dramatic display of stars crashed into impenetrable shadow as I brought my eyes back to earth. Crickets and frogs chirruped and burped while thunderless tropical lightning flashed, and flashed again, behind the peaks to the west.

It was Sunday September 15th 1968. I was to go to the saw mill, which had been built on a rare flat spot at a place called Binaru, the next day.

#1 Some lives were shortened. Cud was killed by Germans in 1917. Margaret died of Spanish Flu in 1918. Mary followed her in 1919 and TB caught Sally in 1928. Old John set a still to be breached family high for longevity by living until he was 92.

#2 Pidgin's ever evolving vocabulary betrayed the contribution made by dock side and bush camp language during the early interface between black labour and white management. *Goapim* for rape (go up im) was one

15

example. *Bagarap* (buggered up), an adverb which described anything, from broken equipment to a flawed idea, that was unserviceable, defective, or useless, was another.

#3 In 1965 Aston University, Birmingham College of Commerce and Birmingham College of Art shared the same Students' Union

#4 Jim and Gordon each became award winning authors. Gordon's biggest *Sun* story in October 1968 was headlined *"Peace, Love and Beauty"* – he had just come back from Haight Ashbury and was full of it.

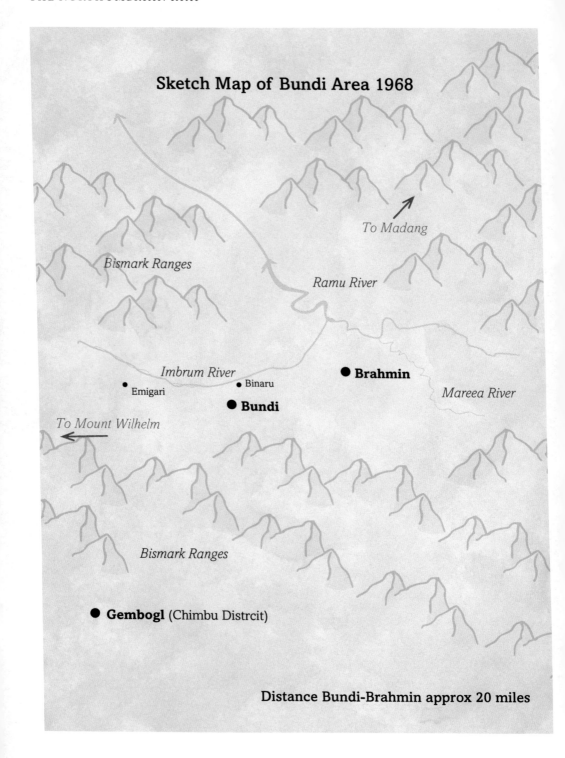

Sketch Map of Bundi Area 1968

CHAPTER TWO

No gat pusim – suibim tasol

"Nothing to do but work.
Nothing to eat but food.
Nothing to wear but clothes."

Ben King

Memory of the first days at Binaru is still obscured by an opaque haze that forced its way between consciousness and perception as soon as I arrived. It is the same feeling which separates a dream from reality. When hearing is dulled by pressure, the vision blurred, and the feet you walk on never quite touch the ground. Nor was reality suddenly restored, as with a pop when a blocked ear is cleared, or an eye refocuses after the tear falls onto a cheek.

I had come down the mountain happily enough. I was impressed, even awed, by the huge trees with their dangling creepers, and very much aware of the dampness of the forest floor. I was pleased when I noticed an electric blue butterfly and glimpsed a rope of red flowers in the vaulted roof, but after being tempted into taking a short cut quickly discovered this was not a pleasant British wood where striking a path could be

19

dictated by whim but the fringe of a trackless forest dominated by pitfalls and sharp edges. The unrelenting unfamiliarity began to numb.

I came to the mill along a path bordering the river. On one side a milky torrent swirled and belched and on the other dark jungle brooded. Turning a corner by a dripping cliff, I splashed through a small stream and like a plane coming in to land made a final approach. The buildings lay ahead. There were machines, logs, and cutting paraphernalia. A solemn group of brown skinned men were standing outside a low hut. They were many and I was one.

A haversack on my back held four tins of meat, four tins of fruit, two sheets and a pillow case – and the only language I spoke was English. Afraid to lose the momentum of descent I strode among them and was relieved when they smiled and we began to shake hands.

Two hours later I was five hundred feet back up the mountain watching this workforce strip a tree and cut it into lengths. Unreality gripped so hard I felt frozen.

The last time I had seen this done was by ruddy Saxons using power saws, and seven pound axes on a pine that was many times smaller. Now a man no bigger than a pre-teen child was chipping at a hardwood log which rang like iron under an axe which was a three pound toy.

Slightly taller men, perhaps five feet high, were pulling a cross-cut saw through the mid-section while a man with a belly as big as a pregnant woman was measuring out the length of the next log with mud-caked feet that looked as wide as they were long.

Another with unusually piercing eyes, he was called Marcus Dam, was tending a small fire on which root vegetables were blackening. Squatting beside him yet another was lighting a newspaper wrapped cigarette he had taken from a hole in the lobe of his ear.

Looking back at the tiny man – his name was Kari – I saw that not only were both his ears pierced but sunlight was shining through a hole in the septum of his nose.

More men struggled out of the bush and built a rough platform from a selection of branches. The foreman, Nicholas Kebma, was the fellow with the belly and he gave orders which set them cutting another log using the bench they had just constructed.

I did nothing but watch. Ants were crawling through the hairs on my legs and, because a confusing twist of misplaced enthusiasm had persuaded me to climb barefoot, small stones had cut my feet twice. The sun shafting through the leaves was pleasant and I could hear the river although I could not see it.

Suddenly there was a flurry of leaping, the crack of snapping wood, and three fourteen foot logs crashed down the mountain while the labourers chorused their descent with high pitched yodels and yells. We followed them down and found they had skimmed just a hundred yards short of the saw bench and lay within easy winching distance.

My home was a wooden hut which stood on short stilts. It had one room, ten feet by ten feet, with two single beds, a cupboard, a table and a chair. The roof was corrugated iron fixed to branches, the walls were planked and the floor was sawn timber too.

Food was prepared in a lean-to by a man whose skin, unlike his colleagues', was a deep copper red. He too had a hole in his nose. The toilet, a typically slim Australian wood and corrugated iron, bottom-of-the-garden, dunny was a seat over a putrid pit.

The sawmill at Binaru. My hut was the tiny, square, black building top right. The labourers lived in the bigger house immediately to its rear.

That night I locked my door. One half of me objected. It said the men were friendly and the Mission's influence must have embraced the saw mill so my fears were unfounded. But as I stood on the doorstep staring into the unfamiliar night I imagined spear carrying cannibals loping through the trees as easily as wolves and feared that I might be their victim.

Reason told me the area was peaceful. Instinct was more interested in the alien darkness, the endless forest, the violent river, and I turned the key. I did not lock it again, or ever had reason to, but that first night I had to do it.

This detached unreality could not last forever. Each day I sloughed a little of that skin until I was wholly adjusted. Nevertheless my position was strange. I was the boss, I was white, and I was alone.

Most Mondays I set out from Bundi with that week's rations on my back while those men who had gone up with me carried down wire ropes, oil, or freshly sharpened chains for one of the saws. Until Friday evening I had no other company and no work other than that at the mill.

Within a month I was able to handle Pidgin English. Being social by nature it would have been impossible not to have made the effort. I would have been speaking halting Hindi if I had worked in a similar situation in India.

At that time it was a maligned language – most criticised by Europeans who thought they could speak it well but could not. I found it indispensable. It helped me converse freely, even delicately, and certainly humorously, with most of PNG's people and for those who like myself picked it up in the bush, not just from other Europeans who often abused it, there were huge advantages.

Its evolution spanned the taking of South Seas labour for Queensland's sugar cane plantations in the mid-nineteenth century, hence traces of Hawaiian and adoption of the noun *"kanaka"* to describe a village man, and then the enthusiasm of Papua New Guinea's people to overcome restrictions created by their 800 plus languages and be able to speak freely, in a syntax which followed their own speech rhythms, among themselves.

When educated Papua New Guineans began to feel sensitive about their pre-contact history they criticised regular use of *"kanaka"*, especially *"bus kanaka"* in pidgin speech. Antagonism grew as university education spread and the word became a political token.

23

The latter should only have been used to describe village people at first contact and some insisted the former was out of bounds too. Nevertheless, most pidgin speakers accepted it was a legitimate description for land owning villagers not unlike the English noun "yeoman".

Village men returning to their communities after a spell in contracted employment, including those who worked at Binaru, described the move as "*mi go kanaka*" which can only be interpreted as "I again became an independent householder".

There were touches of Chinese pidgin in the phrase "*mi no save*" (I don't know) and some words, like the noun "*masolai*" for evil spirit, were imported from Polynesia. Others were German – *Kiap* (bush administrator) was the twisted pronunciation of Kapitan (captain) and then there was English.

This is where there were pitfalls because not all apparently English words were what they seemed. The verb "*painim*" did not mean "find" but "search for" but the most notorious was the verb "*pusim*" which did not mean "push" – that was "*suibim*" or "shove" – but to engage in sexual intercourse.

There were many, many times when a European faced with a flat battery could be heard calling on nearby villagers to help him be unusually familiar with his marooned vehicle instead of giving it a "shove". They seemed to be unaware of the laughter.

"*Maski*", which had come in from Rabaul off the northern coast, was a critical word. Its straight translation was "it doesn't matter" which might be accompanied by a wrinkling of the nose, shaking of a wrist, or a shrug.

But "*maski's*" real meaning rested entirely on context and inflexion. Everything depended on emphasis because at one extreme it could be interpreted as a gentle "I forgive you" and on the other as an expletively delivered "bugger off".

Imagine being engaged in deep conversation with a confidante in which they rest their hand on your forearm and softly say *"maski"*. Literally "it doesn't matter" but in this instance "Don't worry" or "It's nothing". And contrast this with a *"maski"* either forced through clenched teeth or delivered at full volume.

In those circumstances "it doesn't matter" has to be interpreted as "that's it – I've had enough", or if it covers outright dismissal of a suggestion "Get lost!" or "Shove off!" Then there was a quite different inflexion if *maski* was used to suggest "I'm fed up. Let's change this tiresome subject" or even more subtly, "That was interesting – but let's move on".

Few Europeans could speak Pidgin straightforwardly. Some Kiaps would tune their larynxes to a falsetto tone and deliver in sing-song. Many missionaries, especially females, treated it like baby language and spoke in pretty, super-simple, phrases – again in a high pitched voice.

My own approach was to speak normally. This was copied off Max David, an Australian lay missionary who had pioneered the Brahmin cattle station for Bundi Mission, because it meant transition from English to Pidgin was always smooth.

The men who worked at Binaru were either youths or small boys when the first missionaries arrived at Bundi in 1932. These evangelists were followed by others, and two of this group were cut down in 1934 by the Chimbu people who occupied land on the western side of a daunting watershed. They were among only a handful of Europeans killed when the first sections of PNG's Highlands were being explored throughout the decade before the Second World War.

During the struggle against the Japanese there had been military activity along the Ramu River and some Bundi villagers had been employed by US or Australian soldiers as carriers or guides.

The Japanese army had moved into PNG in 1942 with its eyes fixed on using its airstrips and harbours as staging posts for a full scale invasion of Australia. All the northern islands, and almost all the northern coast, were occupied.

At the same time tactically important routes into the heart of the Australian-held South, like the Ramu Valley, and Kokoda Trail above Port Moresby, became established battlegrounds before the Japanese began to retreat and were ousted in 1945. People deep in the Highlands were unaffected by this campaign although a couple of bombs were dropped on the airstrip at Mount Hagen and others were dumped in a range of bush locations where some of the iron was scavenged to make axes.

Lessons learned during the Pacific War, including the strategic importance of a large island lying as a buffer between itself and possible military threats in South East Asia, are commonly held to be the reason Australia was, and still is, prepared to commit to the cost of generous funding for its often difficult and expensive neighbour and maintain stability in what might otherwise be an economically, socially, and politically, vulnerable area.

After 1945 the missionaries at Bundi continued their work but it was not until 1957 that the Australian government staffed a Patrol Post and installed a detachment of police. As soon as the airstrip could take planes, recruiters arrived seeking fresh contract labour for coconut, rubber and cocoa plantations on the coast. Within five years perhaps half of Bundi's able bodied males had been flown from the area, some never to return.

In 1961 the Mission opened its English speaking boarding school, the first in the New Guinea Highlands, and almost every child in the area was from then on able to pass through its doors, some going to High School on the coast and then taking up teaching posts in other schools or work within PNG's civil service. Others would go to university.

Geographic description of location within pre-independence PNG was often inconsistent because it had originally been governed by two colonial powers, Papua by the British between 1884 and 1902 and New Guinea by Germany up to 1918 when the frontier was a largely imaginary line along its central mountain spine. This was dismantled after the First World War but in the early 1970s these historic descriptions still lingered.

Up until September 1975 the country was governed in its entirety by Australia. However, the northern half, New Guinea, was a protectorate managed on behalf of the United Nations while the southern half, Papua, had been administered by Australia in its own right after it was handed over by the British who were not interested in a country more likely to incur cost than generate income – and which was so far from London too.

In these circumstances it should not be a surprise that during the countdown to Self-Government and Independence, when everyone was encouraged to adopt the description Papua New Guinea, the northern half continued to be labelled by many as New Guinea while Papua was still used to describe the south.

The timber we cut at Binaru was being used to build teachers' houses, a workshop, and a huge recreation hall that doubled as a gymnasium.

The labourers were illiterate – it was their children who were being schooled. All but the youngest had been initiated, some of them painfully. Sitting naked on a hot stone was one of the tests, they told me, and being silent when the hole was knocked through the septum of their nose was another.

All walked barefoot and most of the time they wore shorts but nothing else. At night they slept on plank beds with perhaps one blanket if it was cold. They could shoot a reasonably accurate flightless arrow from a cane-string bow and work comfortably all day with a three pound axe. They smoked wild tobacco, enjoyed tinned meat once a month, and ate mainly sweet potato or taro root. Some chewed betel nut and had red teeth.

When chewed, with the help of lime (*kambang*), betel nut (*boai*) juice becomes mildly soporific. The resulting red mess is not swallowed but absorbed orally before being spat out in streams in almost every outdoor location. Newcomers to PNG often thought fresh betel nut juice was blood and someone had been wounded.

Their fathers had killed men in ways most Europeans would think cowardly – perhaps a flight of arrows in the back from a pathside ambush and a coup de grâce in the nape of the neck with an axe.

These men had been taught to kill in a similar manner. All of them had been baptised which qualified them to be Mission workers. They attended church regularly but still took account of the souls of their ancestors and the whims of bush spirits, some malign, which they described in Pidgin as *sangumas*.

When they worked at Binaru they were paid £6 every three months. Inflation adjusted to 2018, this was the equivalent of about £90 – or £7.50 a week – and every fourth week they were given ten pounds of rice, a tin of meat and a tin of fish.

For this they worked as hard as I was prepared to push them, starting about 7am and finishing anytime between 4pm and 6.30. They also grew vegetables on land that had been cleared of trees, which in many ways was their most valuable reward. My pay during this period was £5 a month.

After working for a fortnight on the increasingly familiar saws we came down from Bundi to find a freak wind had flattened the buildings. Everything used to re-build them, apart from the roofing iron, was taken from the surrounding bush.

Small trees were attacked with bush knives or axes and men staggered back carrying posts and roofing poles. Not a nail was used. Joists were tied down with strips of green cane and roofing timber was lashed to supports the same way. Later that week the new roofs were weighed down with river stone and the job completed.

Logs for cutting were pulled in with cane ropes using wooden rollers – just like the sarsens used to build Stonehenge. It might take a team of fifteen just an hour to pull a fourteen feet log, diameter up to three feet, for half a mile. I joined in and enjoyed it. But it was not always easy. On one occasion my demands were judged unreasonable and they withdrew their labour.

It was a Friday and I was organising the carrying of cut planks back up the mountain to Bundi. The method was simple. Every parent with a child at the school, and some elder brothers or sisters too, came down to the mill and returned with a length of timber on their shoulder.

These lifts took place about three times a year, almost always on religious holidays like Christmas or Easter when many people, male and female, old and young, short and tall, big and small, descended and a near continuous line of cut timber began to snake its way back up.

I too carried a plank, one of the heaviest, because it was a challenge. I was impressed by the huge weights these diminutive people could carry and had almost immediately begun to train myself to ignore the pain when carrying similar loads.

Gradually I became able to dismiss discomfort, which was the principal barrier, and so had succeeded in carrying my plank to the stack where it could be picked up by a tractor. My shoulder was skinned, sweat had run in buckets, and I was elated.

Overcome with success I immediately ordered – it was not a suggestion – a return to Binaru to bring up a second load. They refused. The established rule was one lift, one day, and they were not going to break it.

It was their first direct refusal. I lost control. I began to shout. I was so angry I thought I might hit someone. Otto Dirumbi, the man who helped with the flitching saw, thought so too. He delivered an explosive *"maski"* and pushed me away. I turned to look into the calming depths of the empty valley and eventually the spasm, which I put down to an overdose of adrenalin, subsided.

The following Monday just two labourers lined up for work. It looked bad but as more began to trickle out of the bush nothing was said, work followed its established routine, and the following morning they were all there.

Living so close to each other meant we had to share both work and leisure. Later, when I worked for the Australian government, I did not form the same bonds with PNG people – except perhaps with some policemen.

I did not need to because I was married and lived close to other Europeans and even while patrolling deep in the bush local people were impressed by, some might say wary of, my authoritarian position, which was more important in their eyes than anything I might reveal about my personality.

Back in Binaru our world was unusually narrow and so our interests were shared. I was no super-soft white liberal, just one human being who needed the company of others. I knew more about logistical planning than they did and could give directions, which helped them cut more logs more quickly, but they could add practical improvements whenever an immediate problem cropped up.

Nor was our relationship demanding. Above all else I expected them to work and once they realised no heart tugging moan could soften that resolve we shared many genuine jokes.

It was a challenge from Yabanai, a loud man whose father had been a pre-contact fight leader, towards the end of my second month that demonstrated I was on my way to settling in.

We had worked up to noon on an unusually hot day and I was hanging upside down above a circular saw cleaning dust from a chain track. He placed himself beneath me and demanded an extra half hour for the midday break. A quick look round showed the others were watching carefully.

Without getting down I told him as sweetly as I could that his mouth was almost as big as the saw beneath me and if he had all his teeth I would be tempted to cut timber with it instead.

Mori, who was always straightforward, guffawed, the others grinned, and even Yabanai refused to be unhappy that his attempt to test my mettle had failed. *"Mi traim tasol,"* he said, shrugging his shoulders. ("I was just giving it a go.")

We lived together at Binaru where Yabanai had just killed a pig. Here Mori (wearing pullover) works with his sister (who was Yabanai's wife) and Marcus Dam to singe the carcase before it was cooked in a traditional pit oven or mumu.

After three months we moved higher up the mountain to begin cutting new timber. Chutes were constructed by removing obstacles, including stones and small trees, from the bed of natural channels which ran towards the mill. Then target trees were felled by axe. These were hardwoods with huge buttress roots which meant platforms had to be built so the axemen could chip away at a more reasonable diameter high up the trunk.

My attitude to work was strange. I was sweating it out for nothing more than cigarette money in a demanding environment with no one to force me to maintain the pace except myself. I could, if I had wished, done nothing but issue orders at the beginning of the day and rely on verbal progress reports.

Coming from a country in which work effort is usually directly related to the level of pay, I still find it odd that I have rarely worked harder in physical terms than I did at Binaru. Other VSOs have told me they too did little else but work and sleep. Sometimes I lay on my bed as soon as I came back to my hut, waking up later in the evening to take off my boots.

Just before I left I struggled against a self-imposed schedule which targeted two hundred logs at the mill at the time of my departure. As the deadline approached I thought about nothing else and was either tugging at one end of a cross cut saw or taking a spell on a winch that delivered timber to the mill.

At the end of one week I was exhausted, dismissed the men and went to sleep. I woke up on Saturday afternoon, ate some tinned fruit with raw porridge, and stayed in bed until Sunday morning.

The clue to this behaviour was the imminent arrival of a replacement VSO. I was isolated with nothing to do but work and the height of the log stacks and plank piles had become my only measure of ability, pride, and performance.

Disregard of physical danger was another feature of the same phenomenon. In a failed attempt to open the way to pulling in logs from the other side of the Imbrum I had committed myself to a boisterous section of rapids with only a rope tied to my chest.

The current took me under and stripped me of my clothes. When the rope tightened it lifted my head and chest above the water and hauled me upstream. But almost as soon as I surfaced it slackened and so I was taken under again. This cycle was repeated many times before I eventually struggled out.

Otto Dirumbi, a steady, intelligent, man called me over to where one end of the rope had been tied. It had straddled a stone and was frayed almost completely through. He re-hitched it with a shrug. We both knew I would have drowned if it had snapped.

CHAPTER THREE

Eight hundred languages explained

"There is no place on earth where the living is so easy as on these islands. They are rich, laden with food and before the whiteman came inordinately healthy. No one had to work, for the world was full of fruit and vegetables, and in the woods there was enough wild boar for everyone. You would have to call it paradise even though most of you may never want to see it again."

James Michener "Tales of the South Pacific".

It is the wish of many born in urban, western societies to settle in a location conventionally described as idyllic – the proverbial desert island perhaps. To qualify it would no doubt have to be traffic-free, tax-free, and phone free but although life at Binaru enjoyed these qualifications it was no paradise. James Michener had got it badly wrong.

The mountains were oppressive and it was difficult to feel released. Later, between postings in PNG, when briefly working on cattle stations in Australia, the width of sky was so overwhelming I could not prevent myself flinging out both arms to reach for its corners.

Binaru could offer nothing similar. Even when standing on the lip of nearby mountain passes a blanket of trees still obstructed the horizon. There were times when this never ending palisade became as oppressive as a prison wall.

Nor was living there easy or harmonious. Sweat made skin itch, tiny scratches and bites soon oozed pus, the food, mainly sweet potato, sweetcorn, brown rice, and tinned meat, was leadenly basic, and early darkness came down like a curtain.

Nevertheless there were moments when its isolation, its separation from anything but the noise of the river, the passage of the sun, and the progress of mill work, could become briefly tranquil.

The Imbrum was an asset. Most nights I washed in it and felt clean. Sometimes at noon I would plunge into a big pool beneath two large rocks that buttressed a log footbridge – typically arriving under a hammering sun with my skin prickly from sawdust, insects, and oil.

Then with all the style I could summon, because this was moment to be savoured, dive as slowly, and as steeply, as I could.

Under water I would swim to the bottom, stand there with pressure in my ears and flecks of sunlight dancing above me, before rising as gently as possible to break the mirror of the surface. After a hurried pull to the side to avoid being swept into rapids I would sit on a rock. Dry within five minutes, and also refreshed, I was ready get dirty again. The river was always there and some evenings I might do the same thing too.

The tropical moon is rare and wonderful. When full it shines so brightly that colours emerge and individual trees, along with other landmarks, can be seen for up to a mile. The local people enjoyed moonlight too. It was the only street light they had.

The bridge over the Imbrum at Binaru.

When a bright moon stood over Binaru many of the men on the labour line would light small fires and sit out. The first time I saw this Yabanai, who could be clownish, was lying on his back, a fire at his feet, howling like a dog. "Don't worry," he said. "I'm only doing it because I'm happy." *"No gat samting. Mi wokim alosem long wonem mi hamamas tasol."*

At other times they would remain in their hut and sing. These songs meant nothing to me but I liked to hear them. Occasionally they would work all night on winches or other tasks which did not need strong light. They did it on condition they could have the following day off.

I understood this. It was difficult to ignore the pull of that silver glow. Just as someone British might not be able to resist the first long evening in spring so a Papua New Guinean enjoys being released from darkness.

Hunting expeditions are often mounted when the moon is strongest because tree-living nocturnals like possum become an easier target for arrows if they are silhouetted against a bright sky. Dances are also practised and I too found it difficult to snub the moon's appeal. Its light was calm, the heat of the day had gone, and night's landscape was no longer concealed beneath a black blanket.

But I enjoyed dusk even more. The slanting sun could fashion light of a peculiar intensity under which colours became translucent. Grass assumed an emerald luminosity and red leaves became a shining flame.

At such times I would sit on the doorstep to my hut watching men hurrying to beat the deadline of darkness, with firewood and food. An occasional wife (*meri*) could stagger past loaded with sweet potato in a large string bag. Children (*pikanninis*) would reappear after playing in the river – the smallest of them wobbling, brown, and naked.

One evening my *kuk-boi* (cook), Fabian, gave me a ripe *paw-paw* (papaya). Hens would move closer to their hutch as the evening got darker and the *meri* who looked after my pigs, predictably named Aston, Annie and Binarupe, would pad slowly to their pen carrying a bucket of slop. Cicadas chirruped and as the sun fell further the first cricket would strum.

A sudden plume of smoke would signal the men were building a bigger fire to cook their meal and warm the darkness, there would be a final flurry of chopping as the last wood was prepared, a steady murmur of voices and then an occasional laugh. As darkness descended fireflies would begin to wink and I would light a lantern of my own.

On a night like that I might sit in with them after I had eaten. I was able to slip through their door without attracting comment and could take my place on the corner of a bed near the fire without interrupting the cosiness which, like the heat from its flames, extended into every corner of the room.

Once inside I wanted nothing more than to enjoy this conviviality. I would smoke and watch. It was a crudely constructed building, which looked spare, even unforgiving, while empty during the day, but filled with many kinds of warmth at night.

It was like a tableau as bare chested women nursed their children alongside old men who hawked and spat. Perhaps as many as six families, as well as the labourers whose wives were absent, shared that house, but quarrels were almost non-existent.

Around the fire a couple of men would be smoking, while behind them others could be peeling pumpkins or plucking a small bird for the communal stew. Children sat shiny eyed by the flames while mothers rolled string to repair their net bags. Men who were not smoking either talked quietly or lay resting. The light might be helped by a burning cloth hanging from a fish tin filled with diesel or on a handful of occasions by my pressure lamp.

I would stay by the fire for perhaps two hours, demand nothing, and contribute no more than idle conversation or speculation about where we next might work. But when I left and walked back to my own hut, with dew wetting my feet, it was not just the warmth of the fire I was missing.

Even so Binaru was no nirvana. Each morning I opened a medicine box and attacked the latest crop of tropical ulcers. I had my share because any cut inevitably became infected and if neglected would each day drive deeper into muscle.

I might treat a dozen of these, sometimes on just one person, before moving onto diarrhoea and malaria (*skin-hat*). On occasions people who lived nearby came for help too. Anyone who still believes the tropics are paradise should also take account of the many ugly external ailments, including scabies and ringworm, which were the accepted cost of living there.

Diarrhoea (*pek-pek wara* or shit water) was a perennial discomfort that hit toddlers and new European arrivals hardest. Regular hand washing was not common in villages so the latter quickly discovered that until their resident stomach flora acquired the strength to bite the head off invading E.coli bacteria, passed on through any one of a thousand contact routes, watery bowels were a curse.

Stuffing digestive systems with sulfadimidine blockers was the only short term cure and on many occasions immediate embarrassment could only be avoided by clenching sphincter muscles like a vice until the bowel spasm passed. Otherwise any movement, no matter how slight, could result in dignity being abruptly overwhelmed.

The country these people lived in was hostile too. The mission at Bundi had tried for years to link the saw mill to the main station with a vehicular road. Men who dug for countless hours were occasionally helped by a small bulldozer. The net result of these combined efforts was nil. Every rainy season a section was washed away. When I first came to the mill I could ride halfway down the mountain on a motorbike. When I left it was being parked a mile nearer to Bundi.

On some Mondays the bulldozer would, yet again, begin to clear the road. It seemed a futile task. The steep slopes, heavy rain, and unstable soil combined to make its efforts almost useless. The mountains above the Imbrum resisted European impositions as geometrically precise as roads with ungiving determination.

The river could be violent too. In the rainy season it could flood in two hours then visibly subside almost as soon as the downpour was over. One night after an especially heavy deluge it erupted. I was at Bundi but even at that height it was roaring. Muffled thumps from rolling boulders echoed from the valley too.

Next morning we discovered that the familiar riverside landscape had been erased. The path I walked along that first day had gone because the Imbrum had shifted its course. It had scoured a new trench to within ten feet of the biggest saw as well as carrying down a rock as large as a two storey house which blocked its previous passage. This meant that instead of flowing directly past the mill the newly contoured river poured itself coastward on the opposite side of its gorge.

Beyond the buildings the bush was thick and endless. Even so, its effectiveness as a barrier to all types of communication took time to sink in. It flowed like a green tide over every obstacle in its path. Beneath the trees the forest was dark, deep, still and occasionally stinking with rot and decay.

Walking within it, along paths where mud alternated with tree roots that writhed like snakes, the only sounds were the drip of condensation off leaves, the harsh cry of an occasional bird, or the infrequent chatter of a stream. In the lowest valleys even these are dirty and the water flat. Butterflies can be seen but, like the occasional flash of birdlife, are rare.

Leeches (*lik-lik snek* or little snakes), a filthy creature, could sway trackside waiting for an unwary leg. Once sitting on a stone I glanced idly at the ground below and was startled to see as many as there are maggots on a corpse caterpillaring determinedly towards my boots.

They were evaded by standing on top of the boulder and leaping over their heads. In leech country ankles are regularly inspected and the removal of socks could reveal tens of round, shiny black, pulsating bodies

41

that had been hungrily sucking unnoticed.

The tip of a cigarette made them drop to the ground, bloated with blood, and unable to move, leaving the bite still running because the anti-coagulant they inject is long-lasting.

When they attach themselves there is a tiny shot of pain, not dissimilar to a nettle sting, as this innoculation takes hold. It is the only indication they are feasting. I learned to recognise it and also that a leech is more difficult to remove from fingers than the tackiest of snot bogies taken from a truly dirty nose.

There are snakes too but direct encounters were rare. Only once did I find myself in Snake City and that was when working with Max David in the Ramu alongside an army of axemen and a bulldozer to open a new section of road.

Trees were falling regularly and it was my job to cut them into handy lengths so the bulldozer, which was working behind me, could sweep them off the survey line and into the forest.

It was hard to distinguish between snakes and cascading creepers. Some fell into Max's cab and I saw two villagers jog past with a python slung between them that was so long both its head and tail flapped against their legs. They would have eaten it before using its skin to cover their drums.

I was concentrating on a complicated tangle of trees and branches when the man who carried the saw's petrol, oil, and spare chains tapped me on the shoulder. Not yet in strike range, but swaying in attack position, was a pudgy, ugly, white bellied, vexed, ominously named Death Adder. He struck off its head with his bush knife and after it had stopped writhing put it in his *bilum* (small net shoulder bag) to cook later.

That man had another job as well. Bees were attracted to my armpits – it could only have been sugar in my sweat – so when I swung my right arm to re-direct the saw some were crushed and retaliated by stinging. This happened so often it became too much trouble to switch off the engine and remove the stings myself so I held it with the motor still running while he picked them out instead.

In most locations the bush is an obstacle that can only be breached by deliberate effort. No one strolls through rainforest. It is not a recreation park. Appreciation of this is essential to an understanding of PNG's uniquely fragmented social structure and the infrastructure problems it still faces.

Every person travelling between one village and another, even along well-marked paths, would prepare for the journey. In the Bundi area every traveller carried his *bilum* containing tobacco, cigarette lighter or matches, spoon, tin plate, a store of cooked sweet potato and perhaps a blanket. Self-sufficiency was always reinforced by a bush knife and an axe.

During his journey he might ford rivers, walking through some with the current chest high, and climb steep slopes using hands as well as feet. The path he takes could be almost invisible and anything but direct because it is deflected by every obstacle.

On one occasion some of Binaru's labourers spent two nights from the mill, trapped between flash flooded rivers and sleeping beneath a big tree. After their first evening they had nothing to eat except leaves taken from a rank of tulip plants. Later, fording one of these rivers, I lost my footing, and then my haversack, before I fought my way out.

Journeys in PNG are not measured in miles but in hours. Thus a guide may point to village not five miles away in direct line and say "We should arrive in mid-afternoon" – which could mean in about three hours.

One Kiap told me that on a particularly arduous patrol, deep in a remote section of Western Papua, it took him, and his carriers, almost a day to travel just a mile and a half. In this case the obstacle was a thicket of bamboo which they had found their way into but could not find a way round.

On another occasion, when we were taking a small herd of Red Poll breeding cattle from Bundi to Brahmin, the effectiveness of the bush as a barrier between people was further underlined. It was not a long journey, just two nights camped and perhaps forty miles, but we passed through three language areas. Four if a group of only around 150 people, whose presence I had not been made aware of until after we had moved through, were counted too.

I also learned that a herd of driven cattle is always led by a young, most likely first-calved, heifer. Bulls plod along well behind. Faced with a river crossing their instinct is to form a line in which they stand upstream of each other in an unbroken chain and half cover the animal immediately in front.

In this way they reduce their exposure to the current. Calves always enter on the upstream side so if they lose their footing they are swept against a solid line of adults and can either recover their legs or continue swimming.

PNG is credited with more than 800 languages and linguists will confirm they are not dialects but mutually unintelligible, having less in common than French and German or Greek.

The mind boggles that such small, culturally intact, nations could live so close to each other, perhaps just ten miles, but had still to establish sufficient contact to develop a common tongue.

Nor is the rainforest bountiful. Wild pigs are the only large meat-carrying animals and big, well fleshed, birds like the Cassowary or Goura Pigeon are rare.

Hunting in PNG is dominated by the thickness of the bush. There are no aerial, or running shots because visibility is narrow and the hunter has to creep close to his quarry before letting fly from the shortest possible range.

This can be as close as thirty feet and even then to see the creature requires skill. There were occasions when I stood at the base of a tree, straining to sight an invisible pigeon, with a frustrated villager at my elbow saying as quietly as he could: "There, over there" and me asking "Where?" so many times it would have been sensible to have given up and handed over the gun.

Nor is there an abundance of forest food to gather. Sago can be found on low ground but eggs, fledglings, nuts, roots, shoots, grubs, small mammals like mice, and a very occasional fish, which serve only to flavour the main dish, are just about all that mountain bush will yield.

The people were so protein starved – domestic pigs were exclusively killed and eaten at sparse traditional ceremonies – that when cash began to trickle into local economies the most popular trade store purchase by a country mile was a tin of Japanese mackerel.

These cost only ten cents (5p), were packed with much needed oil and protein, and did more than any other introduced item to boost individual, village and national health.

The impact of regular access to *tin-pis* was immediately dramatic. Some bush children could reach maturity up to five years earlier, grew more muscle as well as extra height, and even adults responded by bulking up and acquiring a noticeably sleeker look.

The main food, sweet potato and taro, also pumpkins, maize, bananas, paw-paw, and cucumbers, was grown in gardens which were prepared by men hacking down trees, burning the branches, building protective pig fences, and women planting shoots in the ash covered soil using a digging stick.

Most village women would look after three at the same time. One newly planted, one about to be harvested, and one almost finished. Once abandoned the bush immediately claims back what has temporarily, and at great effort, been taken from it.

Within six months the vegetation cover will be total and soon the site will be obliterated. I re-visited Binaru, which had been abandoned, within twenty months of returning to the UK and could not accurately mark the position of my hut.

Every indicator that might have helped was concealed beneath a wall of shrubs and leaves. Imagine how PNG's people coped with this Triffidian environment when their only tools were stone and fire?

Many villages continue to be surrounded by bush which every day does its best to re-invade and obliterate. To combat this, even on a short trip to the toilet, a Papua New Guinean swipes a ubiquitous bush knife at every intruding shoot. It is a constant war in which the knife, no matter how idly it seems to swing, is always busy.

No wonder, then, that a villager standing on a rare rock outcrop, and looking down on a hamlet not ten miles away that is peopled by strangers, sees the intervening stretch of bush as a barrier that is at once dark, difficult, mysterious and unfriendly.

On trips from Bundi into the Ramu Valley I became aware of superstitions carried by the men who were with me. They were wary of the Ramu people. Not because they were stronger, which because they were small and slight they obviously were not, but because the Ramus were held to be great sorcerers.

Max David, a tall, big bearded, dedicated man of thirty told me this was because the greatest concentration of malarial mosquitoes thrived in the belt of bush lying directly between the two people and the Bundis had rationalised the almost certain acquisition of malarial fever as evidence that, even at a distance, the Ramus could inflict huge discomfort on strangers.

This, combined with the greater pestilence that plagued the hotter Ramu Valley, leprosy, yaws, acute ringworm (tinea), and solid acres of sharp sago thorn, backed by leeches, poisonous snakes and clouds of mosquitoes, kept the Bundis well away.

The powers attributed to the Ramu people were no doubt encouraged by the Ramus themselves, who would have been happy to keep the stronger, more aggressive, Bundis as far as possible from their marriageable women – always scarce in polygamous societies – and their pigs.

Thus, whenever I asked for labour line volunteers to travel with me it was always the same four who put their hand up. None of the others were comfortable about crossing the ghostly stand of bamboos that stood on the further bank of the Wehgi River where the first of the Ramu *masolais,* a malevolent spirit, might, metaphorically speaking, be baring its teeth.

On the trip with the cattle we moved into Ramu country by a different route. Here the boundary was a tumbled pile of unusually large boulders, the biggest crowned with pig skulls. I was told to leave something personal on a flat stone. The Bundis put down betel nut and tobacco leaves. I left a couple of John Player cigarettes.

One evening when we had been out on the Mareea River looking for stray cattle, sunset caught Mori and myself still five miles from camp. He was visibly frightened and as the forest grew darker I could feel him treading on my heels as he pressed closer for physical reassurance and support.

The barriers created by PNG's dense bush and hostile topography are the most obvious explanations for the isolation of its tribes, the preservation of its eight hundred languages, and the difficulties Europeans faced when penetrating its previously hidden interior – and they are real.

CHAPTER FOUR

I'd like to be a Kiap

"The "niupelas" were cowed and huddled against each other so closely they could have stood on a sixpence."

Simbai Patrol Post, Madang District, March 1970

During the eighteen months I worked as a VSO I spent many weekends at Bundi but never felt comfortable staying there. Later, when I became a Kiap, I often felt the same about station life.

Out in the bush, alone with village people, there was no other European presence to stand between myself and the flow of their lives. So I was able, while not submerging my individuality, to be an accepted presence in the same way as a smooth rock does not interfere with the passage of the water flowing round it as much as a spiky one.

However, the introduction of another European, or even too much that was European, triggered conflict between myself and a bush existence, that I could not prevent being expressed through reduced empathy or a shorter attention span.

49

Thus, as I tried to embrace both presences, and do them justice in line with two, often contradictory, cultural norms, confusion would boil in the same way that water becomes agitated as it tries to negotiate a jagged passage of rock.

Other Europeans who worked in PNG have felt the same way. It is unrealistic to expect a person brought up in one culture to be absorbed without turbulence into an understanding of the other, and I found that as long as I did not mix my thinking, and confined my time in the bush exclusively to things Papua New Guinean, I could be happy. However, it was impossible to avoid this muddling at Bundi and so in my final months I spent less time there.

While on-station the only physical recreation was football so on Saturday afternoons I made a great point of dressing carefully in the right gear and playing it as hard as I could. One weekend the team was ferried, four at a time, by plane over the mountains for a game near Gembogl at the head of the Chimbu Valley. The people there were bigger and stronger and the expectation was we would be overwhelmed.

I played in goal because I was best able to catch high balls and was amazed when a penalty was saved and the Bundi team scored most goals. We returned next morning on a crest of emotion because the daunting Chimbus had for generations put the smaller, less forceful, Bundis in fear and a win at soccer – call it a substitute for old fashioned body count – was rare.

Despite, or perhaps because of, my upbringing I remain determinedly irreligious. Nevertheless, my attitude towards PNG's many missionaries was always benign – as long as none of them tried to push God up my nose.

But there was a moment, returning to Bundi that Sunday morning, when

I rebelled. As soon as we scrambled out of the plane to stand within the station's dramatic mountain amphitheatre, our hearing – even though the church was half a mile away – was assaulted by Father Jiezke haranguing his congregation in blood and thunder style.

This high decibel aural attack, not the ancient landscape, dominated our arrival. It was invasive and it jarred. We were happy young men returning to base after an enjoyable night out and Jiezke, who was a veteran, old-school Prussian, was giving them Hell.

I understood very little Gendekar (the Bundi language) but guessed from my Chapel days they were being told, unrelentingly and repeatedly, that unless they walked with God they were no better than wild pigs, cassowaries, or any other creature of the bush.

One of the other passengers was the Kiap's *manki-masta* (house servant) – a man I did not trust and so did not like. Nevertheless, when he groaned aloud in immediate dismay I could not help catching his eye and he instantly knew I was recoiling too.

The motorbike was also used to banish the mental cramps of isolation. Sunday nights could find it roaring up and down the airstrip, sometimes dangerously, as it bounced across the humps on the police rifle range. If the engine was switched off, *kundu* drums might be heard as village people on the opposite side of a valley practised their dancing but the most dominant sound, and a lonely one, on a still evening would have been the bike.

One Monday morning while enjoying the excitement of a gravel spraying ride down the twisting lane towards the saw mill I splattered myself, and the machine, on the front of the Kiap's Land Rover. The bike had a broken back. I had a broken leg and spent the next three months in a thigh plaster. #1

Some of this time was spent at Binaru where the labour line offered sympathy and evening entertainment. Like all Papua New Guineans they had polished the delivery of their favourite oral story and Otto Dirumbi often described a Second World War execution.

The victim was a prisoner taken in the Ramu Valley by the American army for passing information back to the Japanese. Similarly, the Americans used Ramu villagers to track down Japanese snipers. This too was part of Otto's tale and he would offer a graphic account of a Japanese soldier, camouflaged by branches, being himself shot then left hanging from the crown of a tree by the rope he had used to tie himself in.

Turning back to his main theme he explained how a young American, "Captain Jim", had assembled village men and women who were ordered to watch. The Ramu was led out, given a spade, and told to dig his grave.

When it was sufficiently deep he was shot in the temple with "Jim's" revolver. At the moment of execution, frightened women, who had been told to squat at the grave's edge, collectively pissed themselves, flooding the ground below so dramatically it was as if, said Otto, someone had emptied a bath filled with soapy water.

Another popular *stori* covered the arrival of the first missionaries at Emigari in 1932. They were immediately assumed to be spirits of the dead – and therefore both authoritative and superior. Just as interesting was the commitment to memory of minute details surrounding this life changing event.

Not only could every fold in the strange men's clothing be described but also the placement of their feet in relation to a tree root and the pattern of the tendons on the back of one man's hand as he grasped his stick. Martians landing in London could not have been observed more closely.

Each item of debris left behind by these, and other strange new visitors in different locations within PNG, was exhaustively examined by apprehensive villagers as soon as they broke camp. This included faeces which, whatever the location, would be ringed by an investigation committee before being prodded carefully and then smelled.

Eventually the comforting conclusion that the new arrivals could not be entirely supernatural "because they shit like us and it stinks just as badly" would be reached – although this would not have undermined the impact of the obvious, and awesome, material and technical advantages introduced by these first explorers and their immediate followers too.

Common items included iron cooking pots and kettles as well as steel axes and perhaps a two-way radio, guns and an overwhelming range of tantalisingly attractive trade goods which included face paint, mirrors, and money shells.

Another tale, often accompanied by sniggers, confirmed the determination of Christian priests to attack polygamy. Until then the acquisition of many wives was a measure of an individual man's chance of securing economic advancement and improved social clout because a large family labour force could manage more gardens and accumulate wealth by feeding more pigs.

But priests mocked the practice by asking Bundi men if they had more than one penis. Their view was that having just one of these qualified a man to just one wife and if a man with a singleton penis took more than one wife he was being greedy.

Most of Bundi's people became monogamous – not least because it, along with church attendance, meant their children would be offered a place at the Mission's English-speaking primary school and might then be able to move through PNG's ever-improving High School and University system to a well paid job.

While once again working in the Ramu Valley I found myself for the first time accepting mortality. I had risen before dawn and taken a .22 rifle to the top of the airstrip at Brahmin. Wild pigs were damaging the landing area and needed to be scared off. The gun was stood against a fence post until there was enough light to fire.

During the false dawn a thin mist hung on nearby tree tops. Out on the strip I could hear, and vaguely see, the pigs. Up above, the biggest stars were shining in a sky that was gradually becoming dull green as our spinning planet moved the patch of land on which I was standing closer to the waiting sun.

Suddenly, like an explosion, a yellow beam leaped from the tip of Mount Wilhelm, PNG's highest peak. For a long moment its bare rocks, at least 14,000 feet overhead, blazed like a beacon. Then an avalanche of light swept down its slopes, underlining every crack and cranny while I, still in darkness on the floor of a valley many miles away, stood transfixed.

When nearby Mount Herbert began to be washed in pink a crystal sharp view of every summit in the Highland range emerged. The Ramu Valley was still black but advancing day was rushing towards it like a flood. Every fold, every ridge, in the Bismarks was highlighted including indents and valleys that were invisible during the heat of the day.

I had a profound feeling I was an inconsequential human occupying a trivial spot on a revolving planet which was about to complete its multi-billionth, twenty four hour cycle, and once more come face to face with the constancy of an ever-present sun. When I recovered from this mystical plunge the pigs were long gone.

As time at Binaru drew to an end I began to shelve plans to settle in the

UK and debate a quick return to PNG instead. If Paula, who had been a fellow student in Birmingham, remained patient I hoped to marry her in Britain before the end of the year but knew it offered little worthwhile employment for college dropouts who could speak Pidgin English, had learned, while doing bush work, to keep the seat of their pants dry by squatting on their hunkers instead of sitting on damp ground, and roll their own cigarettes.

I approached a mineral exploration company thinking it might offer a bush liaison position but it was put off by my mission history. It was easy to survey the alternatives and decide my best chance of work in PNG was to secure a position with the Australian government as a Kiap or Patrol Officer.

After I left Binaru I stayed for a week at Simbai Patrol Post with Frank Cotton, who for a time had been the Kiap at Bundi. It was much deeper in the Bismarks and first contact with its people had been delayed into the 1950s. Each evening I drank his rum in the contrasting company of an anthropologist and plantation labour recruiter and watched him at work during the day.

One morning a family which had not yet been contacted, its names still to be recorded in a village census book, walked out of the bush and initiated the first ever interaction between Europeans and themselves.

Normally these people would have been approached in their hamlet or village by an exploratory patrol but even in 1970, five years before national independence, they had been missed and, impatient at having to wait, had made the journey themselves. There were six – three adult women and three adult men.

I was with Frank in his office when an excited policeman rushed in to tell him that some *"niupela manmeri"* (new people) were waiting outside and then carefully ushered them in.

They were profoundly cowed and huddled against each other so closely they could have stood on a sixpence. The old man who led them worked hard at maintaining his dignity but even he quailed when Frank and I stood up to shake hands.

People living in the mountains surrounding Simbai are small and neat, with an average height of less than 4'10", which in anthropological terms meant they are classified as pygmies. In contrast we were unusually tall, each of us a long legged lad standing well over six feet, so when we uncoiled their eyes rolled.

Conversation was exchanged through a chain of three interpreters which meant across four languages. Goodness knows what was lost, or added, in translation. The first task was to record their names and their village location then Frank took them round the station.

One of the stops was the hospital where earnest medical assistants injected them many times against goodness knows what. At that stage the women were so frightened their sweat was acrid.

Later the group watched the recruiter's charter planes thundering in to pick up another batch of Simbai's young men to begin plantation labours on the coast. The maximum payload was established by weighing indentured recruits on a dilapidated spring balance hung off a tripod. How was this being interpreted?

During the afternoon the old man was cornered by a young white girl from the Church of England Mission. He sat stiffly, comprehensively culture stunned, as she carefully painted his portrait.

That was just one of many incidents that persuaded me I must become a Kiap. Frank had impressive autonomy and it seemed Kiaps, all of them young men, monopolised much of the action in a country that was already dramatic.

A problem that had still to resolved was that their recruitment, and initial training, was conducted exclusively by the Department of External Territories in Australia and I was committed to returning to Britain and marrying Paula first.

My last days at Binaru had been spent moving a saw to a site where fifty logs that we could not get closer to the mill had been stacked. Leaving it that final time I climbed to a spur directly above the camp and paused to take stock of a place I had become fond of.

The Imbrum thundered past as it always had done and among the log piles chickens were scratching for insects and grubs. The door to my hut was this time firmly locked, while behind it a thin plume of smoke curled from the labourer's house.

Kaspar Gene and his family, tiny figures foreshortened by height, looked up and waved. I waved back, turned, and, with my boots crunching in the stony soil, climbed to where my motorbike was waiting.

I left Bundi on a misty morning in March 1970. The plane was a Cessna 180 and the pilot had difficulty landing. Most of Binaru's *bois* had come to say farewell. I embraced them because they had been good friends and when some began to snuffle my eyes began to water too.

As I flew over their heads and on to Madang I left them standing in their narrow valley before moving onto a much greater swathe of territory, along with its attendant complexities, that I at least partly understood.

A month later I landed in Britain and a fortnight after that was living in a pokey Edgbaston bedsit while working as a builder's labourer on Birmingham's new Municipal Centre in Colmore Circus.

The ganger-man was another Irishman known only, because he was dour, by his surname – Kelly. Most of my work was with a Kango electric chisel chipping out concrete that had failed to meet construction standards, then blowing out the shuttering before puddling in a fresh batch.

My clocking-in number was 556 and the time-keeper, who was a bastard, enjoyed making sure the bonus he built by taking at least fifteen minutes off an idle worker's timesheet was hefty. One of my brothers, Graham, worked there for around six weeks too.

Paula, who was a personnel assistant at Lucas Industries which manufactured car accessories, lived just two hundred yards away. We were married that August. Graham was best man.

All our focus was on securing a quick return to Australia and my attendance on the earliest possible Kiap training course. We emigrated from the UK to Sydney, by plane, in January 1971 to find I had missed enrolment on one of the Australian School of Pacific Administration's (ASOPA) regular intakes by inches and would have to wait until the end of June for the next.

We filled the interlude by working on cattle stations. The first was near Nymboida in north-eastern New South Wales and the second on New England's tableland near Inverell. I rode a horse, learned to butcher sheep, re-acquainted myself with the hand milking of cows, repaired fences and helped Paula with garden work too.

I was summoned to a Department of Territories' interview in Brisbane in May, passed it and the medical, then turned up to enrol at ASOPA on

June 19th. There were thirty eight other young men on the course, most of them enthusiastically social, so the next four months were a young couple's dream.

Our flat was less than a hundred yards from Manly beach, a hidden cove on Mosman's Middle Head was used almost excusively by ourselves and other trainees for weekend barbecues and snorkelling, while ASOPA encouraged rugby matches, cross country runs, and informal cricket because we needed to be fit.

Course work, which focussed on PNG law, history, anthropology, administration and geography, was completed on October 28th after which we flew to Four Mile Camp in Port Moresby to finish off our training and be sworn in. We were despatched to our postings on November 26th. Ours was Minj, which was administrative centre for the Mid-Wahgi Sub-District in the dramatic Western Highlands.

This picture of 1971's June intake was taken at Four Mile Camp in Port Moresby and later used to illustrate a "PNG Attitude" article which suggested the ideal Kiap was a "misfit". No one can deny we look non-conformist and many senior officers tut-tutted after seeing how scruffy we were. Just twenty eight of us have lined up which means ten are missing. (Photographer unknown) #2

#1 The tibia and fibia in my left leg had been shattered and I was treated in Madang by Mr Clezy – a surgeon whose speciality was restoring hand and feet function to lepers by transplanting, or lengthening, tendons critical to open and shut movement.

Their open sores were easy to cure. The only visible sign of their past problem was new skin which healed without pigment and shone pinkly – not unlike a burn. Restoring limb facility was a more difficult, time consuming, task.

#2 The profile of this group of Kiap trainees may not have been typical. The average age was about twenty five, there were eleven who were married, six were born in the UK, one in Finland, one in Southern Africa and another was a Vietnam veteran. There was a cluster of teachers and other civil servants as well as a sprinkling of excited twenty year olds.

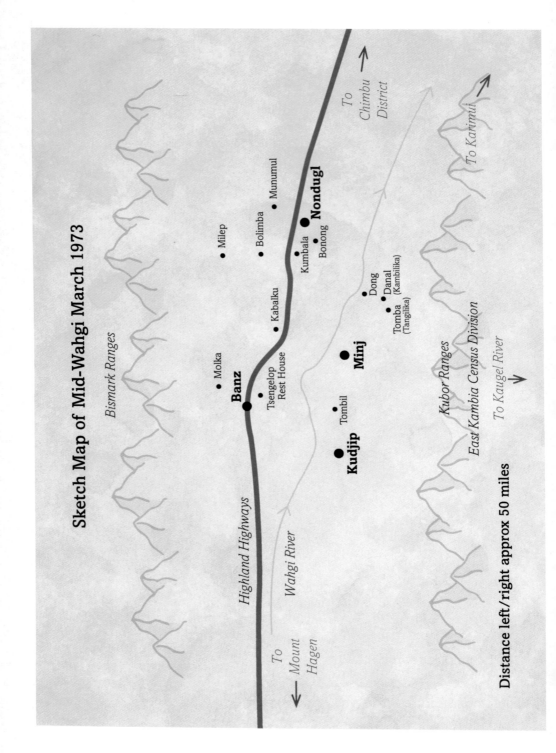

Sketch Map of Mid-Wahgi March 1973

CHAPTER FIVE

Behind East Kambia's mountain wall.

"The people queued to vote and when it was their turn to step forward those who recognised Nopnop's photograph pointed to it. Then the Returning Officer conducting this "whispering poll" ticked off their choice before handing their paper back for them to slot into a ballot box."

East Kambia, 1972

When I was a child I was given a thick adventure book which one of my father's friends had discovered at a Chapel jumble sale. It had been published at the height of the British Empire and, if it had not been burned after I had been sick over it during a schoolboy illness, it may have become a museum piece.

It was printed on rough, slightly absorbent paper, which always smelled musty, and illustrated by streaky pen and ink drawings that were commonplace at the end of the nineteenth century.

Its stories featured sturdy boy buglers who were capable of great personal sacrifice during the Pathan wars of North West India, and intrepid young men in deepest Africa who reliably followed the tradition of Sir Francis Drake by casting improvised fire ships among pursuing swarms of cannibal clustered canoes.

On the cover was a portrait of an apple-cheeked, young white man armed with a rifle who was leading a file of impressively burdened, dark skinned carriers while uniformed soldiers/policemen prodded it along from the rear.

In February 1972 a cameraman could have produced a surprisingly similar picture of a column about to enter PNG's undeveloped East Kambia Census Division. The photograph would not have lied but nor would it have made clear that the shotgun I carried was used only to shoot pigeons for meat, or that the purpose of the government patrol, which included sealed ballot boxes among its many burdens, was to complete the local tranche of a national election.

Neither would the cameraman have foreseen that the result of that poll would mean that the routine presence of a white Kiap at the head of a similar carrier line would, within just five years, be unlikely or even rare.

I had left the Sub-District office in Minj with a senior colleague, Neil Mockett, under instructions to carry a mobile polling station through the villages of East Kambia and collect votes that would confirm the Mid-Wahgi representative for the third post-election sitting of PNG's not yet fully evolved House of Assembly, or Parliament.

It was my first official patrol and its routines were typical of many government-sponsored bush journeys that would be undertaken later.

After climbing through the beginning of a second day, I sat on a cold stone that topped the ridge which divided one watershed of the Kubor Range from the other. Below was a straggling string of about sixty men, the last of them about two hours' walk from the rare patch of grass in a landscape of stunted, moss-covered trees where we had spent the night.

Miles beyond, the Wahgi River coiled through its wide valley and beyond that, yellow with distance, the Bismark Highlands offered yet another of their many faces.

The leading men struggled up the difficult stone wall. The metal box they carried on a pole that was slung between them scraped, bucked, and bumped as they heaved it upwards. Relieved at reaching the summit, they sat on it, pulled out a smoke from their shirt pockets, and together we looked into the next basin.

Carriers on an earlier patrol into East Kambia take a welcome rest after dumping their loads on the crest of the Kubor watershed – estimated altitude 10,000 feet.
© Ian Douglas

Below was a long descent which curved through an unbroken series of tree clad spurs which rolled to the banks of the Kaugel River forty miles away. There were few signs of human habitation – which was striking because the Wahgi Valley behind us was thick with people. Beyond the Kaugel there were no mountains higher than the one on which we sat. Behind them were sago swamps that lined yet another of PNG's big rivers.

Other carriers filed past. Heavy dew had washed their feet, making the soles flash bright yellow. When the last had gone through I heaved myself up and began a descent which took me over several log bridges, through several small rivers, over slanting, slippery sheets of exposed stone and many miles of forest path. I walked, and sometimes ran, once again overtaking men as they splashed and stumbled under their loads.

Finally I scrambled up a small grass hillock and was introduced to a group of waiting Kambians as Her Majesty's representative, a Kiap, by a policeman and an interpreter who had arrived before me. A pair of men came to attention and saluted. One offered a cluster of unusually sweet bananas.

Prompted by the policeman, I called for a pole and soon the Australian flag was flapping over a hamlet of three thatched huts where the patrol would spend the night. Prompted by the interpreter I made sure the Kambians had brought in firewood and fresh food, and on the prompting of my conscience ordered several village men back up the track to help carriers burdened with the heaviest loads.

Neil came in not long after and soon that wet hillock, lying somewhere in thick bush below the Kubor's ridges, was draped in blue wood smoke and buzzed with many voices as food was cooked, tarpaulins hung, and lamps lit.

The village where the first polling booth was to open was just two hours' walk away. We approached it next morning along the banks of a river. Neil and I, bare legged, white skinned, and young walked ahead.

Behind us the interpreter, self-important in a black tunic trimmed with red and yellow hems, then two policemen, smart in their blue uniforms but like all village people who had spent their early life barefoot stomping clumsily in their heavy boots, and finally the carrier line.

Reaching the village required a short, sharp struggle up a steep grass bank. As soon as they could see our heads the assembled villagers began to yodel and the noise level lifted as we came closer.

A group of three men had set themselves slightly forward of the main group and one of these stood slightly ahead of the others. As we approached he swung his shotgun into the shoulder arms position, produced a quivering salute which threatened his stiff black cap, and then advanced with outstretched hand. Luluai Yuak Dju of the Komanka clan, and acknowledged front man of the sparse East Kambian people, had made us welcome. #1

The government too had its protocols so people crowded round the wobbly sapling which was to be the flag pole. They remained at stiff attention while the Australian emblem was disentangled from an awkwardly lopped branch and finally saluted as it fluttered free.

Then came the speeches. Neil told the people he had come to help them select a member of their language group who would sit in a big meeting house in far away Port Moresby.

Yuak said we were welcome as the bringers of justice, salt, and factory tobacco, that he had a taxing problem he wished to discuss with us later, and that many women had fresh vegetables which they were hoping to sell.

The bones of discussion that would dominate the rest of the patrol having been formally declared the crowd disbanded and many of us headed to the river with a towel in one hand and a bar of soap in the other.

Later we would set up polling booths in five other villages and after twenty one nights camped out return to Minj with a total of just over four hundred votes. Activity in these villages did not vary fundamentally from the first. Nor did discussion.

We had been directed to educate the people politically. They were, after all, approaching Independence. This meant we told clansmen whose only access to the wider world was a footpath over a 10,000 feet pass in the Kubors that beyond the Wahgi Valley, and then beyond the mountains east of it, there was a House of Assembly in which elected representatives of PNG's scattered people met to discuss their country's problems and approve new laws.

After repeating ourselves many times it was tempting to think they had been able to absorb this information – but they could not have done. How can colour be described to a blind man? How can national democracy be explained to village men and women whose furthest horizon was the next mountain range and whose clan, covering just over four hundred adults, was the only group to which they felt responsible?

The House of Assembly, a carefully designed, not unpleasant, ferro-concrete building on a hill above Port Moresby's harbour can only have been imagined as a much larger example of the only houses they knew – traditionally designed, wood framed, and thatch roofed.

An understanding that PNG hoped to become a nation of three million people, despite the obstacle of its 800 language groups would have been equally impossible too.

Other similarly obvious limitations, which underlined the poltical obstacles these people were facing at the same time as their country was setting out to become the world's latest democracy, were apparent too. They were universally illiterate and so chose their candidate from a ballot paper carrying photographs, as well as the names, of six protagonists – all of them male.

One of these had chosen to travel with the patrol and hoped to capture the bulk of the 417 votes that were cast. He was Nopnop Tol #2, an important man in the South Wahgi region's political development, but who on that occasion had ignored 40,000 people in other, more accessible, areas of the electorate most of whom, it later proved, had put their tick against someone else.

The people queued to vote and when it was their turn to step forward some of those who recognised Nopnop's photo pointed to it and the Returning Officer, either Neil or myself, conducting this "whispering ballot" ticked off their choice before handing back their paper to be slotted into one of the red boxes.

A handful could not interpret the pictures and many selected a candidate they could not possibly have known. Most of the younger women voted for the only man with a beard, which in Highland communities is thought to underscore good looks.

We could hardly have been directed to take the ballot to a more isolated community. Individuals in the same language group who lived in the Wahgi valley were respected for the political and economic progress they had made since they were contacted by Jim Taylor in 1933, but in the cloud circled valleys of the Kambia the majority of voters were baffled by our ritual with the red ballot boxes and mysterious pieces of paper.

69

Taylor, the first Kiap contracted by Australia to explore PNG's Highlands, was a legend at village level and among his European contemporaries as well. Everything associated with western culture was attributed by local people to his arrival, which, despite the emergence of undercurrents linking European officials, and the missionaries who followed on, with dramatic social upheaval and accompanying ethnic pain, was nevertheless considered by almost everyone to have heralded a huge lift in group fortune too.

His style at first contact was judged temperate – even by the families of clansmen who were shot on the many occasions his patrol was attacked – and this restraint set the tone for universally enthusiastic engagement between Highland Papua New Guineans and Australian administrators through to the late 1960s.

One morning, quite unexpectedly, Paula dropped down from the sky – flown in by helicopter with the Mid-Wahgi's Assistant District Commissioner (ADC), Ian Douglas, who was checking that this section of the national election was making smooth progress. She was six months pregnant and immediately surrounded by excited women who took turns to stroke her stomach.

They had seen their first *missus* (white woman) a couple of years earlier when Betty Douglas had passed through but Paula had a belly (*em i gat bel)*) and this made her doubly interesting – although her stay was brief because helicopter hire is expensive and within an hour she and Ian were clattering over the Kubors and heading back to Minj. #3

Paula. © Graham Forster

Yuak had a problem which consumed him. He outlined it during our first evening in his village and again at regular intervals as well. He said the Kambi people were demoralised because they received little government attention and no economic assistance at all.

Their cousins in the Wahgi Valley had, because they lived in a well populated area where there was an abundance of flat land for airstrips and roads, become rich and sophisticated men while the Kambis anticipated being trapped in an existence exclusively centred on traditional gardening and hunting because they were barricaded in by an almost impenetrable mountain wall.

The Wahgi people, Yuak told us, grew coffee, jangled money in their pockets, wore European-style clothes, drank beer, purchased pick-up trucks, and could buy tinned fish from a trade store. If they were sick they could go to a mission hospital and if they wished could jump on a plane and travel to any part of PNG their pocket might stretch to.

He did not want all this – he knew it was impossible, but he had convinced most of his 747 people that if they moved to much lower, flat ground, at Bol, close to Karimui in the Chimbu district, the already established road system could be extended to include them and with that would come relatively easy access to hospitals, agricultural assistance, casual employment and, most importantly of all, much more money than was currently coming their way.

Yuak hoped the Kambis would then be able to join PNG's expanding, globally linked, economy and was desperate for Kiaps to help by organising a road building project that would connect Karimui with Bol. His plan was clear and almost exactly modelled on immediate post-contact activity undertaken forty years earlier in the Wahgi Valley itself. Patrol Officers would survey the area, tell him where the airstrip should be constructed, then his people would clear the forest and level the land.

But first he needed help with a helicopter pad so the army could fly in a prefabricated medical Aid Post as well as its attendant orderly. He also hoped government funds would cover the period when his scanty labour force forsook its food gardens and built an airstrip instead.

His enthusiasm for self-help, and eagerness to vault the economic blockade imposed by Kambia's mountain perimeter, was almost overwhelming but he was asking too much. In 1972 the Australian government could not, indeed would not, commit itself to an expensive re-location project aimed at fewer than 750 villagers.

Yuak was right to conclude his people had little hope of economic advancement if they continued to be pinned down within their mountain-circled box although we did remind him of the advantages of staying put. Kambian soil was good, the range of traditional foods was greater than we had both seen elsewhere, and the almost unsullied bush was still home to numerous pigeons, cassowaries and wild pigs.

We also emphasised that quarrels over land, which had already resurrected pre-contact clan fighting in the Wahgi, were unlikely in spacious Kambia; inter-village relations were not blighted by random traffic deaths; young girls could not pick up VD from passing lorry drivers; and traditional codes of behaviour continued to be strong.

In other words his sheltered, untouched life should be the envy of his drunken, pox-ridden, brawling, car driving cousins on the other side of the hill – but Yuak was a typical PNG Highlander, whose head was brimming with economic ambition, and so he knew it was not.

We were sympathetic and sensing this the flood gates of Kambian aspiration, which almost exactly mirrored the multiplicity of ambitions circulating at national level too, opened and we listened to dreams of their new life at Bol each evening until we left.

Yuak remained realistic, even when fantasies surrounding a more modern existence were rampant, and one evening quietly asked for assurance we would not "throw away his ideas and leave them in the bush" when we re-crossed the range and returned to Minj.

We outlined them to the ADC. Kambian hopes were summarised in our patrol reports, and were put before the District Commissioner too. But in the cold reality of neat desks, orderly filing systems, and accurate wall maps which showed that Bol was still dauntingly distant from the road-head at Karimui, hopes, which might have appeared realistic while listening to a circle of earnest faces, half seen under a hurricane lamp hung in a creaking hut deep in a remote valley, seemed optimistic when repeated.

Yuak no doubt thinks we discarded them as casually as we might flick away a cigarette butt. There can be no doubt either that his ambitions would have been outlined just as enthusiastically to the next patrol.

It seemed to us that his best chance of avoiding economic petrification was to take his people across the ranges and settle in the Wahgi with clansmen who were their cousins. He, and those who craved commercial excitement, may have already done this, leaving the Kambia to be roamed by hunters, or those who refused to desert their ancestral land, and who may have been rewarded with relative social tranquillity at the cost of a less interesting life.

Much of the time that was not focussed on Bol or ballots was taken by village people keen to settle disputes with neighbours over unhappy wives, inconclusive marriage arrangements, and persistent pig trespass, to whom petty litigation was not just a challenging, often entertaining, pastime but also a demanding art.

Each government patrol since first contact had volunteered to untangle community quarrels over pigs, wives, and minor assault. It was a hangover from a time when Kiap government, anxious to reduce tensions in societies where violence was often used to resolve social problems, introduced an alternative system of mediation.

I found this work difficult because I had neither the cultural knowledge, nor administrative experience, to steer discussion towards an informed conclusion and was often influenced by the most persuasive speaker too. Adding to this frustration was a suspicion that many decisions were ignored as soon as the patrol set off for the next village.

Not long after, I did my best to avoid village litigation, arguing that the people themselves were better able to assess the justice of a complaint. This may have been seen as abdication but informal courts were hard work not least because communication through an interpreter was always difficult – most cultural norms could only be sensed, and a balance guessed at.

At the end of sessions which typically would have been two hours long, bristling with the names of unknown people many of whom had been a long time dead, strange place names, and a confusion of barely sensed cultural imperatives, every decision, even the wrong one, was the result of a mighty effort.

So a plea from an elbow tugging litigant: *"Masta, mi gat kot"* (Sir, I have a complaint) was either met with advice that it would be better to put it before traditional village authorities or a weary shrug if there were no other demands on time.

Back in Minj it was not hard to identify the most important lesson this patrol had delivered to the junior officers conducting it. It was fundamental and it was bruising. Kiaps were the buffer between the administration and the administered. It was their job to pass on government views to the people and the people's view to the government. And if these were at odds, which they often were, it was the Kiap who was tossed in the undercurrents.

They were trapped by near irreconcilable challenges raised by wide discrepancies between national administrative policy and urgent grassroot needs. To have a foot in both camps inevitably meant there were times when, metaphorically speaking, Kiaps had to do the splits.

It was more comfortable to make sure both feet were planted on the administration's side of this line because it paid salaries and controlled career progress. Contradicting this was pressure on Kiaps to be as close as they could to village people and report back what they were thinking – which could only be done through personal contact.

It could, therefore, be difficult, even impossible, to reconcile District Office orders to toe the administrative line at all times and secure the confidence of village people as well.

This Kambia visit had an equally instructive postscript – and not a good one. Government officers entering from Minj invariably carried an unusual amount of cash so they could pay generously for food and distribute largesse among people who had no cash crop to sell.

The previous patrol had been especially generous. But this time many of the carriers were Chimbus – a huge language group which occupied comparatively little land and so relied on ingenuity to maintain its living standards. Not for nothing were they known as the Irishmen of PNG. They were ubiquitous throughout the country because on their own soil jobs, and other economic opportunities, were scarce.

This group has been excellent, uncomplaining workers during a patrol which has faced a number of problems created by unusually heavy loads and the real reason they had volunteered for this difficult task had not been the modest daily wage, or the chance of a mild adventure while moving through previously unseen locations, but to strip the Kambians of what little cash they had through gambling.

In 1972 it was illegal for Papua New Guineans to bet, or own a pack of cards, because their favoured game was *"Laki"* (Lucky) and the tension it could create was enormous. Nevertheless, when these practised Chimbu card sharps returned to Minj they carried with them an unknown, but doubtless significant, proportion of the Kambia's cash wealth with them and it had been taken from under the Kiaps' supposedly watchful eyes.

Hindsight is wonderful. There had been a great deal of late night activity, which had been put down to inevitable socialising, and towards the end of the patrol some of the prominent Kambians, obviously big losers, had shown strained faces.

However, the real lesson, and a nasty one, was that even on a patrol like this, with Kiaps and everyone else living and sleeping within feet of each other, for almost three weeks we had been deceived.

Everyone with a black skin, including our interpreter, policemen, Nopnop and also Yuak the headman, had successfully concealed this large scale, and illegal, betting operation and kept it to themselves.

Eventually the losers complained, not to us, but to the ADC and so we discovered that much of the cash we had handed over by paying generously for food and other small services had been carried out in Chimbu pockets – and some had no doubt been quickly used to buy beer in Minj as well.

The wider message, which had to be profoundly disturbing from the European perspective, was this: If we could be deceived so easily over illegal card schools conducted almost under our noses, what other, more important, things could Papua New Guineans conceal from a Kiap even if he was, as he was expected to be, working with them in their village and not sitting behind a desk?

1 A Luluai is a government approved head man often, but not always, the Pidgin speaking son of a traditional leader. Immediately after contact the relationship between individual Kiaps and village Luluais was fundamental to village advancement.

#2 His village name, Taimil Nopndop Tolmur, had been Europeanised down to Nopnop or even Nop.

3 Queen Elizabeth is described in Pidgin as *"Missus Kwin"*.

CHAPTER SIX

A bonfire of spears and arrows

"Smell this hand," the old man said. "It took out your grandfather's liver and filled his belly with stones." The Tangilka ran to find his axe, the Kambilika fled, and after a break of more than twenty years the two clans were again at war.

Minj, December 1971

The 1972 general election triggered a political earthquake. New parties emerged in the House of Assembly and one of its established members, Michael Somare, was able to construct a coalition government that unexpectedly took charge.

It was a radical change. Until then Australia had overseen Papua New Guinea's development through its main agent, the Department of District Administration (DDA), which was headquartered in Port Moresby, and Kiaps, the most numerous of DDA's agents on the ground, were left largely to themselves as long as they did not stray outside guidelines promoted by their District Offices.

Moresby on the night the new government was formed was hectic. The Australian Administrator, who had ruled in the absence of an indigenous chain of command, hurriedly evacuated his office while files, some no doubt on men who had suddenly become prominent dignitaries, were dumped into waiting transport and disappeared into the night.

Next morning Somare, the new Chief Minister and a man who came from the Sepik River, sat in a chair only just vacated by Australia's chosen representative and began to shape the country to his liking.

While this revolution was taking place, two events which reflected the increasingly obvious, and critically de-stablising, land shortage in the Wahgi Valley dominated work at Minj's Sub-District office.

One, a tribal fight, was handled in typically pragmatic Kiap style. The other, an assassination threat on a white planter, drew in the ADC at Minj, the Wahgi's representative in the House of Assembly, and the people of the Komunka clan in a theatre which confirmed just how radical the overnight transfer in power from civil servants appointed by Australia to elected Papua New Guineans had been.

The armed, inter-clan struggle began when the Kambilika and Tangilka brotherhoods, which occupied adjacent spurs on the south side of the Wahgi, disputed ownership of a promising stretch of garden, and coffee planting, land that lay close to the river itself.

Both clans had been contacted by Australians in the 1930s but exchanges did not become regular until the early 1950s when Patrol Officer Brian Corrigan persuaded each group to come down from the steep, and easily defended, slopes where they lived and move closer to the flatter, more fertile, and vacant ground nearer the valley floor.

Open warfare between the Wahgi clans was even then becoming a thing of the past and before long each of these groups left their mountain eyries, secret caves, and hidden war magic houses, to move onto gentler slopes, some of them close to the Wahgi itself, where they prospered.

No deaths through tribal fighting, improved diet, and progressively better medical facilities swelled their numbers. Employment on local coffee plantations, and then income from their own coffee blocks, made each of these groups wealthy in PNG terms.

The Tangilka owned a herd of cattle and the Kambilikas collectively enjoyed two pick-up trucks. The number and economic expectations of each clan grew yearly. New land was drained and fenced, either for coffee stands or vegetable gardens. Eventually the inevitable happened. A Tangilka and a Kambilika set out one morning to prepare a previously unused patch of land only to discover they had each earmarked the same spot on an attractive riverside stretch called Dong.

The situation was not immediately serious. They were related by marriage and were able to come to a satisfactory agreement. However, their clan leaders were alarmed. They met, raked through collective memories, and the conclusion they reached was depressing.

High up in the mountains where they used to live, boundaries were well defined and beyond dispute. New settlement immediately below the traditional fortress areas had acquired boundaries that were mutually accepted too. But land next to the river was another matter.

It would have been suicide to have been seen there alone in pre-contact days and it may only have been occupied in the most marginal terms during a rare lull in the almost constant confrontations when one clan's ascendancy was unusually high. Dong, in truth, belonged to no one.

Each group reached the same conclusion but the need for more garden land was urgent. So it was both prophetic and alarming when Marie Reay, an anthropologist who had worked from a village near Minj for almost two decades, warned that ownership was traditionally claimed by conquest, and resulting occupation, even though the ground itself may not have been the reason for the fighting.

Before 1953 there had been more than enough to go round. Perennially scarce marriageable women and high value pigs, which were always tempting, were another matter, and theft of these was the main reason for most pre-contact raids and then retreat from previously occupied land by the defeated party.

Reay emphasised, and this was critical, that before Europeans arrived the occupation of land defined its ownership and if an ancestor had seized a parcel of land, for whatever reason and even if for only a short time, and for only incidental motives, then his descendants could, and would, claim those rights too.

It was a recipe for tumult and confusion because veteran Kambilika and Tangilka men could each remember a period when their clan had held land next to the river. When the star of the Tangilka's was high and Kambilikas were licking their wounds on their most easily defended ground, Tangilka men thought it safe to allow their women to graze pigs and manage small gardens there.

But there were also times when Tangilkas had to scurry back to their high forest strongholds and Kambilkas could strut like roosters down below. Both sides could advance accurate claims that they had occupied Dong, no matter how briefly, in the past. The result was an impasse.

In the meantime members of each clan began to move in and many of them may have been cousins. However, the pull of the paternal clan, the phratry, was absolute and the need for it to prosper, even at the expense of relatives and near neighbours, by expanding, and then holding, its economic boundaries overcame any other consideration.

Clan loyalty is unconditional and common identity could seize Papua New Guineans to such a degree that a group of kinsmen on a shared mission moved with the same intensity of collective thought as a swarm of bees, a flock of starlings, a shoal of fish, or a pack of hounds.

In 1974 Paula and I had watched, and have not forgottten, the unnerving focus unthinkingly demonstrated by a line of a dozen Goilala men, some carrying axes, doing no more than investigate a sudden outburst of yodelling in the valley beneath their village. They had poured over a stile in their pig fence and moved down the path to the river as if they had been drilled.

They were running in step, and exchanging thoughts on the most likely interpretation of the noise, while at the same time co-ordinating their stride so that they did not tread on each other's heels. Individualism had been completely suppressed. They were a single, united, and formidable body on an instinctive quest to discover whether its group interest was, or was not, being threatened – and immediately prepared to defend it aggressively if it had been.

Similarly strong forces dominated group thinking among the Kambilikas and Tangilkas and so a deterioration in inter-clan relations, which would underline the depth of loyalty Wahgi villagers still felt, despite many years of exposure to Australian law and a fundamental shift in their economic fortune, to their clan totem was inevitable. This meant re-emergence of the singlemindedness with which they would defend it against any threat, whatever the source, could not be avoided.

The trigger was pulled in December 1971 when an older Kambilika, with memories of earlier bloodletting still fixed in his mind, taunted a

Tangilka in-law. He told the young man he had killed his grandfather in one of many pre-contact skirmishes. "Smell this hand," the old man said. "It took out his liver and filled his belly with stones." The Tangilka could not swallow this provocation. He reached for his axe, the Kambilka fled, and so after a break of more than twenty years the two clans were again at war.

The cautious style of fighting that followed was traditional and while it may have appeared more like carefully choreographed sparring than all out war it was nevertheless overwhelmingly disruptive and could be deadly too.

The clans stood on opposing spurs parading warriors in full fighting panoply (*bilas*) in a vocal and unmistakable demonstration of force while occasionally making tentative sallies across the intervening valley to test the other's strength. Towards the end of the day a bolder rush by Kambilikas bought retreating Tangilkas into arrow range and three were wounded.

This skirmishing ceased when the sun began to set but as darkness fell a Kambilika called Mont slipped through a gap in a hedge close to his house on Dong where a young Tangilka called Kos was waiting. #1 Mont was killed after being hacked three times across his back with a bush knife.

The impact of the ambush was immediate. The Tangilkas, reluctant to raise the stakes by following up one death with yet another, retreated to their most easily defended village at Tomba and settled in for a siege. They had calculated that if they could resist the Kambilika's most determined retaliatory attacks Kiaps would intervene and peace would be restored after suitably high compensation for Mont's death had been negotiated and paid.

Next day angry Kambilkas attacked Tomba. They rushed through its lower section hacking down banana trees, plundering huts, and smashing the artefacts inside. They also seriously wounded one Tangilka man, left arrow heads in the flesh of others, and raped a number of women. If the defence had been less effective there would have been more damage, more rape, and perhaps death too.

The Royal Papua New Guinea Constabulary (RPNGC) detachment based in Minj intervened. It arrested thirty of the Tangilkas defending Tomba, which tipped the military scales in favour of the Kambilikas, and then, fortunately for equilibrium, captured fifteen Kambilkas too. It was there the next day and finally left after removing sufficient fighting men to force a ceasefire.

The situation had cooled but it could never become cold until the Kambilikas had either neutralised their anger surrounding Mont's murder with a Tangilka death or a mutually satisfactory compensation payment had been arranged instead.

Over the next three weeks the Tangilkas faced a blockade. They were afraid to pick their outlying coffee so berries rotted or were harvested by their enemies. Outlying houses and gardens were ransacked. Coffee pulpers, pigs, kitchen utensils and trade goods were systematically removed. Men selling coffee, or wanting to re-stock the clan's almost empty food stores, left the village only in groups and the loss of warriors already in jail was keenly felt because the Tangilkas were outnumbered.

Open skirmishing flared during House of Assembly elections but ballot box commitments meant nothing could be done. Immediately afterwards I was told by Ian Douglas to visit Tomba and scout the situation out.

I drove there with three policemen and was given a long list of complaints as well as names covering the principal Kambilika offenders. Leaving the Tangilkas, we drove to Danal where the Kambilikas were waiting.

"Yes," they said. "The Tangilkas are telling the truth. We did all we have been accused of."

But even as we spoke, a line of Tangilka women, protected by armed men, moved onto the disputed land. Within a finger snap the group we had been talking to had scattered, each to his hut to collect weapons, and at the same time calling on other clansmen to help.

We drove quickly to Dong, jumped the fence, rounded up the women, shouting at them as Kiaps and policemen do, and drove them out. They had come to collect food and as the last ran onto the road with her still empty *bilum* bumping on her back we stood on Dong and looked around us.

It was a clear morning typical of the Wahgi Valley. The sun was bright and the earth still damp after overnight rain. Villages with their neat chequered gardens, gently waving clumps of bamboo, and bright yellow thatched roofs, stood on every spur. The air felt fresh and cool. Droplets still glistened on the purple leaves of a tanket #2 hedge below us.

In the direction of Danal, moving slowly across a broad patch of pale *kunai* grass was a dark mass of advancing men. Because they could not be heard, and because they were packed tightly, their progress was menacing. It was the Kambilikas.

Tangilka women were still running to the safety of Tomba while their men gathered on a spur halfway between them and their village. Some were already dressed in fighting gear. We could see spears and cassowary feather head dresses. Veteran bush policeman Sergeant-Major Siwi pointed to a group of men lined up on the other side of the Tangilkas. They too were armed. "Those," he said, "are Kegerinkabams. They will fight the Tangilikas as well."

That afternoon we raided the Kambilikas in an effort to reduce their numbers. We picked up ten. Some were unlikely to have been directly involved although others were discovered as they tried to hide their arrows. Our best catch was an old fight leader hauled to the ground in front of disapproving Swiss Missionaries.

They were quickly told that it might have appeared un-Christian to chase down old people, like the man a Constable was sitting on top of, but it was veterans like him who instructed young men who were the active fighters, how, and when, to do it.

Next day we returned to Tomba and asked the Tangilikas to give up ten men – which they did. The next job was to round up as many Kambilikas as we could and re-establish military balance. This was difficult. They were determined not to be captured and our efforts were dispiriting, disorganised, and puny.

After several gruelling pursuits through dense coffee blocks, and over humped sweet potato gardens, our collective catch was just five youths and again one lucky find – a resourceful warrior who had openly shot Tangilka cattle.

Help came in the form of a detachment of thirty riot police despatched by the District Office from Mount Hagen. I was immediately unhappy with the squad's arrogant approach. It was staffed by young men who were not mature and visibly revelled in their privileged and punitive position.

Their obvious confidence flowed from the impressive panoply of weapons at their disposal, which included automatic shotguns, tear gas, riot sticks and shields. They also wore steel helmets. They looked fierce but few were Highlanders and therefore had little rapport with local people which put them at a fundamental disadvantage.

Because we had not yet captured any Kegerinkabams we moved to their side of the disputed land. A long-serving police corporal, who was stationed locally and familiar with Wahgi thinking, pointed out a large, freshly constructed building which stood on a crest overlooking the disputed area.

Only days earlier we had slept in the same village hut where he had seized the opportunity to make unrelentingly clear his view that modern Kiaps were weak and useless because most of PNG's newly recurrent instability sprang from their reluctance to use force.

He said the new house had been built as a lookout point, a barracks, from which armed Kegerinkabams could quickly move onto Dong to drive off Tangilkas, and said burning it would undermine the effectiveness of their alliance with the Kambilikas at Danal.

Anything that would make it more difficult for the clans to stage their next fight looked like a good move so we hauled out its contents and set it alight. The thatch flared fiercely and the building was ashes within minutes.

Then we moved onto Dong. Most of the riot squad were combing through the area below and I was sitting by the side of a path with three others. We heard the heavy slapping of running feet behind us and looking back could see a single bowman, arrow already notched, pounding down the slope.

The celebrated riot policemen vanished in an instant leaving a trail of abandoned weapons and discarded equipment. Hoping he hadn't seen me, I slipped off the path and crouched behind some *pit-pit* (wild sugar cane), thinking I might be able to grab him as he ran past.

One of the fleeing squad members ran back and flung himself abjectly at my feet. He was sobbing like a child, with his face in mud, hiding his head with his hands.

Then I looked up at the bare chested man whose hut had undoubtedly just been burned. He was standing ten feet away. His bowstring was drawn back to his ear and an arrow was pointing at my chest. I braced myself because even if I was hit I had the silly notion I might still be able to capture him. We stared at each other for many seconds then something struck the *pit-pit* beside me and he was gone.

He could not have missed so either must have baulked at attacking a Kiap or been afraid of being gunned by the riot squad which had fired several shots in the air.

Sergeant-Major Siwi said he was Kaibelt Dorum – a typically muscular young man whom I met again two days later. We were still rounding up the most troublesome Kambilikas. He stepped out of the bush and walked up to me. He had washed, his beard was combed, and he was wearing a clean shirt and shorts. He took my right hand and put it around his wrist. "I am your pig," he said. "Take me away." ("*Mi pik bilong yu nau. Yumi go.*")

He was not singled out and charged, as were his fellow clansmen, only with riotous behaviour, so there is no record of his house being burned or an arrow being aimed at a Kiap.

After Kaibelt had turned back the riot squad burned another hut on Dong and this destroyed Kambilika resistance. The smoke plumes were read as a signal that the Minj office had decided to take a much harder line. When we passed Danal we called on forty of the men who were there to give themselves up. This time there was no chasing. Those who had either volunteered, or were nominated, climbed without prompting into the back of the truck to be taken to court and eventually to jail.

It was fortunate that Ian Douglas, a big, cheerful, far-sighted man who refused to be overwrought if things became difficult, laughed when I told him we had just burned two houses. Another, less relaxed ADC might have suspended me because "cooking" huts by government officers had been outlawed years earlier and was a disciplinary offence. Ian's humour had been rueful – especially when I protested the fires had been effective. "I know that," he said. "That's why I'll do my best to keep you out of trouble. But don't do it again."

Ian Douglas. © Elizabeth Douglas

The next task was to defuse the situation by encouraging each clan to put more effort into discussing settlement of their mutual problem instead of fighting. Councillor Muga #3 of the Tangilkas had a plan. I liked him. He was a droll, rather slight man who had a habit of rolling his eyes and looking sideways when he offered suggestions that made me laugh.

Not unnaturally he wanted to bring peace to his people. Life was becoming difficult without money; he was still afraid a kinsman, even himself, might be killed; his cattle were being used for target practice by Kambilika bowmen; and many of his clan were keen to leave overcrowded Tomba and return to their outlying hamlets.

This could only be done if the Kambilikas agreed to end hostilities. Muga's idea was simple. Both clans would publicly burn their weapons.

"Good thinking," I said. "Where will you do that?" (*Gutpela ting-ting. Yu laik wokim samting ia long wonem hap?*)

"Minj market place," he replied.

The Kambilikas had to be persuaded. They could lose face if fighting was suspended. Weary as they were they would have still liked to level the score by killing a Tangilka. However, they too needed to revive their economic affairs so eventually they agreed.

I returned to Minj and reported to Ian who thought it was a good idea too. We hadn't a clue what might happen – even if the plan would work. I spent the night before the bonfire at Tomba explaining, among other things, that the next time they set out to cook a frozen chicken it would be a good idea to thaw it first. Then I drank a bottle of warm beer before leaving Muga's fireside and returning to the hut they had given me.

Dawn found the Kambilikas in a less helpful mood and I was disappointed with the number of men turning up with weapons. After an interval which had me bawling orders in a manner that was a backbone to my job, the number of armed warriors began to look respectable and by nine o'clock there were around eighty men, all in fighting dress, ready to carry their bows and spears to Minj.

It is easy to dismiss paint and plumage as decoration. Western soldiers prefer quiet camouflage but the difference between a Papua New Guinean in everyday clothing and the same man in battle dress is awesome.

One is human while the other is savage – and intended to appear that way. The Kambilikas, their skin concealed under layers of ash or soot, wearing rustling bustles of multi-coloured tanket leaves, shells through their noses, with one hand holding a nine foot spear and the other their bow and arrows, were already dancing at a pitch that could take them beyond control – a danger underlined by their unnervingly unfocussed eyes.

I had anticipated this and Muga was under stiff, probably unnecessary, instructions to keep his men out of sight until the Kambilikas were well on their way to Minj. I was anxious to get them started. They had to go first because they might attack the Tangilkas if they could see their backs.

My heart sank when they objected. They did not want to "show the Tanglikas their arses" by running ahead in apparent retreat. Eventually I convinced them that pride and honour lay in the lead position because they would be first to be seen by the crowd of spectators waiting at Minj.

I watched them rush off yodelling when a low cough made me jerk round. Muga stood grinning and rolling his eyes. Behind him about one hundred and twenty plumed, painted, and impressively silent warriors had already filled the road. I visibly started. They must have been hiding close by. His control over them had been superb.

The most alarming moment was in Minj market place. Both clans ought to have blunted some energy during the seven miles they had mock charged, retreated, and mock charged forward again, but they had sung and danced themselves into a super-bellicose state which lost none of its risk as they poured between the excited onlookers that lined the road.

These included Paula, and other expatriate wives, who struggled to keep their knuckles out of their mouths because unlike relaxed celebratory and ceremonial occasions, when the aim of parading warriors was to attract admiration through the most eyecatching display, the mass belligerence that swept past them was raw, and the depth of clan cohesion unnerving too.

Kambilika and Tangilka clansmen were dangerously fired up as they poured through Minj to the market place where they burned their weapons. © Ian Douglas.

There were long seconds when both groups faced each other across the market square and tentative mock charge movements began to flicker. Muga, realising the danger, immediately told his men to sit down and together Ian and I quickly persuaded the Kambilikas to do the same. From then on progress was smooth. Both clans piled their weapons, some superbly crafted, into a carefully stacked pile which stood about five feet high.

Then Muga, and much younger Koilmal, who had been pushed to the front because he was Councillor for the Kambilikas, broke two spears and set the pile on fire. Both groups watched the weapons burn as a deliberately pleasant and informal ADC praised them handsomely for the effort they had made, and then no doubt feeling strangely naked in battledress, but without weapons, they returned to their homes.

Muga winces as heat from burning weapons spreads. Was his initiative successful? Were there later regrets? © Ian Douglas.

Was this a satisfactory result? I was never sure. All that had been done was postpone further fighting, and possibly save lives, until the destroyed weapons were replaced or Dong could be subdivided in a way that would satisfy both clans.

The understaffed Minj office was unable to pursue this problem. The following week another crisis erupted on the opposite side of the Wahgi and attention was immediately focussed on that instead.

Days before their release, prisoners from both clans in jail at Mount Hagen were urged to concentrate on their gardens, and not on fighting, when they returned home. But that was it. No other constructive effort to ease the crisis was made. Sub-District administration was frantic at the time and short-term crisis management was all that was possible. The clans may not have fought over Dong immediately, but unless they were quickly consoled by a mutually satisfactory settlement they eventually will have done.

Australia's post-contact determination to subdue and eventually eliminate inter-tribal warfare had been singleminded, and in the Highlands, where the traumas of the 1941-45 Pacific War were scarcely visible, so overwhelming, it may have persuaded some villagers that Europeans were committed pacifists.

This resolve was so convincing I sometimes thought so myself and needed to be reminded that Britain had only recently fought Germany in two spectacularly nasty wars in which my Forster grandfather had been killed (Passchendaele 1917), my father wounded (Dunkirk 1940), and his cousin killed too (Norway 1940). Within my grandfather's extended family perhaps a dozen half cousins and quarter cousins were also killed.

Compared with those conflagrations Papua New Guineans fought with peashooters – although it was clear that by 1945 Europeans, and others, had learned a bitter global lesson and as a result were determined to avoid adopting military solutions to resolve their own tribal conflicts and hoped, eventually, that Papua New Guineans would follow their example too.

#1 Mountain people in PNG overwhelmingly preferred to kill by ambush – often from behind. Face to face combat with two men locked in struggle was rare.

#2 Tankets are a quick growing croton, not unlike laurel, although their thick, fleshy leaves could be purple, green, or bright yellow. They are often planted to make thick hedges. The youngest, most heavily leafed, top shoots are trimmed off to make male decoration too.

Plain coloured, green leaves were used to cover buttocks on an every-day basis after the stems were tucked into a bark belt. Men who were fighting would use a range of differently coloured leaves in a similar, buttock-covering, decoration. The effect of these, because so many stems were used, was to create an enormous, imposing, rustling bustle.

The Pidgin noun for the routine buttock cover was *arse-grass*.

#3 Villagers in the Minj sub-district were represented by democratically elected Local Government Councillors, not government appointed Luluais.

CHAPTER SEVEN

Life of a European planter is threatened

"Masta," said the would-be killer. "I do not care if they hang me and my father. I am doing this for my children."

Komunka people, Nondugl, 1972

Like many Kiaps I was comfortable working with bush people, villagers, but sometimes found it less easy to empathise with, and understand, the Europeanised products of the system we served.

This was contrary because during our service we met clans and clan members still proud of being able to live in tune with their traditions and while liking, even admiring, them we at the same time challenged their culture and on some occasions undermined their self-respect.

It is true that we Europeans, the Australian government and missionaries, introduced better health, better food, and unusually long periods of inter-tribal peace. But we also encouraged new appetites and in so doing chipped away at established custom and poise.

Clothing is an obvious example. The Wahgi clansman, his elaborate headress bobbing to his step, *kina* shells clinking, and *bilum* (loin cover) flapping softly against his shins, was impressive. But that same man, constricted by European clothing which could include a pair of savagely tight shoes, a crumpled jacket and an off-colour white shirt, could, if his mask slipped, also carry a bewildered look.

In time I was able to ignore this. Clothes are, after all, just clothes. The Wahgis were learning to wear them more easily – just as they discovered, as did my school friends in Slaley and Hexhamshire, how to drink beer without vomiting, or drive pick-up trucks without running out of fuel or putting them into a ditch.

Prominent among these adaptors was Kaibelt Diria, elected Member of the House of Assembly (MHA) for the section of the Wahgi Valley under Minj Sub-District administration. He always wore European clothes, they were always clean, often expensive and usually in good taste.

Nevertheless, I found him mildly odd because he had still to master a trouble-free way of walking in shoes and this showed in a clumping, wide legged gait which may have been exaggerated by a comfortable stomach and shorts that always seemed a little too tight.

His large, and potentially impressive, presence was also undermined by his marginally undersized hat. It had two functions: to cover his baldness and to emulate another carrier of distinctive headgear, Tom Ellis, an authoritative former District Commissioner whom Kaibelt had always admired.

Because I could not approach the MHA (Member of the House of Assembly) without finding him faintly eccentric, I underestimated him. More fool me because he was a shrewd and ambitious man who was able to take advantage of his democratic elevation and stamp his abruptly acquired authority on the post-election Wahgi Valley many times more effectively, and much sooner, than we Kiaps ever suspected.

He was from the Tsengelap clan, which was the most influential on the northern side of the river. Government records indicated he was an orphan reared by Abba Kip, an unpretentious, upstanding old man who had accompanied Jim Taylor on his celebrated 1938-39 patrol over the formidable Wahgi-Sepik divide, who sometimes sold me sweet potato for my pigs, and whose role in the history of the Mid-Wahgi people may never be appreciated.

Kaibelt began his career as a *boss-boi*, foreman over a line of men making roads, and when I asked one of the old Europeans who had once been in overall charge if there was anything visible in the youth to mark him as likely to become the most powerful man in the valley, the only thing of significance he could recall was that if Kaibelt sacked a man the offender was never re-instated.

He went to the first House of Assembly in 1964 because he was a member of a large clan that was allied to a number of others and had secured their overwhelming numerical support. I found his name only once in pre-1964 records. He had been one of five Tsengelaps who had pooled their coffee income and purchased one of the Wahgi Valley's first locally owned pick-up trucks.

He was returned to the House of Assembly in 1968 where he stood solidly behind the conservative, anti-independence, Highlands-dominated United Party, which was the main opposition group.

But immediately after he was re-elected in 1972 he was persuaded to abandon his party sponsors, on whose platform he had campaigned, and became a pivotal member of Michael Somare's more ambitious National Party, one of those which had formed the new governing coalition, after which he was rewarded with the post of Minister for the Department of Post and Telegraphs – later known as Communications.

Kaibelt Diria in 1972 when he represented the Wahgi constituency in PNG's House of Assembly or national parliament. He had just been appointed a senior government minister and was about to be described as the region's "comptroller-general". Kaibelt was knighted in 1983.

This undisguised ambition, cynicism and resourcefulness delivered a chauffer driven car, opportunities to tour other countries on fact-finding missions, and a position in the Wahgi Valley which quickly persuaded the anthropologist Marie Reay to describe him as its "comptroller general".

There are a number of cameos surrounding Kaibelt which underlined the enigmas of the great 1972 adjustment during which the hitherto all-powerful Kiaps, who previously were the government, surrendered their position, not unwillingly but often with bewilderment, to the Somare coalition.

Somewhere around four months after his appointment, the Minister of Posts and Telegraphs told the House of Assembly that PNG's local telephone grids had been linked through Standard Trunk Dialling (STD) and a universal connection system was at last operating nationally.

A Kiap colleague was working from the Tsengelap Rest House #1 when the MHA returned from Moresby. The following morning Kaibelt complained he had tried to ring the Wahgi Local Government Council but been unable to get through.

He was asked if he had used the new six figure number. "*Wonem samting?*" (What is that?) he replied. The Kiap went with him to his home, wrote down the new, three figure STD extension for Minj numbers, and showed him how to get through.

Kaibelt spoke only Iu Wei and Pidgin English and was illiterate – although he had learned to print his first name so he could sign off official documents.

Nevertheless he headed a PNG delegation attending a Tele-Communications Technical Conference in Tokyo during which he was entertained, successfully, over the course of at least one night by two women whose skills had pleased him greatly. I know this because he joked about it in the Minj Hotel while rubbing his bald head and comparing its size and hairless condition to the tip of an enthusiastic penis.

I met him occasionally while out on patrol. He was always polite but was frustratingly uncommunicative too. He controlled his electorate, and control it he did, through his position in Port Moresby and telephone calls, sometimes visits, to the District Commissioner in Mount Hagen.

If a civil servant erred, Kaibelt did not issue a warning before he made sure the transgressor was transferred. His methods avoided confrontation, and most, if not all, his victims were unaware they had been moved on because he could no longer tolerate them in his constituency.

The District Commissioner called a post-election meeting of Wahgi Kiaps and counselled us: "Remember that whatever clothes he wears, whatever car he drives, whatever political party he represents, Kaibelt is not a European." By this he meant that the MHA was a man of the Wahgi Valley, thought in Iu Wei (it translates as "real talk"), and carried ambitions dominated by Wahgi custom which were buttressed by his new found authority as a Minister of State.

We were also, in a move which confirmed just how dramatically the 1972 election had shifted the seat of power, ordered to accept, without quibble or reservation, that Kaibelt was a government minister, therefore the most powerful man in the valley, and to openly acknowledge he carried authority that exceeded the clout previously enjoyed by the District Commissioner himself.

Just after the election I became enmeshed in a complicated, and ultimately tectonic plate shifting, political development triggered by an assassination threat on a white planter, which helped to redefine the role of Europeans who were living, and working, in the Highlands of PNG after being recruited by the Australian government as economic developers – and which at the same time reinforced the newly elevated position of elected Members of the House of Assembly.

Ian Douglas had taken me to Kumbala, an abandoned tea plantation in the Nondugl area, which together with a nearby plot, Bonong, had been sold five years earlier to European-owned companies just before the chill realisation that they would soon need every inch of available land swept through villages in the Wahgi Valley.

When he showed me the blocks that day, Bonong had been drained but was still covered in its original *pit-pit* while Kumbala carried only a derelict bungalow, a handful of tea bushes which were being smothered by re-established *kunai* grass, and a group of Chimbu squatters.

Construction of a plantation, along with its attendant drier, which could have helped to advance nearby local enterprises, had foundered on an obvious economic rock. Ian predicted that each of these blocks would become a political hot potato but did not realise the temperature at which that potato would be cooked.

Dick Thiele, who was described by fellow Europeans as a "bit of a bull" and was unwittingly to provoke the political bombshell that Bonong would become, had, in the mid-1950s, established himself as a planter near the town of Banz, less than a dozen miles away, where he owned a coffee drying factory and occupied an accompanying plantation.

Along with other planters who, after being encouraged by post-war Australian governments, had arrived in the Wahgi Valley at the same time, he confidently expected to live, and work, there for as long as he wished.

When Bonong was put on the market by PNG's Development Bank, which had taken over after the mortgage it had approved had failed, Thiele put in an offer.

Directly above Bonong, which lay between them and the Wahgi River, lived the small Komunka group who were to become his rivals. They were a sub-clan of the powerful Oganas, but a relatively poor band of people whose land boundaries were almost entirely contained within the easily demarcated features of the narrow, and unusually sharp, spur along which their houses and gardens were strung.

Because their land was steep they grew comparatively little coffee, and because their soil was poor their gardens were not especially productive. They had long regretted bowing to pressure from their Ogana brothers and agreeing to sell Bonong for cash and its proximity to their village did nothing to temper their regret.

It lay almost at their feet, large, flat, and fertile. When they heard it was for sale they thought, without question, they would be allowed first option and had raised 2,000 dollars – which was roughly what they had been paid for it.

A track to the contentious plot passed directly through the Komunka village and just beyond it a rotting bridge spanned a culvert. The political touch paper was lit when Theile's son, Richard, drove through to inspect Bonong and stopped to make repairs.

Komunkas crowded the Theile vehicle and Richard, who could understand Iu Wei, realised he was not welcome, and returned to Banz – but not before letting the people know that his father intended to buy the land and that he had wanted to take a closer look at it.

The Komunkas were perturbed. Their leader, Kaibelt Op, was a traditional warrior and he spread the message that if Theile succeeded in buying Bonong he would be killed. It was a dramatic but predictable tactic.

Ian told me to talk with the Komunkas and discover just how real the threat might be. It may have been made in the confident expectation it would never be carried out – but was nevertheless a new, and ominous, development in the already congealing confrontation between the Wahgi people and established white settlers who managed most of the best, and previously unoccupied, coffee and tea growing land.

Late that night I was sitting cross-legged on the grass-covered floor of the long, low-roofed, man's house at Munumul when the Komunkas unhesitatingly confirmed their determination to kill a European planter.

The traditional, men-only venue confirmed the seriousness of the discussion. The hut was filled with smoke, and flames from the fire around which we sat reflected off deeply tarred beams and thatch. Either side of me were a quiet group of senior Komunka men who explained, without theatrics, their land shortage and Theile's threat to their future.

His plans to expand his already large holdings were described as greed and it became clear that if killing was the only way to prevent him undermining clan fortunes by taking over Bonong, they would do it.

"Would you really kill him?" I asked.

For a while they did not answer. Some continued to smoke and one put a new stick on the dying fire.

"Yes, Masta, we would," said a man who was about thirty years old and sitting next to me.

"Who would kill him?" I probed quietly. The policeman, Tippuary, who was with me was listening carefully too.

"I would," said the same man.

I believed him. #2

I tested them with a dramatic description of how the government might retaliate. I suggested that if they did murder Thiele the resulting investigation and trial would leave the clan disordered, leaderless, and much less able to help itself than it was now. I also speculated that the culprit might be hanged.

"Masta," said the group-appointed would-be killer. "I do not care if they hang me and my father. I am doing this for my children."

Leaving them with a promise I would pass their message on, I went to my bed – but not before checking with Tippuary whether he thought the threat was empty. He did not. "They mean what they say," he confirmed. It was well past midnight. The Komunkas continued to talk until dawn.

Next day I called on Richard Thiele and told him the clan would kill his father if he continued his efforts to buy Bonong. Richard, who'd had time to reflect on the incident at the bridge, and wanted to pick his words carefully, agreed they appeared to be unusually determined and that what I had said was not impossible.

I returned to Minj, reported to Ian Douglas, and watched the fireworks go off. The District Office in Mount Hagen despatched senior staff to visit the Komunkas and verify my report.

I was sent to pull a surveyor's chain around Komunka land, calculate its area, and divide it by the number of people in the village. It showed they were chronically short of garden land and must have relied heavily on connections with wealthier in-laws and relatives.

The Development Bank, blind to the de-stabilisation it had created, stubbornly insisted that the Komunkas could only buy back Bonong if they raised six thousand dollars – the same sum as the outstanding mortgage.

Meanwhile Kaibelt Diria MHA was clumping up and down the corridors of power trying, among other things, to remove Ian Douglas, and using the situation at Bonong as an excuse.

He had taken up his cudgel on the Komunka's behalf after discovering, as soon as he returned to the Wahgi after the election, that many of its people were unhappy he had quit the anti-Independence United Party and thrown in his lot with a Coalition which could not seize Independence quickly enough. Electoral fences had undoubtedly to be mended.

Typically Kaibelt did not approach the Komunkas, or the Minj civil servants, but returned to Moresby to take advice from Ministerial colleagues and then intervene directly with top officials instead. It was an approach that was impossible for Kiaps to mirror and ultimately, because it put him at the centre of a tight network of influential decision makers, it would have been more effective.

At the same time the Komunkas called on their in-laws and allies for help in finding more cash. The first response was a money exchange which combined demonstrations of inter-clan loyalty, and staged display, with well crafted deftness.

The clan's men sat at the narrow neck of the spur that linked them with Nondugl's road system. They called out to their kinsfolk for help and listened, theatrically, for the answer. Eventually there was a response. Singing and yodelling could be heard faintly in the distance. It took an hour before the visitors were sighted and another hour before they reached their destination.

The Komunkas continued to sit patiently at the boundary of their land while the visitors advanced, then retreated, and is if to tantalise the waiting people still further sat down to rest as soon as they could be seen. Then they burst into the open space between the groups in a sudden surge of bellicosity #3 and just as dramatically sat down.

They carried with them, woven into large mats displayed on poles, huge quantities of bank notes. These were carefully presented and many Komunkas were moved to tears. The man who was to kill Dick Thiele was sobbing openly.

Help had arrived but it was not enough. Only 1,600 dollars was handed over and although the formal eating of ceremonially presented pig meat to seal the arrangement continued as if all was well the Komunkas were disturbed.

The din from an agitated administrative system was relentless. Helicopters charted by the Department of Lands thumped rhythmically over Bonong and Kumbala so that top men could see that the plots, and the Komunkas, were not words on a piece of paper.

The Development Bank frustratingly refused to accept a revised offer of 3,600 dollars and the District Commissioner sent an urgent message to Port Moresby recommending that the land should be sold at whatever price the Government thought was within Komunka capacity.

In the midst of this Ian Douglas was transferred. Cunning Kaibelt Diria had solicited this favour because the ADC believed access to adjacent white enterprise and expertise was essential if expanding local coffee and tea businesses were to thrive and in pursuit of this had emphasised the financial and structural advantages of continued expatriate presence.

In contrast the MHA, who thought Ian was pro-settler to a degree that prejudiced local people's chances of winning the increasingly critical tug-of-war between expatriates and locals over plantation land, had cashed in twice. He had rid himself of a senior Kiap who thought broad fronted economic development could be best advanced if Europeans continued to contribute to core infrastructure, and re-secured political support in the Nondugl area as well.

After Ian left the pressure died down. The Komunkas continued to accumulate cash and also lost one of their clan, Muli, who drowned while fording the Wahgi on the way to deposit another three hundred dollars in their bank account at Minj. Unlike wealthy village groups they did not own a pick-up truck.

Dick Thiele shelved his plans for Bonong, the Development Bank could find no other buyer, and the land's ownership was still in suspense when I left the Wahgi in April 1973.

Most white settlers were suspicious and some were hostile. The latter described me as a *kanaka* lover, a term with unpleasant connotations, because they thought I had leaned too far towards the Komunkas.

The breaking up of escalating skirmishes between the Kambilikas and the Tangilkas had been simple, if robust, mediation between the two groups by a neutral civil servant and Kiap government was good at that.

But the tumult surrounding Bonong was an earth shaker. It was yet another signal that Kiap administration in the Highlands of PNG was about to end and had unnerved white settlers in the Wahgi Valley because their expectations of being able to live and work there permanently had to be eternally shelved.

A year earlier a District Commissioner had been murdered after he had tried to intervene in a difficult land dispute near Rabaul in New Britain..

The political impact was impossible to exaggerate since it confirmed that possession of a white skin, the bedrock of Kiap authority because it underlined unbreachable administrative neutrality as well as support through the Australian government's formidable technical and financial prowess, was no longer enough to prevent its owner, whatever their station and whatever the circumstances, from being killed by village people.

Then the impregnability of the administration's on-going land development plans, still considered by many to be benevolent, were further undermined when a group of Wahgi Valley clansmen threatened to kill a white planter and were offered official sympathy instead of being punished.

The intermittent murder of European civilians in Port Moresby and other PNG townships since the 1960s had already demonstrated that in an urban environment a white skin was no longer the equivalent of a weapon-proof suit of armour.

The confusion surrounding Bonong revealed that long established white planters in comparatively undeveloped rural areas could no longer consider themselves to be armour plated either.

One morning Paula thought her bump was about to burst. We checked with a colleague's wife, who nodded solemnly, then took a second opinion from a doctor at the Nazarene Mission hospital in Kudjip, who advised a drive directly to the maternity hospital in Mount Hagen rather than return home.

She arrived there knowing no one, the doctor pushed me out of the room, and Daniel was delivered an hour later. When I returned that evening Department rules required me to be with an official driver – in this case Mapa Dei who came from a nearby village. Paula was pleased to see us and Mapa thought the baby had inherited my big nose. (*Em i gat gutpela nus bilong yu.*)

I wanted to wet Daniel's head – it is something uncertain first-time fathers feel obliged to do – so rather than have him feel awkward by going into the posh end of the nearby hotel we went to the main, essentially natives-only, bar instead.

The beer had only just arrived when a plummy English voice demanded to know why I wanted to "slum it". My eyes widened because I was the only European in the room. "Prefer to be among the low life?" it asked – this time with a mocking, teasing touch to its tone.

The speaker was John Kamp, a young man from Hagen who had been educated to graduate level in Australia and was already well known among Europeans in the Western Highlands because he was finding it difficult to be taken seriously, or secure a worthwhile job, after returning home.

He explained, in perfect colloquial English, he was fond of a multi-coloured jacket but no longer wore it because the disappointment of his current circumstances mocked the vividness of long-held aspirations and the technicolour ambition of his dreams.

This dislocation between an established community and its recently returned, most educated, young people was at the same time common in rural Northumberland after the advancement of a new secondary school system at the beginning of the 1960s.

Even in the mid-1950s children attending the two roomed village school at Slaley sat at their desks right through to their fifteenth birthday – unless they passed their eleven-plus, better known as the grading exam, and took their place in the Grammar School at Hexham.

There were so few of the latter that even after similar schools at nearby Healey, Whitley Chapel, Minsteracres and Blanchland were included, numbers covering twenty years since the outbreak of the Second World War could still be counted on the fingers of two hands.

It was not until 1957 that children over thirteen began to finish their last two years at the Secondary Modern, which was at Hexham too, and soon afterwards all children over eleven took this route as well.

In the early 1960s access to both the Grammar School and a new high status Technical School at Haydon Bridge, five miles west of Hexham, became easier and each opened the way to university or college training. Throughout this period most of Slaley's pupils passed their grading exam and one year all four of its eleven year olds succeeded.

The community, not just their parents, was pleased but that was before they had to take account of improved education's impact on family and village structure a little more than ten years later.

Some of these young people, most of them males and especially if they were an eldest son whose family had a farm, returned home as sixteen or eighteen year olds but there were other boys, and many girls, who went to university or college in distant cities, secured a qualification, took a job in yet another city, then married there, and were only seen at home for weddings and funerals.

Those who returned to the community after their education faced difficulties too. Accents had to be modified while they were away, mainly so they could be sure that people whose ears were not tuned to West Northumberland pronunciation could understand them, and so they were accused by some of being hoity-toity or posh.

Many endured the derisory label "College Boy" or "College Girl" for years and for men in particular it could only be overcome through open fisticuffs or by almost total withdrawal.

Hexhamshire and Slaley section of South-West Northumberland in 1960's

This road roughly follows the route of the Roman Wall (Hadrian's Wall)

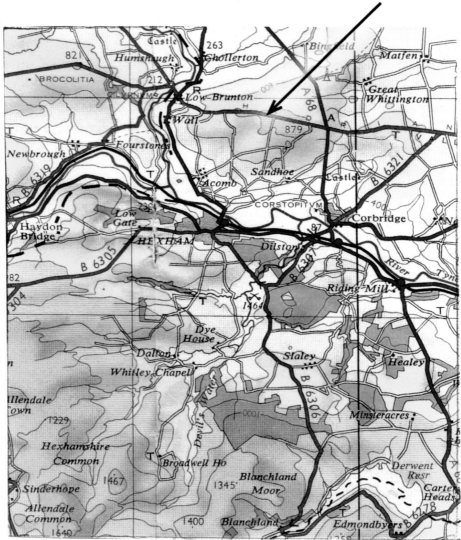

Distance Hexham to Blanchland approximately ten miles

© Ordnance Survey – North East England – Sheet 9

Few college or university educated Papua New Guineans were returning to their villages – not least because there was little, if any, work and their problems were compounded if they married, as young people inevitably will, someone they were working with but came from another of PNG's extraordinarily diverse communities.

This culture gap could prove difficult to bridge. There was no common language apart from English or Pidgin, parents-in-law followed rules established by radically different traditions, quarrels about the direction the upbringing of children should take, and which customs they should adopt, could be fierce – and so initial separation rates were catastrophic.

The fathers and mothers of primary school pupils selected at Bundi to attend High School on the Madang coast were just as pleased at their advancement as those at Slaley but they too would have realised, eventually, that education had wrenched their children from them and the place they would take in their lives would be quite different from expectations nurtured immediately after their babies had been born.

#1 Kiap government required clan groups to build a Rest House in their village which could be used by Kiaps and officials who were on patrol. They were usually two roomed with a private section specifically for sleeping. The main space was used for eating but often served as a meeting place as well. They tended to be taller than traditional buildings so the occupants did not have to crouch.

#2 I have employed a Kiap's discretion by not naming, or describing, this man. He was quiet instead of noisy, committed rather than angry, and while he may have privately regretted the obligations thrust on him by his clan brothers he was determined to follow them through.

#3 Even though the Oganas were delivering gifts, the final charge as they swept up to the seated Komunkas had been spectacularly aggressive.

Some of the bush knife cuts, aimed at exposed necks, were dangerous because if hand and wrist control had not been superb someone's throat could have been slashed.

I often wondered whether the apparent inability of Highland men to express themselves in any way other than unified, and spectacular, group belligerence has handicapped their progress.

The only exception I was familiar with were the Goroka Mudmen whose dance celebrated the strange circumstances of distant post-fight survival instead.

I have wondered too whether Europeans, and then local administrators, were also guilty of encouraging this barely controlled bellicosity because they did not direct moves towards other, less antagonistic, forms of group expression instead.

Mock battles, which could look like poorly disguised practice sessions, were used on most ceremonial occasions – even the opening of new Council Chambers or the appointment of an in-coming churchman.

There should have been an alternative to the carefully choreographed waving of spears and shaking of axes or bows and arrows.

CHAPTER EIGHT

An ill-advised display of Sub-District Office strength

"Masta, what is this thing Self-Government?"

Kaiyer Auwin, Milep Rest House, Minj Sub-District, September 1972.

In 1933 Kaiyer Auwin, like most other young Wahgi warriors, was proud of his strength, confident of his abilities, and belligerent in defence of anything he considered his own. He was the son of a big man in the Omgarl clan and lived near a hamlet called Milep in the tangle of hills behind Nondugl.

Word had reached them that an unusually large group of men were travelling west towards them. Strangers were enemies so Kaiyer, and his warrior age mates, turned out in fighting gear, moved to where they could watch the trail and, if possible, attack. Each man was dressed to appear fierce and, because the interlopers might be dangerous, had been careful to eat food, and respect taboos, which kept them strong.

Kaiyer, who was tall and muscular, had smeared his body with a thick layer of soot and ash. When he finished he was jet black and because of

115

this believed he was less likely to be wounded or killed. Using a bowl of water as a mirror he had put on his shaggy cassowary skin headdress and just as carefully tested the handle of a large wooden shield. Its painted symbol was bold and impressive.

He selected cane arrows designed to kill humans or pigs, checked the strand of bamboo that would string his bow, and with a nine foot, barbarously barbed *kulang* (spear) added to his weaponry, set off with his companions.

As they ran their headdresses streamed behind them and the huge muscles on their calves and thighs knotted, then relaxed, as with the ease of the mountain born, they moved quickly across the slope. Kaiyer looked about him and felt invincible. His clan brothers were awesome in their mud, soot and ochre. He was seized by their momentum. What force could possibly stand before them?

The group hid themselves and waited as a line of strangers approached. They looked for weapons but none could be seen. Some of these men were draped in black and among the others were four who were unsettling because they had red skins. Trailing these were people like themselves carrying what he thought might be pig carcases on poles slung over their shoulders.

They were unusual. They were troubling. Were the red skinned men evil spirits? Were they ghosts? The Omgarls followed the intruders and attacked in mid-afternoon as they prepared to camp.

When the signal came Kaiyer shot off two arrows and with his companions raced madly down the slope. When his ears began to sing with the wind of his descent he once again felt invincible. Dodging between standing trees he raised his spear and began to select a target.

Suddenly a red hole was punched through the back of a clansman who was running in front of him. Blood, muscle, and other mess dribbled down a tree trunk and Kaiyer could see the man was dead. Standing now, his spear arm limp, he saw another stumble past with a huge wound in his thigh, so, still not understanding what had happened, Kaiyer dropped his shield, turned, and ran howling back to the safety of the bush.

Almost forty years later I waited for him to finish his story. A patrol had been taken to Milep and Omgarl leaders had crowded into the village Rest House (*Haus Kiap)* which had become a meeting place.

Kaiyer, now an old man, inarticulate through laughter, tears streaming down his cheeks, and still shaking his head to emphasise disbelief that his transformation from invincible to conquered could have been so sudden, sat on the floor beside me. He lit a newspaper wrapped cigarette, waited till it was drawing, and continued his tale.

It covered all four decades. After recovering sufficiently to respond to friendly gestures from the strangers he was given a white neck ring by Jim Taylor, who led the exploration, told to stop fighting with his neighbours, and on pain of retribution not to let the Omgarls attack other incoming expeditions. #1.

When the clan was considered cooperative a policeman was left with them. Under his direction they cut down bush. They had no idea what they were doing, just followed instructions, but could see they had made a line which dipped through Milep's foothills. #2

Eventually along the road, for that is what it was, and again from the east, came a string of pack horses. These heralded the arrival of many life shifting imports, which with prescient symmetry included penicillin as well as the pox, that were introduced through that first, slim connection with the commercial and cultural tumult that thrummed throughout the wider world. #4

Kaiyer later exchanged his white ring for what he called a Red Penny, another badge of office, and became the Luluai – a village spokesman who helped organise labour to work on roads and airstrips, or build schools and health centres. New Kiaps came and went, all of them increasingly less dependent on the deterrent of their firearms, and the latest in that forty year chain was myself.

He stressed again, and then again, he could scarcely believe the changes he had seen. His people had not fought seriously with neighbours for more than twenty years, they felt free to walk where they willed, and were not harmed when crossing a stranger's land. Their children were numerous and the variety of their food, and standard of their comfort, was inconceivable to an old man such as he. He repeated that if he thought back to the old days, and then considered his current circumstances, he could not believe such a radical transformation was possible.

"It was Jim Taylor who brought this to us," he said. "When he led in his patrol from the hills towards Goroka he pulled after him everything I've described."

"Are you pleased he came?" I asked.

Kaiyer leaned forward and put his hand on my knee. I looked directly into his rheumy eyes.

"Of course I am," he replied. "He brought us all the things we have now, but Masta, what is this thing Self-Government?"

In May 1972 Michael Somare had given the white dominated civil service, and many of the people of his country, a collective heart attack when he announced that PNG would be Self-Governing from December 1st 1973.

Until then his civil servants had assumed it would not be introduced until after the 1976 elections with full independence trailing in sometime after that. However, constitutional right is might and almost immediately the huge weight of government resource concentrated on meeting that target.

A massive propaganda campaign was unleashed that placed heavy emphasis on national unity and collective purpose. Kiaps were told that everyone in their administrative areas had to be reached by foot, four wheel drive vehicle, launch, canoe or helicopter and be instructed, by us, that Self-Government was a very good thing.

It was a contradictory situation. White officers using patrol methods that had scarcely changed since Jim Taylor, which symbolised their style of government, were to tour villages and tell their inhabitants that European administration was about to come to an end.

Older Wahgi people were already worried that a white exodus would signal a return to the anarchy of pre-contact days. Not so widely acknowledged was that after enjoying a lift in living standards, and becoming familiar with some of the skills that lay at the core of newly introduced western systems, numerous younger Wahgis saw continued white presence as an obstacle to lifetime progress.

Nor was it commonly known that some of the most aggressive young men anticipated the removal, by force if necessary, of not only white planters but perhaps even police and patrol officers who upheld a system that suppressed the noisy individual belligerence, which came naturally to many Highlanders, and undermined their chance of building a lucrative local reputation as a traditional strong-man too.

When the villagers of the Wahgi Valley heard Michael Somare's announcement on their transistor radios their settlements had begun to buzz and hum.

Rumour and counter rumour dominated their discussions with fear and greed the contesting emotions in community meetings that could pitch father against son and the cautious against the rash.

It was against this turbulent background that Nigel Van Ruth, the new ADC at Minj, elected to kill two birds with one stone. He had been ordered to launch political education patrols to calm villagers' nerves, but also take account of a lift in law breaking, as well as the swelling undercurrent of anti-planter sentiment sweeping across most of the Wahgi Valley, and so he set out to combine political education with a revived display of Sub-District Office strength.

This meant that in June 1972 Nigel, a big, thick limbed, unyielding Dutchman, assembled a patrol, which was the biggest demonstration of Kiap power to tour the Wahgi bush since Jim Taylor's arrival in 1933 – and was therefore paradoxical because it mirrored exactly the style of administration it was emphatically promising would soon be phased out.

It took 132 days #3 to travel through twenty central collecting points and in that time had direct contact with 20,980 adult people. It was a perplexing endeavour moving through a time of profound political upheaval and, because it lasted as long as it did, had to adjust to events, and then re-adjust, as yet more unforeseen political considerations emerged.

It survived the explosive criminal trial of Nigel, its initiator, for distressing local people, the open opposition of Minister of Posts and Telegraphs, Kaibelt Diria, and attempts by many Wahgi people to use it as a rallying point against the Somare government.

I was nominally the Officer in Charge but for the first month it was run by Nigel whose wish to project it as an overwhelming affirmation of Kiap government was obvious. When we set out it was staffed by one

ADC, two Patrol Officers, two interpreters, three policemen, a council tax collection team that included clerks and an appeals tribunal, three Department of Agriculture staff and two teams from the Department of Public Health who were checking out leprosy, TB and VD.

When the patrol arrived at its first call, Molka village, Nigel strode imperiously at its head to be received by a nervous group of local leaders who welcomed it with a huge assembly of gifts.

There would have been more than a tonne of food, which not only reflected the scale of the patrol but established a pattern too. Ostentation in gift, dance and displays of loyalty to the Kiap were the up-front reaction to an equally emphatic show of Kiap power that focussed heavily on demonstrating unwavering concern over village, and villager, welfare.

Some Kiaps have described formalities surrounding flag raising and attendant speech making as the bullshit and hoped that after these routines were concluded more productive grassroots contact could begin – but on this section of the patrol the so-called bullshit flowed. As a result its real business, which was to stabilise village expectations and align village outlook with realistic fact, was either sidetracked or overwhelmed.

One of Nigel's first refinements was the re-introduction of an armed police drill when the Australian flag, which the patrol was still flying, was lowered at 6pm each evening. So it was no surprise that resurrection of a display which reminded the people of the historic Kiap link with .303 rifles buttressed emerging suspicions that he was keen to reinforce the status-quo – which in turn implied an alternative to the Somare government.

His previous post had been at Laiagam, a remote area far to the west, where the thump of Kiap boots on the backsides of local people had been background music to his management style. He continued this

121

approach in the Wahgi, combining it with an old fashioned take on the maintenance of law and order, which concentrated on imprisoning anyone who stepped out of line.

Many villagers interpreted this as further proof that Nigel was a defender of old style administration and the patrol quickly became a roadshow during which many a Wahgi grandfather, cradling many a Wahgi grandson, chuckled in the child's ear and told him it was just like the good old days.

A mock battle was always staged to welcome its arrival. Entire clans turned up in tankets and feathers to be censused and pay their tax. A suggestion that it might be a good idea to repair a pot-holed section of road would result in a stream of feather, grass, and leaf clad younger men immediately racing to the offending spot with their spades held like spears. They would return excitedly to the camp at the end of the day with the work completed.

Nigel, a gazetted magistrate, also set up a court and began hearing a string of cases, which saw a flood of convicted prisoners leaving the village for jail at Mount Hagen. To maintain this re-declaration of Kiap authority the patrol's policemen slogged constantly to feed his mincer. Any offence, tax dodging, failure to attend the census, assault, minor theft, and petty misdemeanours usually resolved at village level had only one result – conviction.

If an offender did not give himself up immediately after his name was publicly called, his house would be raided at midnight and if that was unsuccessful he would be harried until caught sometimes as much as a week later. Rewards were introduced. Ten dollars a capture. Posses were soon drafted. "If we are hard now it will save time and effort in the next village," he explained.

The stream of detainees continued until Nigel, who was unhappy at losing so much manpower, decided to remand them to the patrol itself and for many weeks it trailed an illegal contingent of prisoners, all wearing official *kalabus* (prison) laplaps, and fed with gifted garden produce. Most worked on road repairs.

It was difficult to assess the impact of the overnight revival of methods that had flourished in the early 1960s on people who at night were debating the implications of Self-Government.

The dominant sentiment appeared to be acceptance – if not outright goodwill. There could be no doubt that at village level the patrol was mainly welcome. Sophisticates, including one young teacher who had fought Kaibelt Diria in the House of Assembly elections, endorsed its methods too. Social irritations that had tormented villagers for some time were eased with the arbitrariness that was a pillar to Nigel's philosophy.

Half-educated youths, too tutored to soil their hands but not too proud to steal money, were handed to the patrol and joined the road squad. Other offenders who had undermined community harmony were also produced. It was obvious that at least one consequence of post 1950s contact was a decline in internal discipline at clan level. Hardworking people were preyed upon by young, often idle, thieves who shared their village life but over whom the traditional system was losing control.

Other sections of the patrol's operation were well received too. The medical team's examination of everyone who stood before it was universally popular and agricultural staff gave practical demonstrations on how to maintain yield by pruning coffee bushes as well as outlining the most effective method of drying beans.

It took a full day for each sub-clan to move through because every family had first to pass the census desk to record births, marriages and deaths, and then volunteer information covering the depth of their commercial enterprises and personal savings, before being passed on to the Council Tax team which took a poll payment from each adult, and then the police who were sifting for troublemakers.

The core activity was an address on Self-Government. Before the updating of their census records began, the people who had been called in that day sat down to listen to a delivery that stressed the need to uphold the law, the benefits of self-rule, and the advantages of growing good coffee.

We emphasised, as we had been instructed, that this did not mean the disappearance of white Kiaps (which we already suspected was unlikely to be correct), that the Australian government would continue to support PNG through direct grants, and that members of the Somare government were capable people who disliked lawlessness and were prepared to be harsh in their pursuit of internal stability if necessary.

If Nigel's initiative had been launched ten years earlier it would have been considered first class in all quarters Papua New Guinean and European. However, there were glaring inconsistencies between the latest shifts in the political climate and attitudes dominating activity within the patrol itself.

Vivid among these was Nigel leaving to meet Michael Somare who was making a series of nationwide, whistle stop, introductory visits. His final instruction was to keep the illegal prisoners out of sight. "Perhaps it would also be wise," he suggested, "to remove their *lap-laps* so they will not be recognised if anyone comes to check."

Another was him being innocent of any thought there might be an angry reaction after despatching a policeman in a Sub-District Office Landcruiser to bring Kaibelt Diria to a meeting at which he intended to expose village opinion that could influence the increasingly confident

MHA's vote in the House of Assembly.

The ADC was without doubt trampling over emerging political sensitivities although the ease with which he was at the same time able to advance other administrative initiatives was impressive. It was also obvious that the political environment he was nurturing would be intolerable to Kaibelt and was ultimately at odds with the patrol's primary purpose, which was to ease in Self-Government, as well.

Eventually the inevitable happened and he overstepped himself. A centrepiece of his patrol technique was to dissuade village people from casting covetous eyes on land occupied by Europeans by demonstrating the government's superior weaponry.

This was an inheritance from contact days when Kiaps used rifles to shoot a pig, or put a bullet through a line of shields, to confirm their exceptional firepower and persuade villagers that peaceful acceptance of their presence was the sensible option.

Assembled men and women were told that if they tried to occupy a plantation, tear gas would be used to drive them off. Jiggling a canister in his hand, Nigel would exaggerate its effects by describing a mob assaulted by so much pain that its collective eyes would dribble down its many cheeks or, at the very least, bulge from their sockets like "a chicken's arse after it had laid an egg".

The climax of this performance focussed on a flare pistol. Describing it as the latest addition to the daunting range of new weapons available to both Kiaps and police, he claimed it could be used to burn houses from comfortably beyond arrow range.

At each venue he whipped it out and discharged a pink ball, which lifted like a tired Roman Candle above the heads of the people, before falling with a hiss in damp *kunai* grass. It was always trailed by an unconvinced, but polite, murmur that came mainly from seated women.

His self-generated crisis came when he pursued this demonstration during a ceremony in which the Tsengelaps were participants, that had nothing to do with the patrol, and had been organised by the Minister of Posts and Telegraphs himself.

His trial in Mount Hagen's District Court was political. He was charged, at Kaibelt's insistence, with unnecessary provocation of the Tsengelap people. Although he was eventually found not guilty his career in PNG was all but over and for the second time in four months the Minj office was without an ADC.

If the Wahgi people had been asking themselves who had most muscle in the new Self-Government era, the MHA or the ADC, the answer had been emphatic. A word in the ear of the Police Superintendent in Mount Hagen, and another to the District Commissioner, meant that despite the scale of his patrol, its improvised courts and the bluster surrounding the flare gun, Nigel Van Ruth ADC had been removed by Kaibelt with only a little more effort than would have been required for the expulsion of an errant child.

After this humiliation it was rare for any senior Kiap, in any part of PNG, to stick their head above the parapet by administering their region with hardline authority that might attract unfavourable comment from local politicians.

It, and similar events in other areas, combined to provoke a hiatus in which a number of long service Kiaps, many of whom had been unremittingly forthright during their early work, decided it was more important to maximise their post-independence redundancy payment and accumulate as many additional service days as was possible instead.

The most cautious stopped in their tracks while many, although by no means all, sat pinned to their office chairs because job survival, not positive administration, had become the dominant mantra. A period of non-government, not just Self-Government, was beginning to emerge as administrative caution, not administrative necessity, ruled the day.

#1 That track eventually became a section of the Highlands Highway, which after much work by local people with shovels, then by drivers with machines, and many successive up-grades was, in the 1960s, able to carry juggernaut lorries from the coast right through to Mount Hagen.

#2 Venereal disease was rife in the Wahgi Valley but could be cured by three successive daily injections with three ccs of penicillin. There was no stigma among the local people, who were relaxed about casual sexual behaviour, and any reference to a course of "three ccs" invariably triggered laughter among young men because the recipient had obviously been a bit of a lad.

#3 The 132 days were not continuous. There was a ten day break, after Nigel was charged and some staff, including myself, returned home for an occasional weekend.

CHAPTER NINE

"You cannot fly the thief"

*"Hurrah, Hurrah, we bring the Jubilee,
Hurrah, Hurrah, the flag that makes you free"*

Marching through Georgia.

Flag symbolism was not lost on the Mid-Wahgi people. The Australian flag introduced by Jim Taylor, and flown in front of their Haus Kiap by every government patrol since, confirmed that "Pax Australiana", with its attendant social and economic benefits, would continue.

In contrast, the new PNG emblem highlighted the re-appraisal challenge being forced on villagers compelled to take a huge collective step in a new direction.

With the ringing example of parliamentary ascendancy over the once all-powerful Kiap still reverberating up and down the valley it was decided to reinforce this message and introduce the new flag as soon as the second, non-Nigel, section of his patrol got underway.

Mount Hagen's Police Superintendent had confiscated its rifles. However, after making a case for the advantages of consistency, the police were once again able to carry them and so in this respect the patrol's new, Papua New Guinea flag flying ritual would be no different from the section that had been conducted exclusively under the Australian banner. It was also decided to fly both flags simultaneously and spring the initial doubling up as a surprise.

I was in the Rest House sorting through census books after arriving at Bolimba, the re-vamped patrol's first call, when Kapuli, an interpreter, came to the door, told me the pole was ready, and asked if he should once again look after the flag before it was raised. I reached behind me and took two cloth bundles off a table. The first was a familiar blue, I hoisted it into his waiting hands, and he turned to go.

"Wait," I said. "There's something else," and lobbed an alien red and black package at him. He groaned, caught it, made as if to throw it on the floor, stopped himself, turned to face me and hissed, *"Bilong wonem?"* (Why?)

"Bring the police," I said and when they came I told them we would soon be raising the new flag, and I wanted it to be treated with the same respect as the old one. "Understand?" I barked. *"Yesa,"* they chorused but there was not much conviction.

In the open area in front of the Rest House a huge crowd had assembled. It was a bright afternoon and the dust it kicked up swirled at waist level. Tall warriors jingled past swigging store-bought lemonade from small bottles and trying to hold onto their weapons at the same time. Their wives sat under the thin shade of three large casuarinas. Toddlers tumbled in the dirt while unmarried girls, their heads crowned with a rig of red feathers, giggled in groups.

Old men with large hats on their bony heads, and little else to cover their scrawny limbs, chewed their gums in the shade of some coffee bushes.

Mature men milled around in their Sunday best of clean white shirt and freshly washed shorts.

In central position was the naked flag pole. Beyond it stood a mini-mountain of food arranged so that the heads of the pig carcases, huge taro roots and an avalanche of sweet potato formed an attractive pattern, highlighted by the contrasting colours and texture of passion fruit, *pit-pit*, bananas and pineapple. This elaborate construction was framed by sugar cane stems – some beaded with live chickens strung up by their legs.

Sitting at its base were the leaders of Bolimba's Danga clan, old Luluais still proud of the badges strapped to their foreheads, modern Councillors, and the man they had nominated to give the welcoming speech.

As we left our hut and walked across the dusty ground towards them a formation of warriors broke from behind some trees and swept towards us flourishing spears and chanting their war song. They stopped about five feet from me jogging on the spot and at the same time passing their weapons about my body – some within inches of my face and throat. This unusual proximity, which was a deliberate test to see if I would flinch, was uncomfortable. I was a long way from Northumberland.

The #1 spear dancing continued for some time. I waited, surrounded by the brittle clack of colliding wood, either looking directly into the eyes of the slightly maddened men in front of me or, for much needed relief, over the swirl of waving feathers towards a green sweep of bush and the rolling mountains beyond. With a collective yell they backed off and laughed as they stood panting.

A Wahgi warrior with his distinctive kulang spear. © Ian Douglas.

The orator began and I stood in the sun with an interpreter at my elbow as he wound his way through the formalities of welcome. When it was my turn to speak I prowled around the inside of the seated circle gesticulating forcefully to drive each point home. The road work that had been earmarked was carefully listed; I also nominated the day each sub-clan should come for census and Council Tax payment then told them about the teams from the Department of Agriculture and Department of Health too.

It was a carefully contrived performance and because everything had to be interpreted from Pidgin into *tok ples* would have taken an hour to deliver. Then I asked the police to raise the flags.

The Danga people were stunned. The women began a keening aye-aye-aye while the men's eyes popped. A sudden buzz among the seated leaders signalled activity. Several advanced determinedly and one stood directly in front of me. I turned to the police telling them, firmly and publicly, they had to hold onto the flag ropes at all costs and that no one was to touch the pole. With the new duet fluttering above us I turned to listen to the man who would make his clan's challenge.

He was unwaveringly direct, telling me he did not want to see the new flag, he called it a thief (*stilman*), on a pole which was standing on land belonging to his people. He did not want to be governed by incompetent black men who came from the coast near Port Moresby, and he was prepared to offer the permanent hospitality of the Danga clan to myself, or any other Kiap, if they chose to remain. He made clear he would like to tear down the imposter on the pole, rip it to shreds, and scatter its rags to the four winds.

I told him the new flag demonstrated his people were no longer bush savages (*bus kanakas*) but sophisticated individuals who grew coffee, owned and drove pick-up trucks, and enjoyed a high standard of living. I stressed Sub-District Office determination to continue the patrol and made clear that, in future, officers of the Chief Minister's Department would be resolute in their pursuit of criminals, encouragement of economic activity and help with the maintenance of roads.

All the emphasis in this extended, relentless delivery was on continuity within the country-wide effort to fuel yet more economic advancement, and progress village wellbeing, at both local and national level. It was a percussive performance – not unlike hammering home a long nail.

He knew he was beaten but was still defiant. "If that is the case," he replied, "the flag can stay but I want you to know I do not like it." He spat the last words. The group waiting to attack the flag pole stepped back, then most of the food was divided between patrol staff and the elderly leaders from other clans who, because they were a steadying influence, had been encouraged to continue to travel with us.

At 6pm, and strictly by the book as Nigel had taught me, I snapped a series of commands at the blue uniformed, rifle swinging, boot thumping policemen in front of me while the interpreter lowered both flags, rolled them up, and took them back to his hut where a fire glowed red and an evening meal was bubbling.

Only a European Kiap could have pulled that off. There should be no doubt the PNG flag, the *stilman*, survived its first outing in that section of the Wahgi Valley because of the authority of my white skin.

There were other, mainly token, attempts to destroy it later in the patrol and these were easily subdued. Only at Munumul, the Rest House for the main settlement of the always feisty Oganas, was a more serious effort made but it failed too.

Who knows what would have happened if it had been torn down? I was worried that if it had, villagers who were not Tsengelap or their allies would have used the incident as a focus for anti-Self-Government, even anti-Kaibelt Diria, opinion. Hostile feelings about his unexpected alignment with the Somare government were still being paraded and by saving the PNG flag from humiliation a swing in that direction may have been curbed because in late 1972 political equilibrium in the Wahgi Valley was fragile.

When patrolling I continued to visit other huts during the evening when fires burned, tobacco smoke was heavy, and the day's main meal was either being eaten or digested, so I could talk informally with the patrol's policemen as well as village leaders and the valuable posse of old Luluais.

I always thought it was better to do that than hole up with a Tilly Lamp and a novel and there was no better way than this informality of picking up some of what was actually being thought and said.

Gradually I became aware that more Wahgi people than I had suspected were unhappy at the contrast between their lifestyle and the standard enjoyed by the Wahgi's planters. This developing rift was founded on the age-old line between the haves and the have-nots as well as the growing undercurrent of resentment over land appropriation and land ownership, which rumbled and grumbled within Wahgi culture like a subterranean volcano.

When European businessmen came, on the invitation of the Australian government in the 1950s, to a fertile Wahgi valley made peaceful by a handful of .303 rifles, handcuffs, jail, and the swinging feet of the early Kiaps and their policemen, the people saw them as potential partners.

They hoped the settlers would be assimilated by their culture so European knowledge, and ability to generate wealth and earn money, would be dispersed throughout the clans.

As was the case on the southern side of the valley they had allowed the government to buy vacant low lying land and lease it to incomers. They did this believing the ground was still theirs, the payment they had been given was rent, and that one day they would be able to reclaim it.

Disappointment began to surface when planters kept their distance, fenced off this land, and were only seen if there was a complaint about pig trespass or other damage. This changed to bitterness, and then resentment as long years proved that most European settlers wanted to concentrate only on their businesses and expected local people to do the same.

Leaders of the Tsengelap clan, who represented a group that had sold land on which three successful plantations were operating, had already made this clear.

"We let the land go because we wanted to encourage the whiteman #2 to live next door. We wanted him to teach us how to become wealthy and to show us how to grow crops of our own.

We love this land. Our people have owned it for generations. We know the names of the small hills, the swamps and the streams. We know where our ancestors are buried and where their villages stood.

The whiteman has built a fence around it. It is a high fence and has barbed wire that will cut our skins if we go inside. We go to talk to this whiteman. We wait for him to come out and sit with us in the sun, but he shouts at us and if we do not go his dogs chase us.

We do not want his money back but we do want him to know that we would like to learn things from him. One day we took him a chicken but he did not return the gift.

We want our land back. We have no wish to be treated as a wild pig by a man who lives on our land. The only time we see him is when he comes to complain that pigs have rooted up his trees. If he can come to complain why can't he come to talk with us in our hut? We want him to go and leave the land to us but he is stubborn and will not listen."

The original statement was taken by Marie Reay in 1968 and repeated to me, when I was camped at the Tsengelap Rest House. It was a first class summary of the Wahgi people's position on land, and its ownership, in the period before Self-Government.

Clan leaders like Luluai Tsike (pale hat: centre) were troubled men when this picture was taken in 1972. They were not hostile to Kiaps, or their style of government, but were wracked with worry about the de-stablisation expected to be triggered by Self-Government and how this might affect their hopes that village issues over the ownership of land leased by expatriate planters could eventually be resolved.

The most disturbing feature of this anti-plantation sentiment was discussion on how land, and the business that stood on it, might be recovered by force. Some planters, and trade store owners, thought written hit lists were circulating. Village thinking was not quite as precise but some names and locations were repeatedly mentioned in these conversations and it was obvious the strings of restraint were no longer as tight as they had been.

Not only were some local people speculating over which Europeans were to be removed but also over how specific plantations were to be re-apportioned to individual clans. This division appeared to have been considered carefully and if I had been asked the direction this sentiment might have travelled in a worst case scenario I would have said the most likely series of events would have begun with the early morning appearance of a group of tribal leaders on a planter's lawn.

He would have been told he had a deadline, perhaps night fall, to remove himself, his family and any belongings he wanted to carry. If he agreed they would enjoy safe passage – but he would have also been told he had to leave his keyring on the kitchen table.

Planters always assumed that one of their number might be killed. It was certainly discussed at village level, mainly among young men, but the Wahgis, although warlike, preferred to minimise escalation during the initial stages of a dispute over land ownership and so a threat, and a deadline would, I think, have been the initial approach.

Nevertheless it was difficult to pin down exactly what the majority of Mid-Wahgi people thought Self-Government might bring because much of what they were saying was either inconsistent or ambiguous.

Older men like Kaiyer imagined it as a new patrol coming in from the direction of the Chimbu river, armed with an advanced weapon, and the ability to subjugate Kiap government as easily as Jim Taylor and his followers had subjugated them.

Another interpretation was apocalyptic with Australia and its representatives vanishing overnight leaving the Wahgis metaphorically naked, with nothing to prevent them from once again taking up their spears and a resuming never-ending rounds of pre-contact inter-clan fighting.

And a third popular image centred around a government-style patrol making an entrance from the east – but this time led by a frizzy haired Papuan #3 from Port Moresby.

137

Fantasising over the expulsion of white people contradicted the wish of many villagers to unite behind Kiaps, and the Kiap system, to maintain the status quo.

However, each was a reaction, admittedly divergent, to the same stimulus which was that de-stabilisation through Self-Government would, whether they liked it or not, be forced on them from December 1st 1973.

The patrol focussed on driving home the point that this was the inevitable conclusion to a process that had begun with the arrival of Jim Taylor, embraced the new inter-clan peace, covered the emergence of the House of Assembly, then Local Government Councils, coffee farming and the education of their children – all of which would continue to move forward.

And when census details covering the last of thousands of families were updated on October 24th 1972, after being in the field for more than four months, I thought it had succeeded in curbing speculation surrounding the takeover of plantations by suggesting that they would not have to wait many years before they could resume ownership by legal, not traditional, means – in other words possession might eventually be transferred through official channels and it would be orderly.

I learned about the intractability of inertia too. Census taking was always instructive. There was no better way to assess the mood, and general wellbeing, of a village group than by working with it to update family circumstances and, if the survey dug deeper, to be told by households about their private economic achievements and future plans.

Census was also a time when an ambitious man would take enormous pride in standing at the head of a line of progressively younger wives and the infinity of children that measured the likely direction of his family's economic fortune.

Polygamy could work. There was ample evidence that many senior wives were comfortable with their younger *susas* (sisters) – not least because the biggest family groups could feed the most pigs and therefore had the means to secure high social standing.

There were also times when a bitter first wife would rancidly denigrate their mutual husband with vanity and selfishness heading her list of publicly aired, and often entertaining, grievances.

And then despite the obvious wealth creation benefits polygamy could offer some couples were naturally monogamous. On occasions they might even be described, despite advancing years, as being devoted to each other, with husband, wife, and children cocooned within a skein of security and quiet affection.

Deaths were recorded by dragging a brutal line through the unfortunate's name, and births, which were always happier, by adding new babies to the family list.

Most names were traditional, beginning with K, like Kunjin, Kulam, Kombo and my own favourite for a girl which was Kundup – also used to describe a pale flower that grew among stone at higher altitudes and reminded me of Lady's Smock, one of the first meadow plants I had been taught to recognise at Houtley in the 'Shire. But some were bizarre and obvious evidence of the impact transistor radios were having too. Tslim Dasti (Slim Dusty the country singer) was one. Elvis and John Kennedy were among the others.

Deaths demanded attention. Was it old age, an accident, was it TB, or was it through pregnancy and childbirth? Scoring a line through the name of a child recorded only at the last census was always sad. As work in one village progressed I was deleting these regularly and my questioning was becoming more insistent.

Eventually I put down my pen, turned to its leaders, who were standing to one side of the table, and demanded to know if there was something wrong with their drinking water. (*"Aiting wara bilong yupela em i nogut tru!"*) They agreed immediately saying it was polluted by shit carried down from an upstream village and confirmed this was troubling them.

The mood was subdued. They were obviously aware of the long term consequences of this catastrophe and because no one was keen to see more baby's names deleted at the next census we cast around for solutions. It emerged that there was no other nearby source of drinking water, and boiling every drop demanded discipline that could not always be guaranteed, so the obvious answer was to up sticks and build a new village close to a spring or stream that was clean.

It was too much for them. I could only imagine the wrench to an otherwise comfortable status-quo this would create. Carefully arranged garden planting sequences would be disrupted. There could be new land occupation and hut location problems to resolve. Coffee currently close to home and easy to pick might become too distant. Perhaps not everyone would go and the clan might be fragmented? The list of problems was infinite.

In the end they decided they had to stay even though the price was the inevitable death of more babies – some of them being nursed even as we talked. That, I said to myself, is inertia. A phenomenon most generally centred on location, or reaction to a disastrous new development, that freezes constructive thinking. It is common to humanity, not just that distressed village group in the Wahgi Valley. I have come across it many times since.

1 A Wahgi warrior's spear dance is designed to raise them to peaks of aggression that can sustain a charge across open ground while under fire from enemy arrows.

2 The Wahgis call Europeans "red man" (*iambang*) because their skin burns in the thin Highland sun.

#3 Papua has always been associated with people carrying a big head of hair.

CHAPTER TEN

A good Kiap but a bad husband

"With ruin upon ruin, rout on rout,
Confusion worse confounded."

John Milton

Out in the bush I had a reasonably comfortable relationship with most local leaders. I could sit in their huts, make my cigarettes while they made theirs, and if a fire died down throw on a couple of sticks without breaking up the conversation.

But back in Minj the fundamental confusion created by the contrast between bush life and station life that I had first felt while cutting timber at Binaru returned.

At home I was a whiteman living in a big, three bedroomed bungalow, who employed Peter, a bachelor Southern Highlander who had been a carrier on the Kambia patrol, to help Paula by chopping firewood and pumping water.

I drank beer in the white patronised section of the hotel and could play snooker at the subscription-only Minj Club. On Sundays I might join a game of golf, tennis, or cricket and often shared conversations with other government employees, coffee buyers and planters.

As time progressed I was finding it increasingly difficult to feel at ease in white company. European conversation about Self-Government was spectacularly uninformed and so I was faced with either raising the temperature by dropping hints about what I had heard in the villages or leaning back and saying nothing.

I chose the latter because I enjoyed the casual bonhomie generated by social drinking and had no wish to undermine it. Sometimes I would look at the mountains, and what seemed immeasurably distant villages, over the top of my beer glass and feel a desperate need to discuss, preferably with someone older and wiser, what was happening out there – but the people I was with could do nothing to help.

The dominant clan in the settlements surrounding Minj was the Konumbugas. A routine joke within the Club was that local people were either Con'em boogers or Ordinary boogers. It was hard to get past that. In the end, and perhaps not surprisingly considering the time I spent on patrol, I found it easier to engage with the Wahgi people and their problems than I did with many of the Wahgi's white settlers. There were times I really did feel caught between two yawningly different cultures.

There were several reasons I was in this valley among tall, handsome, spear toting, feather dressed, Highland people and not on a windswept hill in Northumberland with sheep bleating beyond a drystone wall and curlews bubbling over rush strewn pasture – and one of these was money.

A Patrol Officer's salary was more, much more, than I could hope to earn in the UK and cash did interest me – which made me no different from almost every other European except Missionaries who only wanted to capture souls.

Even the High School pupils I stood in front of, after responding to an invitation from their teacher to contribute to their education by explaining my work, would suck in their breath when, after replying to the inevitable question, I confirmed a handsome pay cheque was important.

They, and the teachers who were influencing them, were hoping I preferred to be altruistic because the idea that Europeans who were interested in money were plunderers was embedding itself throughout the education system.

My counter was that it really was ideal when the job you liked was well paid too. I stressed the advantages of this combination and advised them to adopt this target when they launched their own careers.

I was also interested in earning extra income. In European terms Paula and I were unusually poor. I had earned nothing at Bundi, very little anywhere else, and this showed.

The only non-government – that means un-battered – furniture in our house was a record player and the first pair of overalls that Daniel wore were made from a pink and white striped *kalabus lap-lap* brought home from patrol after Nigel had been arrested.

Despite, in metaphorical terms, walking round in ragged trousers, my ambition was to build a savings pot. We began by selling eggs laid by chickens held in a coop in the corner of our garden for 2.5p (five cents) each and then kept pigs as well.

The latter began with the purchase of three piglets, and bags of high protein concentrate, from the Lutheran Mission. The venture appealed to me because the Wahgi people revered pigs, which took core position in their wealth exchange and compensation ceremonies, and I could not get out of my head the magic fact that when sold live they made almost 50p a pound.

That was an unbelievable sum. A four month old pig weighing about 200 pounds could earn £100 ($200). An inflation index calculator confirms that to be the equivalent of around £1,300 today.

In contrast with village pigs, which survived on low protein sweet potato and other garden products, mine grew like mushrooms. Word spread because their progress was phenomenal and it was not uncommon for a group of elderly clansmen, the tanket leaf *arse-grass* that covered their backsides rustling, to gather by the pen at the bottom of our garden to remark on their amazing transformation.

They thought the growth rates were genetic but the real fuel was their high protein diet. Village people called them "medicine-pigs" (*pik-meresine*), a phrase that carried a whiff of mystery within it.

One of the many people who were impressed with them was Jim Taylor's daughter Meg. Her mother was a Tsengelap so it was not a surprise when she clapped her hands delightedly and told me they were beautiful.

I secured other piglets, and their feed, for an interpreter's family but the experiment failed because the meal cost £10 a 25 kilo bag, say £130 at today's prices, and had to be fed almost ad-lib. Cowed by this expense they could only bring themselves to dole it out in daily handfuls and so their pigs grew at less spectacular, only traditional, rates.

When I cashed my first batch, and counted bills extracted from more folds than I thought possible by men who had no pockets because they did not wear shirts or shorts, I was so excited I brought back nine replacements, and also a dozen turkeys, which Peter, who was eternally cheerful, penned off in a spare corner of his *kuk-boi* accommodation.

He was an ideal employee. He fed the pigs and chickens, sold singleton turkeys and out-of-lay hens at the market, kept grass down, chopped wood for the cooking stove, pumped roof water stored in corrugated iron drums into the house system's header tank, washed dishes, boiled outdoor clothes, and sometimes mopped floors.

He was diligent, unassuming and, despite living in a huge, two-roomed house which could have attracted a crowd of *wan-toks* – clansmen who spoke the same language and to whom he would have been obligated – was only seen and never heard.

He surprised Paula, an upright Catholic, only once when he asked for the stump of new-born Daniel's umbilical cord. He wanted to protect the child by burying it after concluding a traditional post-natal ceremony. I gave him a big pig when we left and the last time I saw him he was tugging it towards a house where one of his clansmen was a *kuk-boi* too.

This search for money eventually backfired because I was selling to local people and this put me in the exploitative camp. It became obvious after I was able to buy a Toyota Landcruiser, a four wheel drive vehicle similar to a Land Rover, from a sympathetic friend at a deliberately low price. It was re-sprayed then polished and sold just two weeks later for a great deal more.

It was a long way short of being overvalued but the village man who bought it knew how much I had made. "You have taken a very good profit out of me," he remarked pointedly in English and left me thinking it might not be a good idea for a Kiap to be trading directly with local people.

That did not stop me buying another, this time at a more competitive price, sprucing it up, and putting it back on the market at what people back home would have called a keen offer. It was not the bargain the first had been. Its tyres were thin and the windscreen was cracked – but it was still a fair vehicle.

The purchasers this time were the Kisu clan from Kudjip and it was immediately obvious they were reluctant to meet the asking price. Eventually they produced their money, which I insisted on counting. It was well short of the total. They hoped I would accept the cash stacked in neat piles in the centre of the circle around which we sat.

I persisted with demands for the nominated sum, eventually they stumped up, and we shook hands. But the atmosphere was charged. I had sold good pigs to happy customers but the Kisus, who had the reputation of being an unusually argumentative group, were well short of being content.

Only days later they returned to re-negotiate. The Landcruiser swept into my drive, parked up, and they demanded their money back. The tyres were thin, they said and the windscreen cracked. They had overstepped their budget and did not think the vehicle was worth what they had paid.

A Kiap would have searched for a compromise; the vehicle was, after all, in good running order and only a third of the price of a new one. However, on this occasion I was a white man trying to skim profit from a tight investment, and the Kisus were pulling back from an arrangement which, according to my code, had been sealed.

They wanted a price reduction. If a relatively small amount had been refunded we may have been able to part with a degree of goodwill but the margin was already meagre. Instead I repeated that a deal had been struck, papers exchanged and money handed over. These were nontraditional arguments and the Kisus thought little of them.

Standing on my lawn, vexed, and perplexed, I had become another exploitative European at odds with local people over money. Eventually they backed into the vehicle and drove off. I too was unhappy. Moneymaking and maintaining harmony with local people was not easy to achieve and cannot, I think, be mixed. I did not trade another.

Uncertainty was compounded by the ever-present conflict between being a good Kiap and a good husband. Almost constant patrolling was a strain because Paula was often alone with Daniel, and one evening I had, unknowingly, driven her to tears.

It was a defining incident in other ways too. I was once again on patrol and camped immediately beside the Highlands Highway at Nondugl where I had just finished a mid-morning cup of coffee when news came in that Talu Bol, the most powerful leader in the area, was encouraging a group of weapon-carrying warriors to threaten a rival group which was beginning to line up in a similarly hostile position only a hundred yards away.

The quarrel centred on the abandoned tea plantation at Kumbala and its Chimbu squatters. I was dismayed because Talu was without doubt a man with a voice and the fight that was brewing was straddling the road. Lorries and pick-up trucks were slowly threading their way through the opposing clansmen and yet another example of deteriorating social structure, and waning government influence, was already hugely public.

He was the "bik-man", or leader, of people living in the eastern section of the North Wall as well as literally being a big man too. More than six feet tall, and with a formidable physique, Talu was second in village clout terms only to Kaibelt Diria MHA— although his base was not overtly political but deeply traditional instead.

Critically he was a fight leader of the old stamp who was said to be still in touch with earth magic. This made him a sorcerer, which meant he could take advantage of village thinking that was inaccessible to a Kiap and made it even more important he called his people off before the first arrows were released.

On top of this he was a hugely charismatic man in his own right who, because he was Vice-President of the Wahgi Local Government Council, was used to being approached carefully by both government officials and the Nondugl people. But that morning he had a Kumbala sized bee in his bonnet and I was not able to persuade him to calm down and call his clansmen off.

It was an impossible situation. A fight was building and instead of dousing the fire Talu was doing everything he could to stoke the flames. He was the problem, not the solution, so I decided to arrest him. Both patrol and locally based policemen, fearful of the consequences, clung to me, pulling me back as I moved forward, and I had to swing my shoulders to throw them off.

I had decided that if I ignored him there was no point in continuing to represent the Moresby government – or indeed working in PNG at all. To my inner amazement Talu came easily, allowing himself to be pushed with the help of just stiff fingers in the small of his back towards the police station, which was only a couple of hundred yards away, then locked in one of its cells.

Next step was to disperse the warriors and decide what to do with the prisoner who sat unmoving in his cell, head always down, and dominating his wooden bench like a brooding monolith. Would he demand to be released? Would there be an attempt to break him out? I decided it was best to take him to Minj – safely on the other side of the river where he would be out of sight.

149

But it was almost sunset before I had squared up patrol activity, could put him in the passenger seat of a Landcruiser, and drive off. After he was delivered to the police station I should have called in, even if for only for a short time, to see Paula but instead hurried back to Nondugl, because patrols camped next to main roads often lost staff who jumped onto passing *passandia kars* (informal taxis) so they could spend a night at home and were often not on hand for work the next day.

I felt bound to set a good example and so returned to camp immediately but Paula, who was once again seeing very little of me, had heard me drive past our house and was devastated.

What can I say in defence? First that my quick return to camp was noticed and second I did not think it would have been a good idea to be absent from Nondugl immediately after a man as important as Talu had been arrested. I had, probably not for the first time, been a poor husband at the same time as I had done my best to be a good Kiap.

He was jailed for riotous behaviour. I remain surprised he allowed himself to be arrested so easily. Was he unable to contemplate a public struggle with a white-skinned Kiap or was he faced with problems, centred on contentious Ogana plans to be sole re-occupiers of the derelict site at Kumbala, he thought might be resolved if he was temporarily off-stage after carefully contriving an enforced break?

To underline this creeping unease, I mismanaged a compensation ceremony arranged between these same Oganas and the Berubugas from Tombil on the other side of the Wahgi near Minj.

They were at loggerheads because a Berebuga had been killed in a traffic accident. He was a passenger in a vehicle driven by an Ogana man; it could have been a cousin or an in-law, but traditional payback rules applied just as surely to traffic deaths as they did to murder and so to avoid an eye for an eye payback for "killing" the Berubuga they had to stump up some cash instead.

I had arranged for the exchange to take place on a football pitch in the centre of Minj Station but underestimated the tension between the groups. It was still festering and nothing could be done to stop them turning up in full fight panoply with each side waving spears.

I had hoped that after publicly receiving compensation the Berubugas would have been able to bury the hatchet – and not in the back of someone's neck. But something had inflamed them, arrows were fired, and an open melee was avoided only because a score or so Oganas, who had been watching from the sidelines, advanced in a determined line, bows strung, and ready to fire.

These men were in shirts and shorts, but had carried weapons as a precaution, and were obviously prepared to join a fight. Parity in numbers was established, the Berubugas responded to this new threat by taking a defensive position, and the risk of Ogana clansmen being trapped inside a circle of spears had been lifted.

I had almost organised a battle and someone, perhaps more than one, could have been killed. More police arrived and the Oganas were shepherded towards the bridge where they could re-cross the Wahgi and go back to Nondugl. This was not easy because pre-contact animosity between people living on opposite sides of the river had been constant and the last thing they wanted was to give the impression they were retreating like lambs.

The new ADC, the third since I had arrived in Minj just over a year earlier, was tight lipped and unforgiving. The Oganas had taken half a dozen Berubuga women with them and next morning I was ordered to bring them back.

The sortie was successful but not straightforward. I drove to Nondugl and negotiated alone. All the important men were there and their welcome was careful at best. We sat in a circle, with perhaps thirty people in it, and reviewed events. It turned out the women were Oganas who had married Berubugas so were not clear-cut hostages. They may even have spent the night with their parents.

This made things less difficult but extracting a positive response was still not easy. Eventually an unseen signal must have been given and I was abruptly told the women were waiting by the Landcruiser so I could bugger off back to Minj and leave them to complete their discussion. It was a reprimand and only just fell short of being an order.

I had also been told that Kaibelt Diria, who was from the same side of the Wahgi, had raised tensions by warning that the Berubugas might seize an Ogana at the compensation ceremony and – this is how it was described to me – "let his blood flow over the traffic accident victim's grave".

If that was the case it could never have been successful and I began to suspect the Sub-District Office's peacemaking efforts had been sabotaged by the MHA, who remained keen to undermine positive Kiap government still further.

I was angry enough to challenge him. He denied it but nothing the Berebugas had said while we were making arrangements had signposted they would use the ceremony as bait to lure Oganas closer to their spears.

So, after a series of early successes, the weapon burning in Minj marketplace, the reduction in Komunka tension over Bonong, and the introduction of the PNG flag to North Wahgi, I was forced into personal stocktaking.

I was also worried about civil commotion, the government phrase for local revolt, on Self-Government Day. The mood in the villages continued to be erratic and I suspected that if there was trouble it would begin at Banz where younger Tsengelaps and Konjigas might decide to take over trade stores or plantations.

If they had, other clans could move in elsewhere, and there would be nothing that an understaffed District Office or the Royal Papua New Guinea Constabulary could have done to stop them – which meant that if the introduction of Self-Government was to be peaceful it would be decided in villages by the people themselves, and only by the people themselves, because if they had other ambitions the government would be helpless.

I would have been happy to stay if I was single but a secure family life did not mix with complex intercession between volatile village people and the new government's shifting demands. Kiaps depended on bluff, reinforced by the implicit authority, and neutrality, of their white skins to maintain control, and too much of what has happening undermined it.

I asked for a transfer from Minj to a position on the coast and was relieved when it came through. In April 1973 it was difficult to balance village expectations with the increasing limitations forced on Highland Kiaps by the advance towards Self-Government.

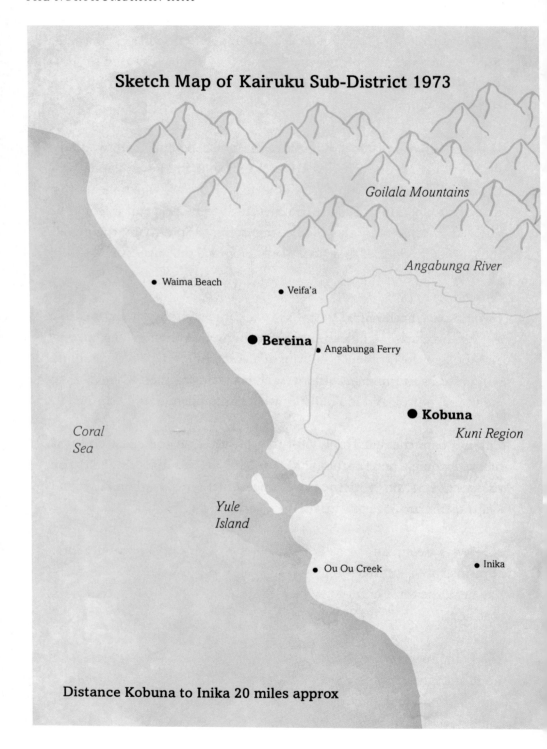

Sketch Map of Kairuku Sub-District 1973

Goilala Mountains

Angabunga River

• Waima Beach

• Veifa'a

● **Bereina**
. Angabunga Ferry

Coral
Sea

● **Kobuna**
Kuni Region

Yule
Island

• Ou Ou Creek

• Inika

Distance Kobuna to Inika 20 miles approx

CHAPTER ELEVEN

Self-Governing Mekeos

"It's too hot to work," they said and having won that argument refused to do any work unless they became bored with not working. The prisoners, not the warders, were in control.

Bereina Corrective Institution, Central District, July 1973.

Life is a cord made up of many threads. One of these is fate and it is often sardonic. I had left the Wahgi because I wanted to escape its many pressures and was transferred to Bereina on the western side of the Central District in Papua where there was no work.

Minj was beautiful. First and most vivid impressions of Bereina, administrative centre for Kairuku Sub-District, were the hammer-like heat, the dust, and the forest of desiccated dog turds that lined its roadsides.

The Wahgi people were handsome, fierce and direct. The Mekeos, who along with the Roro people dominated the population surrounding the Sub-District Office, had made themselves inscrutable and although tall could never be described as doughty.

155

At Minj you might see silhouetted against his mountains an impressive figure with a feather headdress and a spear. At Bereina the Mekeos, who teased their hair into huge Afro halos, were dandies more likely to be mincing in long *lap-laps* through the interminable dust of their flat, and airless, territory spraying casual mouthfuls of ever-present betel nut juice into the roadside grass – their stained lips compounding an already effeminate appearance.

The night air in the Wahghi was scented by frangipani and other flowers. At Bereina it lay like a hot blanket and seethed with the whine of a million mosquitoes. The Sub-District Office at Minj was busy and cheerful. The building at Bereina was a tired, dust covered, backwater ignored by the people and, it was hard to believe the administrative torpor that cloaked the station was so overwhelming, still flew a faded Australian flag.

In our bed we groaned if the station generator shut down before we were asleep because it turned off a ceiling fan and could condemn us to a restless night. And in the morning, already sweating since a lukewarm shower, I walked to work kicking powder over my polished shoes knowing there would be little for me to do when I got there. I felt I was being mocked.

Beyond the heat and dust the fundamental difference between the two localities was the people. Those in Bereina did not need a Kiap. The first Europeans had arrived at nearby Yule Island in 1885 so they had already adapted to white administration, milked out the bits they either needed or liked, and decided to resolutely ignore the rest.

Essentially, and in contrast with those living in the huge sections of PNG's mountainous interior where exposure to Western ideas and technology was still fresh, they, like most of PNG's coastal population, considered themselves more than ready for Self-Government – an attitude which underlined the already critical, geographical, coast-highlands split in national aspiration.

Mekeos lived in large villages which so clearly resisted intrusion they were effectively out of bounds to government personnel. Their focus was a carefully sited platform which caught whatever breeze was available, on which betel nut chewing men, who constantly rattled sucking sticks in the *kambang* gourds that held their lime, rested their backs against carved posts as they regulated activity within their miniature principalities.

The village they ruled was shaded by a long line of coconut palms and the hot dust between each house scored by the feet of naked children and the burrowing snouts of omnipresent pigs.

These people were comfortably off because they were linked by road to Port Moresby, their land was ideal for betel nut palm, and they owned transport which could be loaded with betel nut, coconuts, or vegetables and taken down the rutted road to PNG's capital city.

There they sat cross-legged under the shade of trees which lined its pavements hawking goods laid out in clusters before them. As they talked among themselves in their high pitched, vowel strewn language, and shook their ever present lime gourds, they exchanged with great casualness, and little animation, their carefully presented offerings for ever increasing piles of silver coins.

With money in their pocket, and an empty vehicle, they returned to their villages where they once again tugged at their hair with bamboo combs, chewed even more betel nut, and arranged thin legs under their long skirts on the village platform at the head of its street. Their lives were well sorted.

The material advancement of the Mekeos, and also the nearby Roros, was not flattering when compared with the Wahgis who had been exposed to Europeans, and their economic installations, for somewhere around sixty years less – although it was also clear these coastal people were satisfied with the progress they had made, and the self-sufficiency they enjoyed, while the more ambitious, much hungrier, Highlanders very obviously were not.

Mekeos still lived in villages where sanitation and cleansing was the province of pigs. These were, without doubt, an effective disposal unit. Patrolling Kiaps, who had retreated into handy vegetation, were on many occasions forced, with their pants round their ankles, to swat at over-enthusiastic porkers with a stick – but nothing had been found to remove pig dung which lay everywhere in black and shiny heaps.

They also endured plagues of mosquitoes, suffered from both malaria and tuberculosis, while dirty drinking water continued to be drawn from sluggish rivers or streams.

It was difficult not to compare this with the Wahgi where earth closets were almost ubiquitous and beginning to become sophisticated, very few villages had not been moved to more favourable locations, homes were beginning to be built with modern materials and, in an area where most of the water was already fresh, more villages had installed taps too.

Some comparisons are unfair. Sawn timber and asbestos roofed homes would have been unbearably hot in Bereina but try as I might I could, as long as I ignored the obvious presence of their many vehicles and the substantial financial contribution to village wellbeing made by salaried children who worked in PNG's civil service, see no significant evidence of other material advancement among its people.

It seemed they had resisted Europeanisation with determination and effectiveness. Even their principal cash crop, and its method of disposal, was traditional and definitely more in tune with relaxed Mekeo habits than labour-intensive coffee.

However, if the material progress of Mekeos and Roros was surprisingly modest, their political sophistication was acute. Deliberately, and fundamentally, they ignored Europeans, especially the Kiap. They insisted, and if necessary demanded, he did not arbitrate in village affairs and managed their lives behind a united, impenetrable, and faintly offensive pride.

Only once was I asked to assist in a village matter – a pleasant development after the interminable squabbles that characterised Highland affairs some might say. It was a land dispute and after I opened discussion on the village platform on behalf of the litigant I was told, in acceptable English, by the petitioner's adversary that as the matter had again been raised they would discuss it – but I should not interfere.

The only time village people came voluntarily to the Sub-District Office was to file a request that might be satisfied by government with its money. So calls were made for road repairs, culvert construction, medical aid posts, and water pumps. However, unlike Highlanders, the people would not contribute their labour.

Self-help had worked well in the Wahgi. If water supply funds were limited its people would dig the pipe track but Mekeos expected the government to undertake excavation work too and if village labour was promised its delivery was rarely followed through. It was disappointing to see how many potentially useful standpipes gathered dust in government storerooms instead of spouting water at the end of a village street.

The only regular contact they had with Kiaps was simple administration – the updating of names and numbers or reassessment of political and economic development. Their attitude was always polite but also indifferent. They gave the impression they only raised themselves from their hammocks because they had nothing else to do and a Kiap, or any other government representative, might offer a degree of relief.

My baptism into the operational limitations being forced on coastal Kiaps in the early 1970s came within a week of my arrival after I had been put in charge of a small Corrective Institution and its complement of a dozen short term prisoners.

Every morning these men, each of them wearing a scarlet *lap-lap*, formed a line outside the Sub-District Office while a warder in khaki uniform called the register. Their work was most likely to cut back the station's grass using flexible strips of curved steel.

Most of these prisoners were young men who had been to school. They did not like being in jail and showed it by being awkward. The warders found them difficult to control and this again highlighted fundamental shifts in attitude as PNG approached Self-Government.

Small rural jails were still commonplace and their smooth running depended on the cooperation of the prisoners. Security was at best flimsy and in some cases scarcely apparent. This was rarely abused but in Bereina they were aware they could hamstring a system that was already being drained of morale.

"It is too hot to work," they said and having won that argument refused to do any work unless they became bored with not working. When this came to my attention it was already too late. The prisoners, not the warders, were in control.

In Kiap fashion I read the metaphorical Riot Act, threatening to charge them with being uncooperative if they continued. But they responded by pointing out the many occasions when the Sub-District Office had itself fallen short of the letter of the law – for instance asking them to cut the station's grass even though it put them in public view.

Only days later they accused bewildered warders of trying to poison them and refused to leave the jail to go to work. They were charged with a range of offences after which they agreed to co-operate then ran back to their villages as soon as the gate was opened. It was a mass break-out. The first escapee was arrested that evening but re-capturing the others was more difficult.

Just months earlier a former government interpreter, Erico Aufe, had refused to pay Local Government Tax. He was convicted but the following morning strolled out of jail. While working for the administration he had become familiar with its limitations and was able to evade re-capture so successfully he became a village hero – a cause célèbre.

The confrontation he had provoked escalated. There were a number of fruitless visits to Erico's village, all pursued aggressively in raid style by an Australian trained Police Inspector with urban skills and no appetite for a more subtle, Kiap like, approach.

This could have included a quiet attempt to secure the help of community leaders who may have wanted to rid themselves of a source of aggravation. However, Bereina's top cop was more interested in the application of overwhelming force and so one evening commandeered a Riot Squad to ring Erico's house. Even so the fugitive still escaped, swimming in dramatic style across the Angabunga River, even as shotguns blasted in the darkness.

It concluded when Erico, who when neccesary could plant his feet and stand square, emerged from his house one morning to find himself ringed in by a police cordon and at the same time eye to eye with a .38 pistol. Contemptuous as ever he raised the bush knife he was holding and, confident he would not be blasted, swatted the firearm down with the flat of its blade.

The startled Police Inspector shot himself in the thigh and, even though Erico was arrested in the melee, laughter still engulfed Mekeo villages. He had tricked, then shamed, a white police officer and Sub-District Office rule had been further undermined too. Delight swelled when Erico was found not guilty of breaking jail, released, and only convicted after an appeal to the Supreme Court.

His story was carried by the Australian press which paraded it as evidence of pre-Self-Government turbulence in an already troubled PNG. The latest break out at Bereina reflected this disintegration and we soon learned that one of the prisoners, Nicholas Ain'au Okua, was presenting himself as Erico Mark Two.

He lived where the main road met a transport ferry across the Angabunga River. It was inevitable we would see him because he made no attempt to hide. Bare chested, and wearing a lap-lap, he came to the vehicle I was driving, bid me good afternoon, pointedly skewered a betel nut skin which lay at his feet with a bush knife, and sniggered.

That night when I drove up to his house with Constables Wani and ToWalaun he was still toting his machete. But he was a pale reflection of Erico because, although he raised it to attack position, he retreated instead of advancing and we were able to grab him when he bumped into a house and turned to see what he had hit.

No longer brave, but protesting his privileges, he was handcuffed, taken to Bereina, and locked in a cell. The others gave themselves up over the following week and were transferred to Port Moresby – all with additional sentences. They could have served their original term in relative comfort at Bereina where no smoking and no visiting rules were ignored but, because they could not resist being obstinate at government expense, spent a much longer time at Bomana where all rules were strictly applied.

Bereina's grandly named, and outdated, Corrective Institution was shut down not long after. Its operation had depended on prisoner support and that was no longer on tap.

The dust laden, heat heavy, sluggishness of Mekeo villages continued to be reflected in a slow work rate at the Sub-District Office so I began to look for jobs in the more remote Kuni region.

Out there was Inika – an unusually isolated village with just 142 people. It had been built beside a river which wound through heavy bush to the Papuan coast. It had no roads, no airstrip, its nearest point of contact was Kobuna Mission Station about five hours' walk, or twenty miles away, and could only be seen from the air.

If passengers on an over-flying plane were observant they would see that around Inika there were unusually large areas of cleared land. Despite its inaccessibility it boasted an impressive cattle herd, purchased with the help of the Development Bank, which in stock quality terms was first class.

I had visited the village during an Area Study Patrol to update an official assessment of its economic progress and was the first Kiap its people had seen for four years. I went a second time to see if I could help with the cattle by bringing out those that were ready to sell. They had been bred from pedigree Brahman bulls, were long, with broad backs and huge hindquarters, boasted hides that shone with health and were a delight to the eye.

One of the cows was barren and three of the first calves had grown into huge three year old bulls which were breeding indiscriminately with their mothers and half-sisters. The village had since learned how to castrate so three full grown steers were running with the herd too.

It was agreed that the barren cow, the young bulls, and steers should be taken to Bereina and then trucked to Moresby and be sold. Also the stock bull needed to be replaced before he bred with more daughters and more bush needed to be cut down to create new pasture too.

The latter was easy and when, by chance, I flew near Inika two years later, the pilot obligingly made a detour, and we could see that more trees had been cleared.

The villagers yarded the animals, we sat on a rail admiring them, then spent an exciting hour drafting them into two groups. The main herd was released and disappeared into the shade to find water.

We left the cattle that were earmarked for Bereina to stand overnight and I returned to the hut I had been given to read HE Bates' "*Fair Stood the Wind for France*", occasionally lowering its pages to stare at the river or an infrequent woman paddling back to the village in a vegetable-laden canoe.

As dusk approached two small dinghies chugged around a bend and, buoyed by a ragged cheer from the quickly collecting villagers, turned to run ashore. A pair of youths gave up the tillers and began unloading provisions which they had purchased after selling fresh vegetables in Port Moresby. Soon there was a small pile which included drums of paraffin, bags of rice, and sugar.

Later that evening, sitting on the village platform, eating a mush of fish, pumpkin and yam, I learned more. The Inikas originally lived in mountains further inland but on the urging of a priest had re-settled on more fertile land near the river.

Then the Department of Agriculture had bought timber rights covering a huge area of nearby bush and the village had been given around £10,000 in compensation. Some of this money had been spent on an Izuzu Colt pick-up which had broken down after 235 miles – only a little more than twice the distance between the nearest road and Moresby. It was entombed under a mound of *kunai* thatch at Kobuna after being abandoned because the clutch had burned out. #1

Some of their windfall had gone on the dinghies and the rest on a huge party. It looked like Inikas had wasted their money. The celebration was justified because it would have been unthinkable for them to have not shared their good fortune, and build reserves of goodwill, with their neighbours. But the cash spent on the vehicle might as well have gone down the toilet and there was a good chance the two outboard motors would soon go the same way too.

Next morning we set out to drive the yarded cattle to Kobuna. They refused to go. Although they were used to being handled their instinct was to return to the herd. The young bulls were first to break out and, leaping over tree stumps and ditches, thundered back into the forest with their raised tails trailing like plumes.

I was not dismayed. I was enjoying Inika after arriving with a mosquito net, blanket, spoon, tin opener, and food tins in a style far removed from a Highland patrol with its attendant formalities. #2

It was not an especially difficult journey because the country was flat. The main feature was the fording of three rivers, one of which, the Dilava that came down from the nearby Goilala mountains, was cool enough for a swim.

Kiaps, like everyone else who lived and worked in rural PNG, could stomp prodigious distances through rough bush. Most regular journeys would be covered within five hours but there were occasions when more effort was required and even the toughest legs began to weaken.

When this happened the only response, especially in mountains when yet another 3,000-4,000 foot climb was the immediate challenge, was to focus on pushing one leg in front of the other and keep moving forward.

The mindset became automaton. Even policemen joked about settling into a blind rhythm in which they did no more than force their boots through yet another stride in a sequence that had already covered tens of thousands and might still require thousands more.

One of the problems when making a journey for the first time was not being able to pace the effort. Guides did not wear watches and efforts to link arrival to sun position could be frustrating too. Attempts to drag out a guess on the remaining distance in miles were just as futile.

Experienced stompers found it best to give up asking how far there was still to go, maintain their focus, and treat their eventual arrival, whenever it happened to be, as a welcome surprise.

Soil surrounding Inika was fertile and during my two spells there I ate and slept unusually well – most of the food, which included fruit, delicious *galip* nuts, and fish, was prepared by the villagers themselves.

We rounded up the cattle again and let the main herd go. This time we built a chute with bamboo and branches to channel the target animals onto the Kobuna track. It was partially successful, four cattle including the barren cow, two steers and a bull went the way we planned while the others leapt the obstruction like antelopes and were once again free.

This four were pushed on quickly while the villagers were told they would only be able to cash their finished stock if they drove the entire herd to

Kobuna, loaded the surplus animals onto a waiting truck, and then came back with those they wanted to keep. They were also advised to kill the remaining young bulls and trade their meat.

Did anyone ever go back? Did the Inika people cash any cattle by selling them to be killed in Moresby or were they absorbed into the local exchange economy like gigantic pigs? If a curious visitor does turn up at that distant village they may still hear its people chanting the Rosary in its square at dusk – a gesture aimed at pleasing the priest who persuaded them to move their home. #3

The only other group I was able to connect with were Rugby League players. This game cast coastal Papuans as Jekyll and Hyde. Apparently indolent and seemingly short of motivation, they were transformed if they had an oval ball in their hands and a forest of arms was ready to haul them down.

They became hard muscled battering rams of barely controlled ferocity that took huge delight in crashing bone against bone and a grim seriousness in smacking flesh against flesh. This was a pleasure I shared. After a week in Bereina's Sub-District Office I was ready for anything and found relief in the flattened bodies I trailed behind me before eventually being tumbled joltingly to earth.

The joy was simple. You took a ball and were asked to make ground. You could either pass to someone better able to move forward or tuck it under your arm, gather speed, and turn your shoulder, pelvis and thigh into the hurtling body trying to scythe you down.

One bouncing off was marvellous and if a second crashed down it might just be possible to summon up enough reserves to fuel a third destructive collision before being tipped over and bounced jarringly off the parched ground.

I was familiar with Rugby Union. While with the Cobras in Birmingham I had played with, and against, men who either were, or later became, internationals. There I had picked up some skills but for sheer flesh tearing, skin ripping, blood running, sinew twisting, bone crushing, sweat pouring, chest-heaving robustness I have not played anything to compare with Papuan Rugby League.

The Roros were best. They maintained a warrior tradition typical of the South Seas. They had paddled war canoes and scattered brains using wooden clubs so face-to-face combat on a rugby field was cultural meat and drink. They had strong clan systems and Rugby League was their substitute for battle.

The partisanship of spectators confirmed this. They did not mingle. A village would claim one touchline and their opponents the other. Each score would be greeted either with dancing or jeers. If the game was tense insults would be traded between touchlines too.

I was never singled out for a sly punch, nasty gouge or kick but there was always a queue of would-be tacklers and if a collision was shirked the result was painful. I had to match speed with more speed and drive with more drive before disappearing under an avalanche of bodies.

Frustration relieved I could turn up for work on Monday still wrapped in a cushion of physical tiredness and muscle ache that had not completely eased. After I left Bereina the only thing I missed was rugby matches. I shared camaraderie with the players and both on, and off, the pitch I liked them.

But back in the village their parents remained distant and if their sons had not included me in a fierce game that we both played well Bereina would have been an intolerable posting.

#1 There were similar problems in Minj where vehicles with an estimated value of about £100,000 (£1.3 million at today's prices) had been abandoned, standing rusty, child vandalised, but not fundamentally broken because their owners had almost no knowledge of basic maintenance or mechanical repair.

2 I usually took miniature tins of Chinese curry sauce into the bush. They were a safeguard because I could slop the contents over food that was difficult to look at too closely and still be able to eat it.

#3 Just one animal, the red steer, eventually reached Bereina and it may have been some time before it was sold. Despite repeated prods aimed at the OIC it was still lingering in the Department of Agriculture's stockyards when I moved on.

CHAPTER TWELVE

A calamitous seepage of will

"There is a tide in the affairs of men
Which taken any way you please is bad
And strands them in forsaken guts and creeks
No decent soul would think of visiting"

Vibart: "Moralities".

The Assistant District Commissioner wielded great power over the local people in his Sub-District. His attitude could also dominate the lives of white subordinates and other government staff. The happiness, or unhappiness, of a station like Bereina could hang on his preferences or whim.

Willingness to extend the hours in which the station generator ran, so records might be played at a late night party, could make the difference between families being able to enjoy social diversions or being dominated by heat imprisoned despair.

At Bereina the relief provided by the "liberty vehicle", an elevated but resonant description of a government Landcruiser that could be driven on Sundays to a nearby beach, was immense. It offered the only regular opportunity for expatriate wives and small children to leave their heat stifled homes, and scorched gardens, to enjoy breeze on an open beach, picnics in palm shade, or a tumble in surf.

On the sands delighted children shrieked, their mothers relaxed, and so their husbands did too. Days highlighted by a dusty walk to the Post Office to pick up mail, pulling children from the betel nut skins, discarded soft drink bottles, dog turds and other rubbish that littered the way could be tolerated, even forgotten, if this break could be anticipated.

We were not without resource. At Christmas three families hired a flat decked, double canoe, organised some accommodation, and spent almost a week holidaying on nearby Yule Island.

One weekend a colleague surpassed himself by borrowing a powerful motor launch along with water skis and a towing line. But the weekly trip to the beach at Waima, where we might spend hours just standing with sea water up to our necks, was the mainstay.

Then a nervous and uncertain ADC arrived at Bereina and, sensitive to the possibility there might be pre-Self-Government accusations he was favouring whites over local staff, ruled, to our distress, that government vehicles could not be taken for private use on Sundays.

We were desperate. One weekend I sneaked away a two-wheel drive pick-up instead of the four-wheel drive Landcruiser road conditions demanded and attempted to take my own, and my neighbour's, family for a dip in the sea that was so important it was almost psychological surgery.

Like a fool I buried it in a mud hole under a midday temperature of a hundred degrees. Leaving my neighbour's wife, and two squalling, prickly-heat wracked toddlers in the thin shade of a lonely bush I sweated with Paula, who was again heavily pregnant, to reverse the vehicle from its stinking wallow.

Two hours later we had emptied the petrol tank and moved it back just ten feet. We were caked in fermenting mud, our hands torn after ripping up wood and grass to put under the back wheels, and she was exhausted.

I walked back to Bereina cursing the unreasonableness of a service which could incarcerate its overseas staff by preventing them from driving thirteen miles once a week to bob around in the sea.

What employer, I muttered to myself, could condemn the foreign families that were still important to national wellbeing, to the little prisons that were their homes for week after week and still expect morale, and work output, to be high?

But most of all I cursed the thin-skinned ADC who had the power to inflict so much that was unnecessary on us – and even more so on our families. To deprive us of access to mild relief was wicked. Still caked in mud I clumped into the station, collared some petrol, another vehicle and a driver, and returned to rescue the stranded women.

That night Paula was angry, I continued to swear, and was still stotting when I went to work on Monday morning. We were imprisoned by our temporariness. It was impossible to justify the purchase of our own four wheel drive vehicle if its principal function was a 26 mile round trip each weekend.

White station staff were faced with two choices. They could either accept the ADC's decision and stew near their homes on Sundays, or take a vehicle without permission. We chose the latter and were not challenged by the local people we worked with.

The timidity of the ADC was in obvious contrast with the huge effort made throughout PNG in the 1960s to provide on-station leisure facilities aimed at encouraging, and sustaining, the presence of in-coming European personnel and their many skills.

Hundreds of short-term prisoners had laboured to re-direct water and build swimming pools. Golf courses were created, and then kept in shape, again by *kalabus* labour, and sites for tennis courts were dug out too.

This had happened in Bereina but the swimming pool had cracked while the dilapidated tennis courts were almost threadbare. The Club, which tried to maintain them, may once have been an epicentre of white privilege but when we were members it too was shabby because its fabric was breaking down.

Nevertheless it was still important, not just to government staff who gathered there to gossip and swig beer, but to Europeans working, or with businesses, elsewhere in the district. One of these was Bruce Hides, a slight, sun-dried, man who owned a modest plantation in the Kuni – just above the Catholic Mission at Kobuna.

It would be difficult to describe Bruce as an expatriate because he had been born in Port Moresby in 1914 when many Europeans expected to settle permanently in PNG and had lived there all his life.

His elder brother Jack had been one of the best known pre-war explorers of Papua's interior, the equivalent of Jim Taylor in the Highlands, but Bruce, after a spell in the army during the Second World War, had settled down as a businessman, with his wife, Dulcie.

He ended his life in PNG as well because after driving to the Club to watch the regular Sunday evening film – it was *The Virgin Soldiers* – he was caught in a downpour on the way back, his vehicle left the road, and he was overwhelmed by pneumonia.

The tension Paula felt in Bereina increased with the advancement of her pregnancy. The baby was due at the end of October but even as she waited by the airstrip for a plane to take her to hospital in Port Moresby her labour pains began.

There was no alternative to a dash by Landcruiser to the hospital at Veifa'a Catholic Mission where the nuns immediately took her in but not before warning she might catch an endemic infection because she would not be immune.

Ruth arrived quickly and easily but only days later Paula became unwell – creased up on a sporadic basis with abdominal pains that were later put down to a malfunctioning gall bladder. Nor was it easy to nurse, and comfort, a new baby in Bereina's relentless heat.

Self-Government Day celebrations were to be staged on December 1st. The lead up was un-alarming. Dr John Guise, Deputy Chief Minister, arrived at the beginning of November and castigated us because we still flew the Australian flag. There were no ulterior motives. It was not misplaced stubbornness. None of the local people had been critical and when a sparkling new PNG flag flew in its place the only reaction was silence.

He also told the people we had dragged from the shady side of the trade store to listen to him that Papua uniting under the same independent government as New Guinea was a good idea and was shocked into silence when one of the assembled men told him without equivocation it was not.

Elsewhere there were conflicting undercurrents. More Highlanders were said to be resisting the flying of the PNG flag at the same time as others began to squat on European owned land.

And there were, without doubt, more demonstrations of anti-white hostility around coastal towns on the New Guinea side of the island – some as simple as a lift in the number of people threatening to throw stones at Europeans in passing cars.

There was a huge two-day clash between Highlanders and Papuans in Moresby too. The Australian press suggested this was a symptom of pre-Self-Government tension. Those on the ground said it reflected emerging economic and social strains that were not immediately political but were nevertheless likely to be hugely damaging in the long term.

Then we learned, some of us with an ironic shrug, that the political spotlight would be shining on Bereina on December 1st. Josephine Abaijah, regional member of the House of Assembly for the Central District, which included Port Moresby, was promoting an obtuse political platform in which an independent Papua separated from New Guinea.

She had gathered support in many coastal villages, including those surrounding Bereina, and so it was among the venues shortlisted for a declaration of secession on Self-Government Day when she would raise independent Papua's new flag.

On November 30th the ADC returned from Port Moresby and summoned his staff to his home. There we found him in agitated conversation with Bereina's new senior policeman, Sub-Inspector Anton Gawi. He outlined government fears that Josephine might be using the demonstration at Bereina, and other near simultaneous gatherings along the Papuan coast, to stage a coup.

He explained that only nine policemen, and half a dozen white Kiaps, stood between the status-quo and her conquest of the Bereina area. "To make herself the government she only has to rid herself of the current one – and in this neck of the woods," he said, tapping himself dramatically on the chest, "that is me." Then, like a general planning a campaign, he outlined the station's defence.

Next day most of the Europeans rolled up at our house, chosen by the ADC because it had the best field of fire, and most of them, as instructed, carried rifles or shotguns hidden in blankets. When these were lined up on our spare bed they made an impressive pile but, like their owners, were a motley lot. A resigned Kiap, who had been an army sergeant in Kenya, was posted to the nearby Radio Room and told to lock himself in.

I was instructed to attend the ceremony and if its intentions became hostile rush to the Radio Room, pass on my observations, and then dash to the safety of my fortified home. It was hoped Lofty – who was not a tall man – would have time to contact Moresby before a baying mob began to break down doors and we would be rescued after an RAAF Hercules, carrying a cure-all Riot Squad, flew in to save the day.

It was hard to be serious about this charade and I was not put out by my frontline posting. Unlike the Waghi, where the scent of impending village disturbance was pungent, my Bereina antennae had still to develop a twitch. A highlight of that ridiculous day was Dulcie, Bruce Hides' ever-cheerful widow, who had taken over the running of the station's trade store, arriving in her best frock carrying a bottle of gin and a handmade .22 rifle. She was a veteran of enforced isolation and, no matter what the circumstances, wasn't going to miss out on a rare chance of company and conversation.

Another was rattling the burglar wire on the Radio Room window to see Lofty, who had lived through a real colonial emergency, shake his head and mutter "the man is mad". He too could not believe the ADC had evacuated his home and, among other things, panicked his wife into scrambling without a shred of dignity into the back of an open Landcruiser to seek armed protection in another.

176

The last highlight was meeting a relaxed Anton Gawi just before Josephine arrived, him looking hard to see if I was worried, and guffawing conspiratorially when he realised I was not.

Josephine had her way. She declared independence for Papua in front of not much more than one hundred mildly enthusiastic people, and almost as many newsmen and cameras, then returned to her vehicle and left.

The high point was her new flag. She carefully explained its symbolism and its colours – which were essentially red on blue. This, she emphasised, was because Papua's most common Bird of Paradise had a red tail while the bird on the national flag had a yellow tail – and was most likely to be seen in the hated Highlands of New Guinea.

When she left, the crowd – which had not been much bigger than attendance at a typical Saturday market – dispersed. Sleepy Bereina may have been the only sub-station in the country to have flown three flags in a little over four weeks.

The people at the ceremony had been relaxed. I had watched from the front row and no one suggested I was intruding. After walking to the Radio Room to tell Lofty he should come back for some tea, we passed a score of news cameramen with film footage to spare encouraging children to cheer excitedly into their lenses. They must have been disappointed. Animation was something the afternoon had obviously lacked.

The real point, although they had missed it, was that Bereina's expatriate civil servants, who no longer had confidence in the protection and privilege, secured so effectively in the past through possession of senior administrative positions and a white skin, had surrendered the station to Josephine's Papua Besena movement and hidden themselves indoors behind a barricade of guns. #1

Michael Somare's government had decided not to make a fuss over the arrival of Self-Government, although bars had been closed and police presence elevated. As a result it may have been PNG's most peaceful day for some time. The only serious incident was in the Chimbu, not far from Nondugl, where a policeman had been killed by a flying stone after interrupting an illegal card game.

There had been no movement against white property and perhaps the noisiest moment of the day was when Paula rid herself of her frustrations and railed against the ADC who had entertained his captive audience with vivid accounts of the civil chaos that had trailed the collapse of colonial administrations elsewhere. That was between frequent trips to the window to peep through its frosted louvres. She said he was not just a fool but a frightened fool. It was impossible to disagree.

It was Lofty who later underlined the importance of the will to rule. He had seen it evaporate immediately before the British left Kenya and thought he was witnessing a repeat in PNG over the closing months of 1973.

He had just come back to Bereina from Moresby feeling dismayed after an incident in which, as directed by the District Commissioner, he had tried to evict squatters from a cattle ranch. The initiative failed because he had been threatened with bush knives and warned he would be killed if he did not get back in his vehicle and drive away. He had radioed the DC for instructions, confidently expecting to receive back up, but was told instead to return and try to speak to the people again.

"Damn it," he said. "Either the DC wants the men off that land or he doesn't. If I go back I could get chopped. Why should I risk my skin? We can't talk them off because the only way to get them to move is force them off. If we can't force them off they can stay there." The squatters squatted on. The will, or the skill, to remove them was not there.

Situations like this highlighted a growing post-Self-Government divergence between perceptions at field and administrative level. Older, senior Kiaps either thought junior officers in the field could act as they themselves had in the past and immediately solve a bush problem by demanding their preferred course of action should be taken – or were reluctant to challenge village people, who had fallen in with the new mood and were pursuing ambitions the government did not want them to, through additional force in case it offended new, and unfamiliar, political sensitivities that continued to surface.

In this instance the determination of the squatters to stay put had either not been appreciated at District Office level, or Lofty did not have the skill to persuade them to move on without having to fall back on a heavier, more confrontational, approach which, if pursued, may not have solved the problem either.

The view among junior officers at Bereina was that local people had sensed administrative hesitation at District and Sub-District Office level and were taking advantage of it by digging in on issues that they would not have felt able to before.

And these thoughts, still seen by many senior Kiaps as either hugely disappointing or mildly subversive, were almost immediately reinforced by an obvious, and calamitous, seepage of will at Bereina itself.

It boasted a particularly fine grass airstrip on which DC3s landed daily and returned to Moresby filled with passengers and cargo – most of which was dried fish, fresh vegetables or betel nut for street markets. This traffic was a fundamental prop to the Sub-District's economy. On occasions there could be three on the ground at the same time.

The Department of Civil Aviation was autonomous. Nothing it said relating to airstrip safety could be countermanded by pleading or negotiation. It was responsible for the impressive safety record of PNG's airstrips, many of them unusually hazardous, as well as disciplining civil pilots, and overlooking the maintenance of civil aircraft too. Its word was law.

After a routine check at Bereina a DCA inspector pointed out that three coconut trees on its western end had intruded into air space required for take-off and landing and that a row of banana trees had invaded the fifty feet of cleared ground required at the edge of the strip too. We were given a fortnight to remove them.

It should have been a simple task. We would cut down the bananas, lop the coconut palms, and then refund their owners – but these plans were thrown into immediate confusion when they refused to cooperate.

We checked records and found each tree was on land that had been purchased by government when the airstrip had been built. I set out one morning with a group of prisoners to remove the bananas and was confronted by villagers, all carrying bush knives, who were so angry they were spitting like cats. I passed the problem on to a higher authority, the ADC, who avoided confrontation by doing nothing.

The Civil Aviation Inspector returned on schedule and immediately lowered the airstrip category from A to C which meant that nothing larger than specialist short take off Caribous, Twin Otters or Norman Islanders could land. DC3s, mainstay to the region's transport system, were blocked, and so its economy came under immediate strain.

Scheduled Norman Islanders with a maximum payload of just 1500 pounds could not cope. Betel nut and people had to be driven piecemeal to Moresby, mail came in only three times a week, trade store stocks dwindled, and passengers jostled over the nine seats available on each plane while once there had been forty.

The ADC spoke to the squatters. They were obdurate and sullen. A new garden was ploughed out to make up for the twenty bananas that would be dug out. They refused to be tempted.

The people of the area gathered in the Council Chamber where they were told that the cussedness of a vindictive group of trespassers was holding the local economy to ransom. They agreed, said they would support us when we took out both coconuts and bananas, and shook their heads in amazement when the ADC said he would only do it if the squatters agreed. The will to rule was nakedly thin.

Bereina became animated. Delegations from nearby villages arrived to tell him that the squatters were outcasts, beyond redemption, and because they could not be shamed into restoring the local economy the government should take direct action – knowing it had solid local support.

Despite this unprecedented public endorsement he still sat on his hands and his resolution became even weaker when he learned that the handful of people at the centre of the dispute were threatening to ask Josephine Abaijah to intervene.

Perhaps she would have been prepared to make political capital out of twenty banana and three coconut trees, although this was doubtful because popular support to have them removed was too high.

But the truth was that after Nigel Van Ruth's court case few senior Kiaps were prepared to risk annoying an MHA and so simply by mentioning Miss Abaijah's name the squatters had guaranteed the continuation of spectacular government inaction.

I had been in Bereina just six months when I wrote to the District Commissioner pleading for a transfer. My reasons included the lack of work, the indifference of the Mekeos, non-provision of a "liberty vehicle" and the demoralising absence of Departmental will over the airstrip debacle.

There was another, more personal, motive too. Our children were suffering from prickly heat or sweat rash. It erupts when the skin can no longer cope with constant sweating and is typified by a stinging sensation not unlike being attacked by a thousand nettles when the first beads emerge.

Electric fans helped but no one living in Bereina, not even babies, could avoid breaking into a sweat at some stage. Daniel was scratching his chest raw while Ruth, still in her cot, complained incessantly.

The DC was sympathetic and on February 4th 1974 we left Bereina for the mountain posting of Tapini in the Goilala sub-district. It was just twenty minutes away by plane but could have been in a different country. Its air was cool so the rashes vanished within days, and I was so quickly surrounded by work that I soon forgot the never-ending, heat bound, ineffective days that had to be endured at Bereina.

#1 Josephine was a product of the London Missionary Society's education system and as a child I had been asked on more than one occasion by Slaley's Methodist Chapel to collect money on its behalf. Some may even have found its way to Papua and funded her schooling.

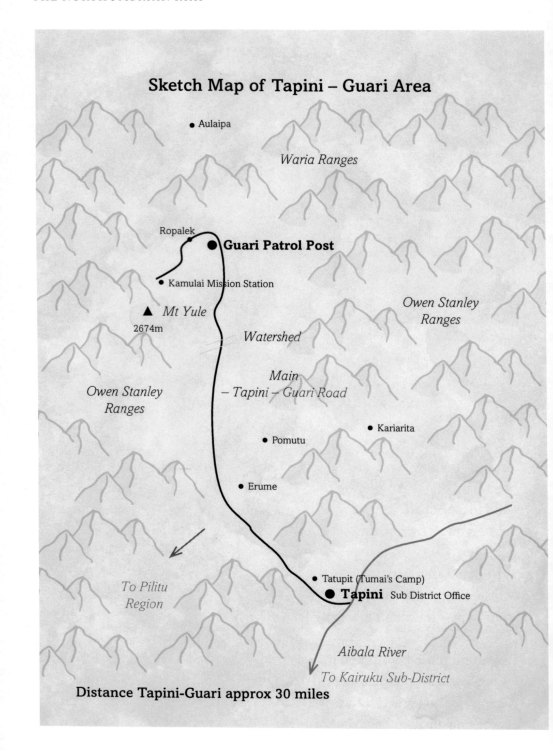

Sketch Map of Tapini – Guari Area

Aulaipa

Waria Ranges

Ropalek

● **Guari Patrol Post**

● Kamulai Mission Station

▲ *Mt Yule*

2674m

Owen Stanley Ranges

Watershed

Main – Tapini – Guari Road

Owen Stanley Ranges

● Kariarita

● Pomutu

● Erume

← *To Pilitu Region*

● Tatupit (Tumai's Camp)

● **Tapini** Sub District Office

Aibala River

To Kairuku Sub-District

Distance Tapini-Guari approx 30 miles

CHAPTER THIRTEEN

Only the grass-man should be convicted

"One of the ways a young Tauade could build his reputation was to creep into the hut where a Kiap was sleeping and lower a raised axe to within an inch of the man's neck before slipping back out again."

Goilala Sub-District, Central District, February 1974.

Tapini looked good. The air was fresh, the station was neat, sure confirmation Kiap morale in the Sub-District Office was still strong, and the house we were allocated was not only large, and well maintained, but set on its own within wooded ground above the airstrip.

Just hours after arriving I was on its veranda sharing a beer with Jeff van Oosterwijck, the temporary ADC, who suddenly asked, "What job do you want – the cash office or the police?"

My mind raced because I had objections to both. Work at the cash desk was sedentary, predictable and had to be meticulous, but to be put in charge of a police detachment was daunting and I was apprehensive about a working life dominated by snappy salutes and the synchronised thump

185

of carefully polished boots.

However, there had been frustrations in the past at having an ambiguous hold over the police whose on-call presence was fundamental to effective Kiap-government.

They also tended to be in the thick of most of the administrative action and I was still looking for adventure. The answer, advanced with a touch of apprehension, was "the police".

Jeff, who in different circumstances could have been mistaken for a deep thinking San Francisco hippy, nodded and next morning I took the Tapini Detachment's salute. The Sergeant later told me I had been standing in the wrong place.

It had been left to fend for itself and was scruffy. Fortunately a new senior Sergeant arrived three weeks later. He too was keen to pull it together so we – that is a neat and thoughtful Sergeant Gabume and I – pounced on Constables who came on parade with dirty boots or without shaving.

Next job was to replace worn uniforms, inspect houses to replace broken furniture and kick-start minor repairs. More work on the typewriter updated arrangements covering overtime and leave entitlements, then there were inspection parades and the re-introduction of routine drilling. Weaker policemen were transferred and one was recommended for dismissal.

The result was a full detachment of fifteen, all properly equipped, all living in well maintained homes, all in good uniforms, all aware of the importance of good off-duty behaviour, and all keen, because prospects for promotion were also being dangled, to work as well as they could.

It was Michael Nuglai, one of the Constables, who said living at Tapini was like being a housefly trapped in a fish tin. The station clung to steep ground at the top of an airstrip which followed the length of an almost perpendicular spur that was itself a minor feature in a landscape dominated by scowling buttresses and plunging slopes. The terrain was even more unfriendly than Bundi.

Mountainsides towering over the station forced you to raise your head if you wanted to enjoy the sky, and there was a river, the Aibala, which could only be seen from the air. Vision on all sides was obstructed by forest-clad rock and on days when cloud descended, and lay across mountain tops like a soggy wreath, Tapini was locked in a stone box sealed by a soft, grey lid.

Its people, the Tauade, were notorious throughout PNG. Back in the 1920s Bruce Hides' brother Jack had shot dozens as he crossed and then re-crossed their territory. Unlike the Wahgis, who immediately recognised the advantages of capitulation, they were persistently hostile and because they specialised in ambush, even after being contacted many times, were exceptionally dangerous too.

Collectively they, along with those administered from nearby Patrol Posts at Woitape (Fuyege) and Guari (Kunimeipa), were described as Goilalas and, along with the Kukukuku of the Morobe District, were among the best known – more accurately notorious – of the tribal groups in PNG because they found it unusually easy to kill. Within them the Tauade and Kunimeipas were most feared.

It was because of this that bush-savvy Kiaps, not regular police officers whose methods were less flexible and so less effective, continued to be in charge of police activity across the Goilala sub-district, even though the Tapini office was just eighty miles from Port Moresby and the Police Department, which abhorred role confusion, was never comfortable with Kiaps continuing to be in charge of police operations in areas that had been de-controlled and opened up to civil activity.

Goilalas were a short, moderately sturdy, people who were less able than Highlanders to build a cash crop economy because the land they occupied was so hostile. Some grew fresh vegetables which were back loaded by plane to Moresby but the revenue was not huge and so the majority found it hard to move from their original village sites or feel encouraged to modify their restrictive culture.

Many escaped subsistence living by migrating to Moresby where, from their shanty town bases, they waged never-ending, and bloody, feuds with squatters from the Highlands – most often those from the similarly overcrowded, under resourced, Chimbu.

Murders by axe or bush knife were regular on both sides because even in this urban environment traditional payback rules demanded tit-for-tat exchanges which generated a never-ending cycle of death.

The roots of this rivalry had been debated for years. The most convincing came from the Office of the Crown Prosecutor which said the main struggle was over control of garbage collection and the opportunity not just to pick up valuable European cast-offs but to identify homes, and businesses, that could be most easily burgled too.

The plunder was immense and garbage collection teams were used as scouts. The Goilala were the first to benefit and the lift in their shanty-town living standards was substantial. But when the collection contract changed hands a new bidder employed Highlanders, many of them Chimbus, and, as is often the case in wars enmeshing larger nations, the primary cause was economic.

Goilala culture had also produced the infamous Peter Ivoro, who was sentenced to death in 1970 and very nearly became only the second

Papua New Guinean to be hanged since the end of the Japanese war. He set out on his path of destruction in Port Moresby after laying his hands on a .22 rifle. The trail of killing began with random sniping at unsuspecting women by their washing lines, and ended with the murder of two European men and the fatal stabbing of a Papuan girl.

There were many others including Karto Kartogi who was convicted for murder at almost the same time and was thought to have killed fifteen other people including two Europeans. Goilalas were undoubtedly special and just their presence could make many of PNG's people feel uneasy.

The more I learned the more wary I became. They had killed each other on the grass mound immediately outside the Patrol Post office at Guari, within Tapini's jail, and at the door of its Court House with a Judge, wigged and robed, standing just paces away. They murdered with shotguns as well as axes and the conviction rate was thin because they were masters at covering up.

There had been a murder in the distant Pilitu region in 1973. The corpse carried a number of axe wounds but no arrests had been made. The long walk from Tapini was a problem and a Kiap was not on-site for three days.

However, the investigation had been desultory, so threadbare that the location of the fatal ambush, which may have opened a useful line of enquiry, had not been visited, and this casual approach was disappointing.

Unrelenting post-contact suppression of murder was a keystone to Kiap government's success and softening of this resolve looked suspiciously like further confirmation of the general slide in national administrative will.

I was warned one of the ways a young Tauade could build his reputation was to creep into the hut where a Kiap was sleeping and lower an axe to within an inch of the man's neck before slipping back out. This enthusiasm for axe work did not mean they could not laugh – some were bright and cheerful – but an ability to be instantly personable was rare. Mission presence, dominated by the Catholic Church, was widespread but they were reluctant Christians too.

Priests said they had a deep love for their immediate family, especially the children. However, many men could be cruel to their wives and it was not uncommon for a husband to scald a wayward spouse with boiling water or assault her with the handle of his axe.

There were occasions when Tauade villagers could be seen being happy but acceptance that a sudden, brutally efficient, murder was pivotal to their management of community affairs could not be overlooked – and as a result some of the sub-district's people lived in near perpetual fear.

One of the problems was deeply knotted village relationships. Family trees constructed in an attempt to disentangle the complicated affiliations that could obscure a murder investigation revealed regular marriages, as did 19th century census records back in Northumberland and over much of Britain too, between full cousins added to which there might, as a result of polygamy, be a multiplicity of common half brothers and sisters to confuse the mix.

With their record of savagery it is not surprising that the pacification, or conquest, of the Goilala area, particularly the Tauade and Kunimeipa people, was savage too. Exploration patrols in the 1920s listed their casualties to arrow or axe in half dozens and if these are correct then unreported Goilala losses from returning rifle fire must have been immense.

Patrols conducted through the 1930s still lost carriers to ambush, often directed at the rear of the column, and sometimes patrol staff were killed as newly recruited guides fell on their victims from within.

Whereas records indicate initial contact with the Chimbu and other Highland people was secured after the deaths of comparatively few tribesmen, most often on the occasion of their first and most dangerous assault, the pacification of the Goilala was achieved only after a long struggle which persisted until just before the Second World War.

Even in the late 1940s routine intra-Goilala aggression, especially in the most difficult sections of the Kunimeipa region, had still to be broken and priests are adamant that the man who eventually cudgelled villagers into abandoning everyday murder was a Kiap as hard, and uncompromising, as themselves.

He was Roy Edwards #1 who together with a band of similarly tough-minded policemen, an iron will, and an ability to live in the bush for months at a time, reduced them through his own aggression to what might be called truculent tractability.

He made the elimination of routine murder a priority. If a village refused to help him identify a killer, he shot some of its pigs. If it refused to give his patrol food, he took what was needed and destroyed gardens when he left. If he still encountered resistance he burned houses, if a community continued to hold out he found other ways to make his presence a burden, and if a man delivered to him as a murderer refused to confess, Edwards would intimidate the suspect by burying him up to his chin or use firebrands to burn his skin.

His reputation grew and eventually he had only to declare an intention to set out for a village to persuade its people to meet him on the road with the murderers already restrained and confessions ready. Fathers Abel and Morant, who worked at Kamulai in the Kunimeipa, insisted that

191

although his methods were brutal the Goilala owed him a debt because he broke the back of a never-ending pay-back spiral.

Killing had been an almost daily occurrence but even though four murders were reported at Tapini (population 26,000) in 1974 the number was still declining, and in the Kunimeipa, which had been notoriously reluctant to abandon regular execution, the murder frequency had become intermittent. "It needed someone as savage as themselves to break them. Hundreds of lives were saved," they concluded.

Edwards, described even at the time as a rogue officer, was, however, too extreme for the Moresby administration and in June 1950 he was jailed for six months for common assault.

One of his interpreters was the son of the headman at Tatupit, the village which stood on a spur above Tapini. He was Tumai Mumu. When I knew him he was an old man – but still recognised as one of the important leaders in the area.

He had a long, lugubrious face which was saved from sullenness by a tilt in the way he carried his head, that reminded me of a cock sparrow, and eyes, which although deeply shot with blood, still held a twinkle. A flat scar covered one side of his face. I never did discover its cause. It could have been a burn or he may have been flayed by a glancing blow from a bush knife.

Tumai was a murderer of great renown. His stealth and cunning were legendary. Even when patrolling in the Kunimeipa with the feared Roy Edwards, it was said he would slip away and quietly axe, apparently just for the hell of it, a helpless woman in her garden or a man returning tired, and unsuspecting, to his home.

I do not know how he escaped discovery. It may be his reputation saved him from informers or perhaps he interpreted only what he wanted Edwards to hear and deflected information that was dangerous to him? The more I enquired, the more victims Tumai seemed to have notched up.

Perhaps like an outrageous Robin Hood his legend had grown beyond him and he was attributed with unsolved murders he had not committed. What is certain is that he killed with indiscriminate random the length and breadth of the Goilala, and that for some ambushes he had used early government patrols as his base.

One day when we were talking in my office, I asked him how many people he had killed. "Men or women?" he queried. "Men first," I replied. He showed me two clenched fists, raised his feet off the floor and gripped all his toes, then showed me his right hand with all the fingers hidden and only the thumb extended. "Twenty four," I said.

"And how many women?" He did not answer. He pushed forward an already drooping lower lip, raised his shoulders in a long and exaggerated shrug, wrinkled his nose, and flapped both hands vacantly. His gesture was dismissive; it indicated that the numbers were huge, he was not disturbed at losing count, and nor was he interested in being pressed into further detail over the trivial matter of dead women. He might as well have said "Fucked if I know".

Much of the work undertaken by Kiaps was difficult because they represented an alien culture that had been imposed on the people with whom they were working – and nowhere was this cultural gap more obvious than during an investigation into a murder.

In the early days the aim of the Administration was to reduce their regularity by punishing the culprits. But the Goilala people had developed methods of obscuring both motive and method to such a degree that a murder might go undetected, or even when discovered the

193

actual murderer may not have been punished even though someone, the appointed *grass-man* or decoy, might have been successfully prosecuted and sent to jail.

Almost as soon as I arrived at Tapini I became entangled in an enquiry so complicated that no matter how hard I strained to grasp the intricate cultural concepts that dominated the investigation they still danced mockingly, like spiteful wraiths, just beyond my line of understanding.

Oulaine Papaite had been axed four times early one morning as she knelt over a noisy mountain stream to wash soil off the sweet potatoes she had just dug up from her garden. Opu Anuma had given himself up and confessed to her murder. But he admitted to striking only one blow. He was resolute on this. So who then had struck the others, and why?

The attack was appallingly viscious. Oulaine died because someone had cut her spinal cord with an axe; as she lay face up someone had struck her brutally just below the left eye; another axe blow had severed her collar bone; and yet another had bit into her neck spilling almost all her blood. Opu admitted only to the first. He also said that he had killed Oulaine because her brother, Maia, had beaten his sister, Katai, with a stick, breaking her collar bone and splitting her left cheek.

The investigation was difficult. Opu's and Oulaine's families were intricately related and trapped in a complicated internal feud. Nevertheless it ploughed on and eventually Oulaine's nephew, Tuta, revealed she had quarrelled with Katai so persistently the family had decided the only way to restore domestic peace, and ease a number of sexual tensions, was to rid themselves of her.

Once this decision had been made Tuta's eldest brother, Tatai Kurua, had sealed an assassination contract with Opu and three other men by asking them to cut a portion of pigmeat with their axes before smoking

194

a ritual tobacco they called kukumara.

According to Tuta, the four men had been summoned to a hut and told how, and when, to ambush Oulaine. His brother had passed them the tobacco, which had been cut carefully with an axe before being smoked, and so the contract had been sealed. Only Opu was to give himself up and promised a reward after his jail sentence was completed.

Kukumara, a tool used to commission a murder, was new to the current staff at Tapini, but a search through office files unearthed a report by Bill Graham, who suggested an influential village leader, Tau Inam, had been murdered in 1969 after being lured to his place of execution near Kanitata by conspirators bound by ritual smoking of the tobacco. Bill had added that anyone who co-operated with Kiaps, or the police, after smoking kukumara could be executed too.

I consulted Tumai. Now his killing days were over he enjoyed exposing the subterfuge of younger men less experienced than himself.

"Four men were involved," he told me. *"In the Goilala many men will kill one man. You must understand that with a pig it would be different. A man can use several blows to kill a pig and it would carry no consquence. But humans are special. Usually one man is marked to strike the victim first. This blow should be the killer. Then while the murdered man is shaking and turning the other men will come and strike him once. They strike once then run away. And then the man behind them strikes. It is the first man who really kills the dead man. The others just cut him with their axes."*

He then went on to describe how kukumara – he too emphasised that it had to be cut with an axe – could be used to commission a murder. Later, during the Supreme Court trial of Opu, and three other men who had been arrested, he was arraigned as an expert witness and repeated this in just as much detail.

I found it odd watching Tumai, who had stained his hands through the cold blooded murder of many victims, passing on this information to another old man, in wig and gown, who was a pivotal representative of the culture that had undermined the system within which Tumai had built so much of his formidable reputation.

Michael Nuglai thought he was a convert to law and order. I did not. He might not have been able to stalk helpless, almost random, prey any longer but could still be wicked. The squirming of the prisoners in the dock no doubt delighted him.

Evidence that had been assembled in the meantime resulted in Opu's three accomplices also being charged. The next step was to secure a formal remand through the magistrates' court but it was soon clear their arrest had touched a tender local nerve.

That night the President of the Local Government Council, Kaga Lava, who taught at the local primary school too, picked up a shotgun and appeared to make determined effort to kill the brother of one of the most important witnesses, Kepara Lamoro, who had seen two of the men who had just been charged, Tatai Kila and Aia Paimere, fleeing the scene of Oulaine's murder.

Kaga had burst into a house on Tapini station, levelled the gun at Kepara's brother, but was quickly overpowered by two other men so it discharged harmlessly through the floor.

He was already a problem. He drank heavily, bullied local people continuously, and had been protected by previous ADCs who were keen to avoid arresting, or disciplining, a Council President, because it could undermine national plans for the advancement of Kiap-free, more democratic, regional administration and perhaps put a black mark on their service record too.

And Kaga had thrown his weight behind the alibi of Tatai, one of the alleged murderers, which, depending on your point of view, meant he was either colluding in a cover-up or keen to protect the reputation of an innocent man. Kiap bosses in Moresby prefered the latter explanation and frowned heavily in my direction.

Two days later Meto Wanuwe, the fourth man to be charged with Oulaine's murder, was found almost dead in the cell he shared with Council President Kaga and the three men who were his co-accused. He said they had persuaded him to hang himself and coldly watched as he began to choke. He was near enough dead when discovered for suspicions that he might only have been trying to gather sympathy to be dismissed.

Murmurings out in the villages continued. The District Commissioner's office was told and its instruction to Tapini was to back off, ignore evidence that suggested otherwise, accept that Opu was a lone killer, and restore village tranquility. Perhaps it thought the Goilala district would be more stable if only *grass-men* were convicted and murder accomplices remained free?

This directive was reinforced when the ADC returned after a long illness, took over from Jeff van Oosterwijck, and after telling me I was a wet behind the ears junior upstart #2 who had upset the delicate balance between the about to be self-governing and those about to quit government, ordered investigations to be suspended.

This was done and critical attempts to dig out more information ceased immediately even though the Crown Prosecutor's office insisted that the trial of the four men had to go ahead.

The plunge in fact finding endeavour meant young Tuta was no longer as confident about repeating his testimony as he had been and other witnesses were suddenly reticent as well. Only Opu was convicted, and sentenced to fifteen years, while those who had stood with him in the dock went free.

I was rescued from humiliation by the Judge whose verdict was an unusual "Case Not Proven" rather than "Not Guilty". In his summing up he was careful to say he had not seen enough evidence to convict Opu's co-defendants but he had nevertheless found their defence remarkably unconvincing.

My posting to Tapini meant that for a year I was submerged in sudden death even though nothing in my past had prepared me for it. In the 1950s and 1960s Britain was a peaceful country and Northumberland a backwater.

There had been huge excitement in Slaley in December 1957 when a Newcastle taxi driver was found shot and stabbed on nearby Edmondbyers Moor. Norman Silk, who farmed Spring House, had been moving sheep in his livestock wagon that morning and one Sunday afternoon detectives called to ask him if he had seen anything suspicious.

It was the same day that his son, Stuart, was celebrating his eleventh birthday and I was one of the boys at the party who were gripped by this drama. Only days later we found some bloodstained snow – it had almost certainly been left by a lame animal – but nevertheless carried it carefully home and asked the first adult we saw if it was necessary to call the police.

Then in July 1966 a man had been stabbed just below the Black House crossroads to the south of Hexham. It was our second murder in ten years and, teenagers now, we would drive slowly past the verge where the body had been found so we could appreciate the tragedy implied by the area of grass that had been trampled flat.

#1 I met Roy in 1973 although I did not know he had been a Patrol Officer and was unaware how influential he had been. He was a hard, spare man who ran the Ou Ou Creek plantation on the Hiritano Highway between Port Moresby and Bereina. He and his wife kept a crocodile in their garden pond and a donkey that sheltered in their kitchen when the afternoon sun was hot.

#2 Internal Kiap culture could be deeply hierarchical – reflecting the evolution of the Department of District Administration from paramilitary structures during the Pacific War.

A District Officer, who might be gazetted as an Assistant District Commissioner, was near the top of the pile. Next in line was the Assistant District Officer (ADO) followed by Patrol Officers and Assistant Patrol Officers who had still to complete two years' service. The District Commissioner was God.

CHAPTER FOURTEEN

Running a Goilala Gauntlet

Amuna wiped muddy hands on his shorts and produced an empty shotgun cartridge from his shirt pocket. "I killed Panai with this," he said.

Pomutu village, Goilala Sub-District, 1974.

I was still shaving when big boots pounded the veranda. Constable Apua was at the door and obviously excited. He was a remarkable policeman, a devout Christian from Ioma in the Northern District, and most decidedly one of Christ's warriors on the blue-uniformed side of Good.

When he came to attention I feared for the survival of whatever lay beneath his feet, but that morning his salute was a shade less correct and his excellent English a little more hurried.

"Good morning, sir, there has been a big trouble at Kariarita."

"What kind of trouble?"

"Someone has shot their chief."

"Is he dead?"

"I think so. They say they have left him where he fell down."

Half an hour later I was sitting in the back of a Landcruiser with Sergeant Gabume. Beside us, as we braced ourselves while it pushed its blunt nose up the steep road from Tapini and swayed round hairpin bends, were five other policemen and an interpreter.

It was a beautiful morning. The sun was bright but the air still chilly. The mountains were clear with each fold distinct in the low morning light. As we travelled cloud whispers hanging on the tops began to lift but a thin layer of mist still lingered on the rolling roof of trees that almost hid the river in the valley below. Huts were clustered among stump strewn gardens and smoke from newly lit fires was rising in thin plumes.

Down in the valley a long exchange of urgent yodelling echoed. Pigs rooting by the roadside galloped in front of the vehicle before darting through a hole in a hedge where they honked indignantly as we passed.

Government officers were allowed to shoot pigs if a road had to be protected from their foraging but not many were because there were few easier ways of antagonising the local community.

Gabume knew this. "You should have shot them," he teased.

"Huh," I snorted. "What was that shouting about?"

"Just spreading the news. Just spreading the news."

Panai Koiai, leader of the Kariaritsi community, had died in his wife's hut. He was spread eagled on his back with arms flung wide. His head was pillowed on someone's folded clothing and a bag of money had been tucked into his right hand.

I crawled through the narrow door and began to look around. The floor on which he lay was strewn with mats and blankets. Net bags hung on the low walls contained female clothing. At his feet were the still-warm ashes of a fire.

Beyond this sleeping area was a partition broken by a small doorway. This second room had been used for sleeping too. The ceiling, less than five feet high, was formed by loose lengths of split timber on top of which pineapple sized pandanus nuts were stored.

The light was temporarily blocked as Gabume crawled in. Together we examined the body. We noticed burns to the heels and back of the ankles but the main wound was a neat hole in the right side of his chest. Rolling him over we could see that skin on the left side of his back was puckered by tiny lumps. I nipped one. It was hard, cold, and squirmed beneath my fingers. "Shotgun," I sighed. Gabume nodded gloomily.

We crawled back out and for a second sunlight made us squint. A sombre group of men were watching from a nearby doorway. I turned to Gabume. "Any witnesses?" Apua pushed forward a very old man, a traumatised, wide-eyed, three year old boy, and a surprisingly resilient eight year old girl.

"Is that all?"

"Yes, sir."

After talking to the old man and Aito, the girl, a picture emerged. We were looking for Amuna Ipoi who had come in the night to visit Panai's wife, Ke'ere. Their noise had woken Aito who was sleeping with her brother in the room furthest from the door. She had pretended she wanted to urinate, stepped outside, and then scampered over to her father's hut to tell him what she had seen.

She said Panai had grabbed a stick (it turned out to be a shotgun) and come to the hut. As he came in Ke'ere crashed out and bolted. Panai had torn some thatch from the roof, used the fire to light it, and raised the torch to search the cavity above the rafters.

Amuna, who had hidden himself there, reacted by thrusting a shotgun into Panai's chest and firing it point blank. Shot through the heart, Panai fell to the floor with his feet slowly burning in the fire. The din woke up the old man, Mavi, who staggered out of his hut to see Amuna, still carrying his gun, crawl out of Ke'ere's hut and sprint into the bush.

It seemed straightforward. We checked that Panai's house had been slept in. When I asked for Panai's shotgun I was told his deputy, Kaita Kamo, had taken it and was trying to hunt Amuna down. Apua raised his eyebrows and coughed. "I think you should know this Kaita has already served ten years in prison for the murder of two men." It was obvious we had to find Amuna before Kaita killed him.

There was a surge of new excitement. I looked up and heard someone asking "Is he really dead?" I walked over to Gabume who told me that the young man grinning vacantly beside him had just killed a man in a nearby village.

"Was the dead man Amuna Ipoi?" The answer was "No". Amuna had not been found, so instead, Alama Kaita, who continued to grin nervously, had killed an old man called Gitai Ino to pay back Panai's death and had come to give himself up.

Panai had to be taken to Tapini for a more formal medical examination so we wrapped him up, tied him to a pole, and asked Alama, his avenger, and another man to carry him to the Landcruiser, which was three miles away.

I gave Apua a cartridge clip for his rifle, telling him to look out for attempts on Alama's life, and to lock him in the vehicle until we got back. A constable was left in Kariarita with instructions to detain Kaita Kamo, the shotgun carrier, if he returned and to keep his ears open in case more revenge killings were being planned.

Sergeant Gabume completes his notes during the investigation into the murder of Panai Koiai at Kariarita.

With Gabume and the two remaining constables I moved down the valley to find Gitai Ino. The hamlet at Erume was deserted. No mourners, no other people, no fires. A search uncovered two spent arrows and a score of untended pigs but no body. We climbed back to the road in darkness.

Gabume and his men were left to sleep in a nearby hut and move down the mountain at first light searching for Gitai on the way. I returned to Tapini with Apua, a still cooperative Alama and an increasingly stiff Panai. Next morning Apua set off to another valley to bring in Ke'ere, the erring wife, who was an obvious target for pay-back as well as an important witness.

She had to be protected and this was most easily done by charging her with adultery, putting her through the local court, and keeping her safely in jail for six months until the heat surrounding her midmight liaison had cooled.

Alama was left in jail and with the Detachment's most durable Senior Constable riding pillion on a straining trail bike, we whined up the mountain from Tapini. We were to be followed by a tractor and trailer. The priority was to find fun loving, shotgun toting Amuna.

Bakaia – the man gripping my waist and giggling every time we hit a bump – was the son of a police sergeant, came from the Waria Valley on the northern side of this same range of mountains, and was a first class bush cop. He was square, short legged, could walk for hours without resting, and was not just bi-lingual in Motu and Pidgin but could speak Tauade too.

As we levelled out on the ridge top below Tumai's village the old man hurried stiffly towards us urgently waving his arms. I stopped and saw Bakaia was grinning in anticipation. Tumai fired off a rapid burst of *tok-ples*, smiled, patted my hand, and walked back to his hut.

"What did he say?" I asked.

"Amuna is hiding in Pomutu village."

"*Tru?* (Really?)" I exclaimed, raising my eyebrows. This information had saved us hours.

"*Tru,* (Yes really)" affirmed Bakaia, grinning again.

We sat at the road edge by a designated meeting place and waited just ten minutes before Gabume led his small column towards us. They had not found a body.

An old man stepped out of the bush. His shins had been flayed raw and were still seeping lymph. He spoke in Tauade explaining that his legs were skinned because the previous morning he had sprinted for his life through tangled *pit-pit*. He was a relative of Amuna Ipoi and as soon as he and his family heard Panai had been killed, they had fled down the mountain to escape.

Just on dawn they had lit a small fire but as they warmed themselves two men carrying bows and arrows had attacked them. The old man had taken off in a limb flailing straight line stripping the skin off his shins in the process.

Stopping on a hummock to catch his breath he saw his son fending off attackers with a spear while his daughter-in-law and grand-daughter made their getaway. One of the men fired an arrow, his son threw his spear, then hurled himself towards the river after the womenfolk.

Only one member of the group was left – the even older Gitai Ino. He had hobbled with painful stiffness across the clearing for the safety of the bush. The two armed intruders watched the younger man disappear then, with a whoop, one turned to chase down Gitai who was still shuffling desperately in an effort to escape. The fugitive was pushed over when he was overhauled and then axed in the back of the neck. I asked the name of the attacker.

"Alama Kaita," he replied.

"And the other?"

"Mana Ivoro."

He was told to wait until we returned that afternoon and to make sure his family was with him so we could protect them at Tapini.

When the tractor arrived with more policemen and an interpreter we climbed into the trailer and set off for Pomutu. We had to stop at a drop-rail gate which the driver was told to leave it open so we could save time on the way back.

As we bumped along the road began to climb. We moved into cloud then through never-ending stands of gloomy *Koroka* (pandanus) palms with their ever-dripping, spear-like, leaves.

The mist thickened until we were contained in a world bound entirely by the spinning rear wheels of the noisy tractor, withered *Koroka* leaves that clacked against each other like a witch's fingernails, and moss covered trees we could see only as we pulled slowly passed them.

When the road ended we jumped down. The interpreter barked a question at a group of Tauades who were stepping out of the fog. One man swallowed before answering.

"He knows where Amuna is hiding."

Glaring fiercely, Kiap style, I jerked my chin in the direction of Pomutu. He made a decision, walked quickly down the narrow path, and we followed.

Our group was silent as it squelched along the misty track then crossed the open, even muddier, square of Pomutu itself. Each hut was a shapeless blot half hidden by cloud. The village was deserted: no children, no chickens, no pigs, no dogs. The only sound was the suck of mud under our boots and the chink of buckles or webbing harness.

We ducked through a tanket hedge, moved up a path which twisted through open ground where even the grass was still and heavy, then stopped by a small pig fence made of roughly piled branches layered between upright stakes.

Beyond it was an orange tree, its fruit still green, and some low shrubs. Beaded spider webs almost obscured their leaves. Among the bushes, squat and low, was a hut. Its thatch was black and a thin tendril of smoke hung above it. The door was shut and it too was silent.

We moved into a huddle and whispered.

"Was Amuna in there?" The man we had met at the road end nodded.

"Has he still got his gun"? A moment's silence then another nod.

Gabume posted a man at each corner of the rectangular fence then told our guide to go to the hut and tell Amuna to throw his gun through the door.

He took me by the shoulder and together we knelt behind the fence as our messenger padded forward. He crouched with his head just under the eaves. Condensed mist dripped onto his back as he called softly. There was a muffled reply. He called again and we could hear the door being opened. He went in. A hand appeared holding a shotgun by the barrel. It was stood upright then pushed so it fell towards us.

"Tell him to bring it here," I said.

"Is Amuna alone?" asked Gabume.

"He has a woman with him."

"What woman?"

"His wife."

Gabume beckoned to Bakaia and together they stood on each side of the door.

"You can come out now," he said.

Amuna crawled through the opening, stood up, wiped muddy hands on his shorts, then walked over to me, pulling an empty cartridge case and two live cartridges from his shirt pocket.

"I killed Panai with this," he said. "I will come back with you to Tapini."

We formed a square around him and set off through the shrouded bush back to the tractor. There had been an incident at nearby Guari some years earlier in which a murderer was walking between two policemen as they made their way back to the station after her arrest. She was axed by two men before the constables could intervene. Since then there had been attempts to ambush other suspects on their way back to Tapini too.

When we reached the trailer Amuna was told to lie against the headboard. We hid him under blankets then Gabume, Bakaia, and myself sat over him covering those parts between us with haversacks. The tractor driver, who was unhappy about being caught in a revenge attack staged by Panai's family, watched anxiously.

He twisted in his seat so he could talk to us directly. "They'll be waiting for him," he promised.

He was ordered to stop only for the old man with the flayed shins. It was beginning to get dark.

We arrived at the gate we had left open. It was shut. I half stood to have a better look, sat down again, loaded Amuna's shotgun and cocked the hammer. Each of us anxiously scanned the nearby wall of trees. The interpreter opened the gate and we charged through.

Later, after I had been at Kariarita to see Panai buried, and was sleeping there, Kaita Kamo, tall, strong, lean, and fierce, the man who had been hunting Amuna, told me he had closed the gate and lain in ambush.

"I did not see you," I said.

"I was there," he replied. "I knew you were sitting on Amuna. When you stood up I was going to shoot him but when you sat down I could only see you at the end of my gun."

I counted my blessings. Few Papua New Guineans are aware of the width of a shotgun's spread.

Not knowing this we had driven on and picked up the witnesses for Gitai's murder while I climbed onto the trail bike and set off for Tatupit to see Tumai. I wanted to find out where the body of Gitai might be.

He was pleased we had found Amuna and rocked back and forwards smiling to himself. But he was pessimistic about finding Gitai, saying the body had probably been hacked to pieces and thrown into a deep pool. I left him and went home to my wife, my children, and my supper.

Next morning Gabume and another group of constables returned to find Gitai's corpse while Bakaia hurried off to Kariarita to bring in Alama's accomplice, Mana Ivoro. I spent the day at my desk interviewing witnesses, taking statements and then charged Amuna and Alama with wilful murder under Section 3 of the Queensland Criminal Code.

I also wrote a Pidgin English instruction to warders who were in charge of a jail that was a roof to both Amuna and a man who had searched the countryside to find him, failed, and so had killed another man instead. #1

Sitrong Toksave Tru Bilong Ologetta Warder Insaet Long Kalabus Tapini.

Tupela man Kiap i bin chargim ol finis long ol i bin kilim i dai wanpela man na ol i stop nau insaet long kalabus bilong yumi.

Nem belong tupela: Alama Kaita na Amuna Ipoi.

Harim Gut.

Bepo long Alama em i kisim remand bilong em, em i wok long traim mekim i dai dispela man Amuna Ipoi. Tasol Alama em i no paindim Amuna finis, na em i kirap nau na mekim i dai finis narapela man alosem wanpela smol papa bilong Amuna, nem bilong em Gitai Ino.

Orait mipela polis i no paindim finis long bodi bilong dispela lapun man Gitai. Alosem mipela tingting planti nau.

Mipela ting ting olosem – aiting ol kanaka i laik trikim yumi long Alama em i kilim Gitai na Alama i go nating insait long banis kalabus na em i stap klostu long Amuna na bihain em i traim kilim finis Amuna insaet long kalabus iet.

Alosem em i strongpela toksave tru long tupelo man Amuna na Alama. Tupela I no ken lusim rum bilong ol long wanpela taim. Em i strongpela toksave tu long ol wok olosem katim diwai bilong fia or samting bilong tomiok or naip, ol kalabus i gat taim finis ol i mas mekim outsait long banis kalabus. I tambu long naip or tamiok i stop finis insait long kalabus iet.

Mipela no save finis long dispela samting tasol moabetta samting no gut i no kamap insaet long kalabus bilong yumi.

Em tasol sitrongpela toktok bilong mi.

It said Alama and Amuna could not leave their cells at the same time. Also, all work requiring axes or knives, like cutting firewood, could only be done by prisoners serving sentences and even then only outside the jail.

We had to be aware of the possibility Alama might only have killed Gitai so he could be locked up under the same roof as Amuna and then kill him as well.

It was better to be safe than sorry. An incident similar to the one we feared had erupted some years earlier when a murder suspect was killed by a prisoner from his victim's clan as they both split wood.

Apua arrived next day striding alongside the surreal figure of Panai's wife, Ke'ere. Her appearance was strange because her clothing had been ripped into rags and she had covered herself in a thick layer of white ash to make sure we understood how deeply she was mourning.

After she was safely locked up I took the bike towards Kariarita and arrived at the venue in time to see Gabume climb onto the road.

"Find him?" I asked.

He nodded and pointed to a blanket swathed bundle slung on a bamboo pole that was being carried by two villagers.

"Any visible wounds?" I was keen to find out if Mana Ivoro had axed the old man too.

"No, we couldn't find any. There isn't much left of him. He's been mostly eaten by pigs."

And so it proved. Someone had thrown Gitia's body over a cliff above the river, where it had lain caught on some bushes and been almost devoured.

Next day Bakaia arrived with Mana Ivoro who was charged with the wilful murder of Gitai too.

Good bush policemen (Apua to the left and Bakaia right) were essential to effective Kiap government. Their role has been criticised since Independence but few who worked with them doubt most were collectively motivated by a genuine wish to preserve the dramatic post-contact lull in village violence and inter-tribal strife and were prepared to make a great deal of personal effort to sustain it. Interpreter Louie Girau stands behind.
© Graham Forster.

Committal procedures through the District Court, an obstacle that always had to be negotiated carefully, were successful and there was follow-up work too. A pair of constables had been left in the Kariarita area and as a result two men from Panai's clan were given six months in the Local Court for continuing to threaten members of Amuna's family. Kaita Kamo, the shotgun-carrying revenge seeker, was fined £15 for being in possession of an unlicensed weapon and it was confiscated.

When I left Kariarita after Panai had been buried I thought that if Amuna was given an adequate jail sentence all would be well. If Kaito, and other members of his clan, were denied pursuit of their payback tradition, the alternative route to justice had to be satisfactory for them too.

So we were alarmed to hear the Supreme Court representative would be Judge Lalor. Once a crusading Public Solicitor, it was said that he had never stopped championing the public.

Just before his arrival at Tapini he had acquitted, to the accompaniment of deep groans throughout the Public Service, a group of Highlanders from Mount Hagen who had been charged with hacking a man to death while he was handcuffed between two policemen. He said their arrest and interviews had not followed correct procedure.

We need not have worried. The Judge swept aside evidence collected to show that Amuna and Panai had been rivals for some time. Instead he concentrated on this section of Amuna's Record of Interview.

"We both saw each other at the same time through a crack between two pieces of wood. I had already put a cartridge in my gun and I was ready to fire it. I saw Panai load his gun. Aito saw this too, Panai took his shotgun ready to fire. He said, 'Aito you come quickly and hold my torch.' I knew that Panai was going to shoot me so very quickly I shot him."

It made clear that he had loaded his shotgun before Panai had loaded his, which made him guilty of technical assault and destroyed his plea of self-defence.

Judge Lalor also noted that Panai, who was right handed, had been shot through the right side of the chest which meant he could not have been aiming a shotgun and was most likely to have been holding up a torch instead. Amuna was given fifteen years – the longest sentence he had handed out.

Alama, who had said Gitai was so old his murder should be seen as inconsequential, was given ten years because he had been provoked by Panai's death. Mana Ivoro was acquitted because there was not enough evidence to support a murder conviction.

This account could confirm that Goilalas are, or were, mercilessly cold blooded and struggled to be compassionate. However, that was not always the case.

In vivid contrast to their indifference towards people outside their family circle they cared so deeply about individuals closest to them, many Westerners, especially those who have recently become disinterested in the wellbeing of members of their immediate household, might feel embarrassed.

Evidence of this came even while we were searching for the body of Gitai Ino. A group of four huts appeared to be completely empty but Bakaia, who was smiling, called over to show me an ancient woman entirely swaddled in a nest of dried moss.

She was too frail to move and had been made as comfortable as possible. She was deeply senile and well beyond the stage most British families would have considered tending her on a daily basis.

Later, when conducting a census in the Kunimeipa, I was confronted with an elderly man suffering from yaws. He was immaculately turned out, wearing a super-smart black jacket #2, and in good physical condition too.

This could only have been the result of all round love and dedicated nursing because it would have been impossible for him to have looked after himself. The disease had not only mutilated his fingers so he could not grip a spoon, it had also stripped him of his lips which meant it would have been difficult for him to hold food, especially liquids, in his mouth.

Adding to his woes he was blind and had lost his nose as well. Despite this he was amazingly alert and held his place in the family line as they stood in front of me. He would have to have been described as content.

Nor was there anything in the attitude of his family that suggested they were doing anything unusual or strange. I had the impression he was consulted on family affairs, had status within the group, and may even have, on occasions, been deferred to.

This divergence in attitudes has to be put down to the responsibilities felt by people who may have no concern for others living less than five miles away but are enveloped in a contrastingly concentrated, mutually supportive, family unit.

This intensity has been diluted among westerners who instead widen their collective responsibility by accepting ever more remote ethical concerns while at the same time neglecting, even adandoning, aged parents and on occasions difficult children too.

The concept of mutual, all-encompassing, family care throbbed a powerful deep red in Goilala villages while in Western culture it is being diluted to a barely detectable pink wash.

1 This text is proof, if it were needed, that Pidgin is not at its best in written form because important emphasis through inflection and tone is missing.

#2 It must have been stolen from a European house in Port Moresby and been part of the loot that regularly found its way back to Goilala villages. On one occasion, while searching for an escaped prisoner near Guari, I came across a full dinner set. It fell short of the cruet and a gravy boat, but almost everything else was present.

CHAPTER FIFTEEN

A family reckoning

"I knew you were sitting on Amuna. When you stood up I was going to shoot him but when you sat down I could only see you at the end of my gun."

Kaita Kamo, Kariarita Village, Goilala Sub-District, 1974

After the murders at Kariarita it became even more obvious that shotguns were a problem in Goilala Sub-District. Owners had to present themselves, and their gun, to police so they could renew their licences, and because a gun that was unsafe could be confiscated I destroyed as many as I could.

It was not especially difficult. Barrels were often pitted, the stocks loose and the trigger mechanism rusted. Ownership was common so it was not hard to make a case that, because there were so many, they were a threat to public safety.

They were also a danger to increasingly scarce Birds of Paradise because these could be picked off from treetops with much more accuracy than when they were hunted only with bows and flightless arrows.

The people were forbidden to shoot them with a gun but the plumage was prized by villagers throughout PNG who had a strong abstract link with the birds and imitated them conscientiously in their dances.

Almost every male performer at these *sing-sings* wore Bird of Paradise plumes in his headdress. Immediately after contact decoration levels were relatively modest. Photographs taken at Nondugl in the 1950s, where men cherished the two, enormously long, tail feathers of the Black Sicklebill, confirm they were content to wear just two or three – with four so rare it immediately signalled the carrier was a man of unusual wealth and importance.

In the early 1970s displays highlighted by six, even seven, of these graceful feathers were common. Like all Bird of Paradise plumes they were stored carefully between dances in crushproof, bamboo sheaths. Nevertheless some faded, or were broken, and for this to be countered, and the number of Black Sicklebill feathers displayed at Nondugl's sing-sings to have more than doubled in just 20 years, must have meant more birds were being shot or that the people had suddenly become significantly more skilled with bow and arrow.

It was impossible to attend large dancing demonstrations like those at Mount Hagen and Goroka, where thousands of astonishingly intricate headdresses were on display, or even much more modest ceremonies at village level, without speculating about the glaringly obvious demands being made on the Bird of Paradise population and the likely contribution of the shotgun to the bobbing seas of impressive feather decoration on view.

Wi Kupa from Kabalku in the Wahgi Valley helps a senior clansman prepare his headdress so they can earn useful cash by staging a "wedding" for a group of Japanese tourists. The importance of Black Sicklebill Birds of Paradise to their performance can be judged by the number of carefully preserved tail plumes standing to their left. Each pair represents one bird.

220

To my surprise the ADC objected to efforts to curb shotgun use. I was upsetting too many people and they had begun to complain to Louis Mona, the local MHA. I was told Kiaps had to keep their political noses clean.

But I did not back off and so opposing ideas on yet another contentious administrative issue exposed a rift between myself, and some of my immediate superiors. I was sure I was right because it would save lives. Even so it was made clear I was being paternal and the days when Kiaps took positions on public wellbeing which directly upset village people, and triggered avoidable complaints to democratically more powerful MHAs, were over.

Shotgun permits had originally been distributed among well-placed people like Luluais or ex-policemen as a reward for loyal service which might, for example, include prompt completion of a new section of road. But they quickly became coveted status symbols – and not just because of their obvious superiority over bows and arrows when out hunting.

It was also abundantly apparent that Goilalas, a people not averse to murder, appreciated a shotgun's withering lethalness and knew that possession made the owner more intimidating than an individual who only carried an axe.

Not surprisingly men from almost every village, and every walk of life, would, if they could, beg, borrow wheedle, cajole or steal, shotgun ownership. Records showed that in 1974 about one in twenty Goilala men held a permit and 330 guns had been registered within the region's borders.

Confident that there could be no challenge if the weapons were genuinely dangerous, and sure in my mind that if there were fewer guns village people were less likely to be killed, I continued to confiscate those that were unsafe and refuse to allow the purchase of another. In this way perhaps thirty more were smashed and entombed in the concrete foundations of a new building.

The ADC intervened again. The MHA continued to be upset at my tenacity. Did I not know, he said, that I was treating villagers like children and shotguns like dangerous toys? When I repeated that such common ownership was a threat to public safety he sighed and insisted my attitude was out of place in a country that was about to become independent.

It was making Australian administrators unpopular at a time when PNG was moving through a sensitive stage of political development and so, for the sake of stability, I, along with other Kiaps, should make no fuss, raise no dust, lie low, work quietly, and if in doubt do nothing.

Life could undoubtedly be difficult for senior white Kiaps working for the first time under unfamiliar priorities identified by a black government – especially if they were also being watched by muscle flexing MHAs maintaining a keen eye on the barometer of their electoral popularity.

But it was hard not to think that increasing acceptance of the 'lie low and say nothing' mantra that had begun to dominate rural administration throughout PNG was at the same time being reinforced, almost exponentially, by an ongoing uplift in ultimate monetary gain through enhanced redundancy payments and not just informed awareness of new tensions and sensitivities that were emerging in the approach to political independence.

Many permanent white civil servants were unhappy at having to give up their work and be replaced by senior black officers.

To compensate for the unexpectedly sudden end of their careers, and also lift morale, they had been told they would receive, after they were laid off, a payment calculated in multiples of their present salary – which because it was reviewed annually offered obvious rewards for those able to stay in position longest.

A modest annual pay lift of £250 could, for the most senior, emerge as an additional £2,500 when the final cheque was written. Small wonder, then, that pocket calculators flicked incessantly in almost every government office – and the process was repeated, often to a chorus of delighted expostulations and oaths, each time there was a pay rise.

Adding to the incentive to dig in for as long as possible was a superannuation scheme within which the ultimate payment was determined by the breaching of pre-identified time obstacles.

If a payment of only two and half times the amount contributed after ten years' service increased to three times after twelve years there was clear motivation for a man in his eleventh year to survive into his twelfth by every means at his disposal.

It was obvious these officials had accepted their career in PNG was no longer open ended and were taking comfort from a strategy based on acknowledgement that the depth of their post-PNG wellbeing rested on being able to survive at their desk for the longest possible time.

My attitude to the wisdom, or otherwise, of allowing shotgun ownership levels in the Goilala to be maintained at current high rates continued to be reinforced by field observations, which within six months identified a man with a hand mutilatation that could only be explained by a shotgun being pushed away from his body just as it was being discharged, another with infected pellet wounds pockmarking his face, and yet another shaking with shock after a shotgun aimed at him had been deflected.

Nevertheless there was unrelenting insistence that continued confiscation risked reducing the Goilala sub-district to ferment and yet more warnings I should be cautious about the advancement of positive administration.

Being in charge of a Police Detachment required me to assess the constables and submit reports, which meant I could advance, or retard, careers. One was dismissed while two others faced internal disciplinary charges.

To compensate I did what I could to progress the advancement of Apua, Bakaia and Michael Nuglai. Their conduct was ideal but may not have been noticed because in police service terms Tapini was a backwater.

Eventually Apua was able to attend a course which, if completed, would have given him two stripes and the option to attend a Sergeant's course a year later and I hoped I had made enough noise to allow Bakaia to add a stripe to the one he had already earned.

But the first success was through Michael Nuglai. He was a Chimbu who moved with the head lowered determination of a bulldozer. Physical as Michael appeared to be – it is always an asset for a policeman – his muscle was deceptive. He was a philosopher as well.

He had joined the force after failing exams at Goroka Teachers' College. He told me he had not studied books but had instead paid long and exhaustive attention to a detailed assessment of beer.

During his first years as a policeman he had shed this habit and gone through a period of devout Christianity during which he said he "really believed". Then he was disciplined for two internal offences at nearby Woitape, which lay on his Record of Service like an unbreachable dam over which promotion could not flow.

After three months I had watched him long enough to realise he was under promoted and also discovered he had been charged with damaging police property after coming home from work to find a drunken station employee pissing in his living room.

Michael had tried to sling him out but had missed the door and damaged a wall instead. Then he had been disciplined a second time for giving the offender a verbal blasting as he staggered away. I could not quash the convictions, but could try to obliterate them, and was rewarded with his attendance on a course from which he emerged as a Sergeant.

He often went with me on patrol where he again demonstrated his appetite for explanation and discussion. When I told him Independence was inevitable because it was against nature for an old man with grey hair to suckle at the breast of his mother, the response was that many people in PNG's mountainous interior had only just begun to move out of nappies.

We could talk at length, invariably in Pidgin, but this did not prevent him launching into metaphysical discussion about the existence of Man which could begin with comparing us to ants in an ant's nest unaware of the forces which shape our lives and end with him casting his search for explanation so wide he was understandable only to himself.

His Christianity had toned down because he could see flaws in interpreting its doctrine too literally and in the end afforded it no more status than a rule of thumb guide to the pursuit of a useful life. I thought it was an impressive conclusion to have reached just thirty years after being born into village culture and then exposed to proselytising missionaries as a child.

Apart from murder, shotguns, and police paperwork, my other dominant field activity in the Goilala was – as was the case with every other Kiap whatever their location – road making.

Metaphorically the region was a vastly ridged mountain island connected to the coastal mainland only by airstrips. Its internal road network clung precariously to valley sides that in places were crevasses and sometimes the bench was so narrow the only way to be completely sure all four of a vehicle's wheels were safe was to risk scraping a door handle against the gelignite blasted sides of a cliff wall.

These constructions were miracles of rule of thumb technology and personal persistence. Most had been surveyed by French Sacre Coeur priests, like Abel and Morant at Kamulai, using homemade theodolites. After being armed with operating permits and as much explosive as Tapini's Local Government Council could pass their way, they would blast their way round mountains and then, after rock falls had obliterated parts of the roads they had built, shovel their way back again.

Sacre Coeur fathers Abel (Kamulai: right) and Duffey (Tapini: left) discuss road making practicalities in a Mission workshop. Each carried a gelignite blasting permit.
© *Ian Douglas.*

Those lengths that could be hacked out with pick and shovel were given, in six chain contracts, to villagers for £20. These roads wound in, down, out, up, and along valley sides because they had to follow contours if they were to sustain a gradient of no more than one foot in twelve. There were occasions when, after negotiating a particularly ferocious spur, a road could swing in exactly the opposite direction to its destination.

The aim was to link every village with Tapini and priests continued their efforts even though the only vehicles on the station, perhaps six in all, belonged to the government, a mission, and two European trade store owners.

Their vision spanned the 20th century and looked into the next. They hoped Tapini, and therefore all of the Goilala including Guari and Woitape, would eventually be linked to Moresby and become part of a national transport network that embraced PNG's northern coast as well.

They also hoped their efforts, and those of the Department of Agriculture, to raise beef and grow salad vegetables for the Moresby market – at that time all flown out – would be buoyed by direct road delivery and village earnings would expand.

These projects would have daunted anyone but a priest. Goilala terrain had even intimidated a government which had successfully used similar civil engineering skills to construct the Highlands Highway, which in economic terms justified the cost and effort of its creation on an almost daily basis.

Single minded concentration on road building was an integral part of Kiap folklore too and there was a story, often repeated on Patrol Posts after a couple of weekend beers, which, whether apocryphal or not, underlines this focus.

It takes place in a remote corner of the Western Highlands sometime in the 1960s where a busy senior Kiap has reluctantly pulled local clansmen off a road-building project so they can turn up at an airstrip in full traditional dress to impress a visiting dignitary.

The assembled lines of fiercely painted, weapon carrying, warriors wait patiently as a touring High Commissioner winds his way through a typical round of clichés and superlatives.

At his side, dour and glowering, stands his Kiap interpreter still seething at the loss of a valuable road-extending opportunity.

The visitor concludes his speech with the inevitable "I am so glad to have had the chance to see your wonderful country and meet you wonderful people; God bless you all."

The Kiap completes his interpretation by concluding: "The important man is very pleased to have seen you all and he thinks your land is fertile. But he wants you to know, and he says this with all seriousness, that after taking a careful look he has had to conclude that your roads are no bloody good."

Their massed feather headdresses nod solemnly as villagers accept that the effort they have put into road building must be even greater.

The construction of roads is, after the imposition of the Pax Australiana, which curbed endemic inter-village warfare, the Kiap's biggest achievement – although their introduction inevitably trailed mixed results.

One of the unwelcome cultural adaptions they provoked had surfaced at Minj where a group of youths from three clans had combined to form the "Class Six" gang named after the driver's licence coding for heavy vehicles.

As lorries loaded at the coast grunted up the steep section of the Highlands Highway near Kabalku that was known as Skyline Drive, these young men would climb onto the load, slash the canvas, and if they liked the look of its cargo would tip off crates and boxes for partners hiding by the roadside.

Profits were high because cost was low, risk added to the excitement, and their standing among youths of their own age soared too.

It was obvious roads would eventually invade every corner of PNG. In the short years since 1968 there had already been big changes. Binaru, the natural bridging point over the Imbrum River below Bundi where I swam while working on the Mission sawmill, had been earmarked as a pivotal point of construction for the Madang-Mount Hagen Highway.

And, no doubt provoking grumbles from "Class Six", the Skyline Drive at Kabalku was to be sidelined by a new, multi-million dollar, valley bottom section of a re-directed Highlands Highway.

National plans also included linking Port Moresby to Mount Hagen, Lae, and Madang – which would mean, as Sacre Coeur priests fervently hoped, a national trunk road cleaving through the formidable Goilala mountains too.

Papua New Guineans in established communities were not the only ones facing new pressures in the early 1970s. Increased social mobility and therefore the almost overnight appearance of people with no connection to local structure, was at the same time disturbing villages in South West Northumberland.

Up until the end of the 1950s the only people who had not been born into these tight knit neighbourhoods were teachers, policemen, clergymen, shop owners and professionals who could afford to buy the grandest houses.

But improved road access, almost universal ownership of a family car, and an ever-widening range of employment opened the way to mainly middle class people, all of them strangers, some of whom had moved in from distant cities like Birmingham and London and who tended to work on industrial Tyneside, only around 20-25 miles away, as well.

Initially these "in-comers" entertained the local people because their approach to everyday living was so strange, but by the beginning of the 1980s they were so numerous, and so overwhelmingly middle class, longstanding attitudes previously dominated by people who could just about recite each other's family history were undermined.

There was structural damage, as well as benefits, and principal among the former was soaring house prices because local newly-weds could not compete with middle class people able to arrange large mortgages for village homes and so were forced to live elsewhere.

This triggered yet more dismemberment of established extended families and introduced an ephemeral, commuter culture because many of these arrivals moved on to other transient destinations like Milton Keynes or Welwyn Garden City as breadwinners threaded their way through a carefully planned sequence of lucrative promotions.

A benefit was a surge in the number of children attending the village school and a near universal lift in concentration on academic achievement – although ultimately this too helped to undermine family frameworks as more village children earned places at university.

Station life at Tapini was good which meant Kiap's families found it easy to be content. The sun was pleasant instead of punishing, there was a well-maintained tennis court, a deep swimming pool fed by a mountain stream, and a fine hotel with a terraced bar.

The comprehensively stocked trade store was run by a busy European couple and planes landed regularly to deliver newspapers and mail from Port Moresby, as well as frozen meat and other supplementary food ordered by telegram or radio.

There were three other white families with young children so socialising with peers was not a strain, the hydro-electricity supply was constant, and there was work for wives in the Post Office too. In PNG terms it earned a four star, even five star, rating.

Home life was given additional spice by the arrival of one of Paula's sisters, Rosemary, who not much later married a man who worked for the Department of Agriculture in Lae.

Then my brother Graham, who was returning to the UK after a year and a half's voluntary work in the nearby Solomon Islands, flew in too. He had bummed his way to Wau, on the other side of the Owen Stanleys, then talked himself onto a charter plane carrying building material. There were no seats so he made do with a toilet pedestal and arrived with his backside deep in its lilywhite recesses and knees tucked under his chin.

However, new undercurrents were beginning to undermine bedrock acceptance that no matter what was happening elsewhere a Kiap's family was, despite its fundamental isolation, always secure – even on outstations like Tapini which were surrounded by village people who woke up to the threat of violent death on an almost daily basis.

A Kiap's domestic life was unusually demarcated because bush work could not be shared with wives whose principal obligation was to adapt to the administrative demands thrust on their husbands, accept or endure the restraints and restrictions of station living, do their best to fit in, and earn extra money through service work if it was available.

The assumption that wives, and children, were safe was not ingrained. In pioneer days most Kiaps were single. Wives were not allowed into uncontrolled, newly contacted areas and when the men who were stationed there did marry they were often sufficiently senior, in years as well as service, to work from a sub-district, even town, base with the husband patrolling a desk and quelling paper warfare instead of being absent from home for weeks at a time.

I was recruited as a married man, as were many contemporary contract officers, and as we were allowed further from administrative centres, and posted deeper into the bush, our work became more exciting.

The strain between this advance, and responsibility for the safety of our wives and children ignited when I was told to take over the Patrol Post at Guari.

My delight was in clear contrast to Paula's dismay. Even by PNG standards it was a lonely station with accommodation for only one European officer, the Kiap, who ran it with the help of an office clerk, four policemen, an interpreter, a tractor driver and as many casual labourers as there were funds to support.

There was an airstrip but the only regular flight, which brought in groceries and mail, was on Wednesdays and it was often clouded in by mid-morning too. An unstable bush road connected it with Tapini and another, particularly difficult and dramatic, was the only link to the nearest Mission at Kamulai.

It stood at 7,000 feet and although the Kunimeipa people were more volatile than the Tauade they were generally easier to work with. From the standpoint of my job I could not have been happier.

But Paula's heart sank. She had already been through Guari where she had seen that the radio and electricity generator were broken and the insecure house was in poor repair.

She had two children, one almost three years old, the other seventeen months, and was expecting her third just four months later. Even at Tapini she was worried about only being able to fly to Moresby in medical emergencies during daylight hours and the low cloud that often barricaded Guari's airstrip meant it could be shut down during the day too.

Compounding these fears, the nearest radio, and the simplest medical help, were at Kamulai which was ten miles, or an hour's drive, away on a road that frightened her and she knew I would be on patrol for perhaps a fortnight every six weeks or so leaving her alone and unsupported.

She refused to come. I began to argue but was silenced as her long suppressed anxieties over elementary family safety flared. Had I not, she said, taken out a Wahgi Valley patrol with Nigel Van Ruth that had left her without a husband for the thick end of four months?

Did I know that she often had to listen in her bed at night, both at Minj and Tapini, while prowlers roamed our garden and scouted the veranda?

She reminded me that both her babies had arrived early and her third might too. She also warned that Daniel's Pidgin would soon be better than his English and his education was beginning to suffer as well.

I protested that I loved the work and the pay was good. She silenced me again. Did I know, she asked, that during our entire time at Minj she had been afraid of driving, or being driven, on Highland roads in case someone walked in front of her vehicle and she was killed in retaliation?

Did I know, she persisted, what it was like to see her children suffer from prickly heat, an occasional mystery illness, or be deprived of liberty vehicles by foolish ADCs?

And then she delivered the coup-de-grâce. Was I aware, she asked with her jaw firmly set, that while I was single-mindedly pursuing the murderers of Oulaine Papaite, and arresting more suspects than some village people were happy with, one of the station's retired police sergeants, who had been alarmed at local reaction to the conviction of Kaga the Council President, had taken her aside and advised her to keep her children close because there was a risk there might be *"trabel"*?

"What does 'trouble' mean? What might people do to persuade Kiaps to pull in their horns?" she demanded. "Would I have been intimidated? Could Daniel be assaulted? Might he have been kidnapped?"

I had to take this seriously because ex-Sergeant Toro was no gossip. He held the Queen's Police Medal for gallantry and was an intelligent, and worried, observer of new social undercurrents that were surfacing in pre-independence Tapini.

I knew she found our life challenging but had not realised her fears ran so deep. It was clear that I, a Kiap, enjoyed most of PNG's excitement while Paula, a Kiap's wife, had to shoulder the bulk of domestic worries hoisted on an outstation home. She was determined this insecurity would not continue and told me she would never, ever, live alone at Guari.

Our approach to life in PNG reappraised, and also resolved, she returned to Britain on February 22nd 1975 with our two children. Crates were packed and transported to Moresby. I was to take up the posting, living as a bachelor, and then fly to Britain after resigning from the Chief

Minister's Department that August.

I kissed her, and our children, goodbye and accepted my final appointment, confused by yet another bout of contradictory feelings. Family had to take precedence but the solution had been radical. There was to be no career for me in PNG.

CHAPTER SIXTEEN

Critical signs of fundamental decline

"You're a Kiap," she cried in accusation. There was a moment's silence before nearby black voices responded with "What's wrong with that?"

Port Moresby, 1974.

When I was a VSO at Bundi, and so new to PNG that my newly bared legs were lobster pink, I asked a Kiap what it was like to be in charge of a Patrol Post. He mumbled, thrashed his arms in an effort to hasten a summary of his feelings, smiled self-consciously and mumbled, "Well – it's a bit like being a …King."

In the moments that I could laugh at myself that is how I felt about being in charge at Guari. It did not matter that after midday this kingdom was invariably obscured by cloud so dense it could waft through windows in my living room then drift in tendrils past the fireplace.

The fanfare that heralded my morning arrival at its tiny, two man office came not from the polished throats of brass trumpets but the gaping gullets of two donkeys, which were survivors of pre-airstrip days when

Kiaps came in from Moresby carrying their supplies on pack animals.

At the office I took a salute from a pair of grinning policeman instead of ranks of palace guards and then directed hovering lines of court minions, or in this case the station's labourers, to their tasks.

The prancing charger was a mud spattered, trail geared, Honda 90, the ermine cape the tatty pullover I wore first thing in the morning, throne a dilapidated office chair, and staff of office the notebook in which the names of absent labourers and those who offended national law were recorded.

And I ruled Guari more or less as I pleased because the posting, which was also my swansong, was to be a short five months and I did not have an ADC breathing down my neck.

When, ten months after leaving Binaru, I had landed with Paula at Sydney Airport and immediately ran off to bang on the door of the Australian School of Pacific Administration in Mosman to beg admission to its Kiap induction course this was exactly the situation I had been hoping for. Working as OIC on an isolated PNG Patrol Post not only confirmed unusual freedom it also carried a whiff of romance.

Even so, my assessment of the situation facing pre-Independence Guari was sober. I did not think Patrol Officers who would replace me would be able to secure enough funds to keep the road link with the Sub-District Office at Tapini open. It was already disintegrating and neither the money, nor the machinery, needed to make immediate repairs were at the station's disposal.

And there were other indications that the post-Independence Day wellbeing of Guari's Patrol Post might already be hanging on an unexpectedly slender thread.

The Kunimeipa's villages were a refuge for criminals, usually unmarried young men who fuelled the region's theft-based secondary economy, who had burgled one house too many in Port Moresby and were on the run from the city's police.

Communication between Moresby and the Goilala was wretched but one Wednesday the mail plane delivered a telegram confirming that a well-known local offender, Peto, had broken jail. Enquiries revealed he was back at Ropalek, the village below the airstrip, which was also home to most of the station's labour line. He was arrested and because there were no cells he stayed with one of the policemen in his home while we waited for a plane.

But Peto was a man whose code had been forged in Moresby, not in the bush, so he could not resist escaping during the night. Next morning his fellow villagers were sacked from the road line and told they could have their jobs back as soon as he returned to custody. Peto gave himself up and stood bail at £20, which was a huge sum, but forfeited it forever by absconding yet again and disappearing to goodness knows where.

There were other signs that Kiap government at Guari was disintegrating. A local leader, Suiz, was seen jostling a protesting airline pilot in what looked like a hostile opening, and ultimately destructive, manouevre to reinforce a combative claim that his family owned the land on which the airstrip had been built and had still to receive a worthwhile payment.

And his son David, a young man who, I suspected, had made himself good company to lonely Kiaps who had worked at Guari before, and on the strength of this had been able to carve out an unusually privileged position, refused to let us continue to dig out sand from an established pit by the roadside, claiming it belonged to his ancestors and he had still to give permission.

It was a groundless attempt at obstruction because land up to fifteen feet on either side of a road was controlled by government, so a tractor was sent to bring back a load. Next morning this fresh heap of sand had been scattered and lost. It would have been difficult to have been faced with a more direct challenge.

The following day I went on Patrol and came back a fortnight later to discover my house had been burgled. Only food had been taken and my concern increased when I was told sand, which was mixed with cement and clay, to make the station's housebricks, had not been collected because the tractor driver was afraid of confrontation and no one was prepared to make a counter-move on the Chief Minister's behalf.

Another load was brought back and an hour later David, who was being interviewed, bolted as soon as he suspected he was about to be charged with entering government property. He too honoured Moresby, not bush, rules.

This defiance could not be ignored so a search warrant was secured and we discovered his house was stuffed with government furniture, perhaps acquired over some time, ranging from a wood burning stove, and an iron bed as well as saucepans and chairs issued only to the police. These were loaded onto a trailer and sent to Tapini.

Men from David's village were sacked from the road line and told they could have their jobs back if he reported to the office the next day. He did, but when he was charged with breaking and entering he fled yet again, diving almost horizontally through a forest of legs and a door that should have been locked, before disappearing over the mountain tops in exactly the same way as Peto.

This was alarming because harassment, aimed at government in general and the resident Kiap in particular, would, if it was not suppressed, undermine the reputation of post-independence Guari and make it difficult to persuade the PNG-born officers, who would inevitably follow on, to be enthusiastic about a challenging appointment.

Initially fewer patrols might be undertaken because no OIC was going to feel happy if their house could be burgled while they were away, but eventually the Patrol Post might acquire a no-go label, and never again be fully staffed, which meant fewer funds would be channelled through it and less money would find its way to village people's pockets as well.

These gloomy thoughts reinforced the decision that the future of the Tapini-Guari road should be committed to luck and good fortune, and effort concentrated on the link between the airstrip and Kamulai instead.

It was clear to me, and this might have been considered heretical at the time, that the long term advancement of the Guari area was more likely to be led by the Catholic Mission than the Sub-District Office.

It had already built, and staffed, a number of schools, the largest of these at Kamulai itself. None were being managed by government and there was no trade store at Guari either. In contrast there was a shop at Kamulai which distributed general merchandise, clothing, soap, kitchen utensils, tinned fish, tobacco, and other goods which were essential to the comfort of teachers, policemen and other in-coming personnel, to a network of village stores at bulk prices.

Kamulai also ran an aid post, which was able to cope with ailments or injuries beyond the experience and skill of government orderlies working in villages, as well as being home to the only two-way radio in the Guari area and direct contact with both Tapini and Port Moresby.

To confirm its position as the single, most positive, economic force the Mission had also, with the help of funds from PNG's Development Bank, launched a project that introduced villagers to the practicalities of raising cattle and in addition to this owned, and operated, two air compressors which drove the only pneumatic drills available for road construction.

In truth the Mission at Kamulai was, in almost every aspect except policing, formal administration, and its pursuit of regular Church activity, the model of a vigorous Patrol Post.

Relationships between Kiaps and missionaries on a trans-PNG basis had at times been strained, which perhaps made this unorthodoxy look extreme. Nevertheless I could see no better way of making a contribution to the long term welfare of the Kunimeipa people than making sure the road link between Guari airstrip and the mission station remained open for as long as possible.

This being the case almost all the station's effort was concentrated on widening the narrowest parts of its ten mile section, improving its drains, and trying to shave some of the severity off its most dramatic hairpin bends. To succeed called for blatant fund adjusting. Our Departmental slang for this was "spivving", and although it was not only unofficial, but also illicit, a Kiap's ability to "spiv" funds was acknowledged as an essential bulwark of Patrol Post administration.

Simply explained the method was this. Central funds allocated quarterly for airstrip and house maintenance could be diverted into unbudgeted road-making if claims covering regular maintenance continued to be filed even though no work was undertaken. Then, by paying wages at just 40 per cent of the going rate, a permanent line of at least thirty labourers on the Guari-Kamulai road was sustained for almost five months.

Funding had also been boosted after a senior clerk in distant Konedobu, the Moresby headquarters of the Chief Minister's Department, was persuaded to vote an additional £750 to the project too. The wage bill over the five month period was around £4,000 while the official road fund allocation totalled just £1,750.

Kunimeipas from Ropalek village take their midday
break from roadmaking. © Ian Douglas.

This was not working by the book but was nevertheless typical of what might be done on any pre-Independence Patrol Post that had a pet project to push through.

While still stationed at Tapini I had travelled to Moresby to attend the Supreme Court and one evening found myself at a party. It was alcohol-free and attended primarily by Papua New Guineans. The cross-section was wide. One of the guests was a Chimbu I had played football against at Gembogl in 1969 while another, Father John Momis, was front man for the Bougainville separatist group and already a political giant who was putting the Somare government through yet another of its periodic tough spells.

Others included Ignatius Kilage, first Highlander to be ordained into the Catholic priesthood, and Meg Taylor, Tsengelap daughter of Jim, who was the Chief Minister's private secretary and someone I had known for some time.

There were three other whites. Two were husbands to local wives and the third, a large and vocal female academic from the Australian National University, was a fully subscribed member of the power-groupie clan.

University staff regarded Kiaps as prize game and on this type of social occasion I had learned to keep my occupation to myself because it could, especially among those who saw it as an obstruction to post-colonial liberalism, trigger an abusive response.

Eventually she rumbled me. Her delight temporarily silenced the room. She had discovered someone she could rend and tear. "You're a Kiap," she cried in accusation. There was a short pause before nearby black voices responded, "What's wrong with that?"

She gulped in surprise and then summarised a visit she had made to Laiagam in the Western Highlands. "I spoke to this Kiap," she stuttered. "I was in his office. It was an arsenal." #1

It was a good start and at the University might have provoked a storm. Father Momis silenced her with a single, gruff, retort. "They need guns at Laiagam," he growled. She sat stunned with her mouth opening and shutting like a fish.

Academics, many of them white, at the University of Papua New Guinea almost unanimously held Kiaps in contempt and cited them as relics of outdated administrative arrangements, which meant their criticism of the Kiap system, especially the Europeans employed within it, was overwhelming.

Their overview was that a typical Kiap was an arrogant, culturally ignorant bully and students, who were about to become the new elite, were encouraged to adopt this view and express it any way they pleased – including verse.

"The Kiap shouts at us
Forcing the veins to stand out on his neck
Nearly forcing the excreta out of his bottom
He says "You are ignorant"
Every whiteman the government sends to us
Forces his veins out shouting
Nearly forces the excreta out of his bottom
Shouting "You bush kanaka"
(University of Papua New Guinea, Port Moresby: Circa 1975.)

While in Moresby in late 1971, before being flown to the Wahgi Valley, I spent an evening on the University's Waigani Campus where a series of student led theatre presentations were being staged. Criticism of Australia for delaying its departure and continuing to impose its style of government on PNG's village people was an overwhelming theme.

Most of these playlets, which were written by undergraduates, featured a Kiap who was presented as a comic figure in exaggerated colonial dress, whose clumsy cultural insensitivities, and general incompetence, were a source of huge amusement and derision.

Signature Kiap phrases included "bloody stupid bush kanakas" and there was no doubt that within these performances Kiaps were deliberately cast as pantomime villains and their script carefully tuned to deliver the widest possible range of laughter and scorn. When the "European" in the big slouch hat and heavy boots came on stage I half expected the audience to collectively yell "He's behind you".

We could, without doubt, be culturally clumsy, not least because PNG's many traditions were so complex that the adoption of a universal template which covered its endless parade of language groups was impossible. But most Kiap effort was dedicated to persuading people not to kill each other and then building roads which opened up their communities to improved health, education and economic advancement as well.

Critics of Kiap government also pointed to the management style adopted at Guari when denouncing it. Perhaps its system is best described as creative expediency backed by benevolent, but arbitrary, rules.

It is worth saying that Kiaps were rarely cruel, that within the bounds of natural justice they were rarely unjust, and that they regularly sidelined regulation not for their own gain but to accelerate progress in the area where they worked.

The upgrading of the Guari-Kamulai road was an example of this. Many protocols were ignored, and if these breaches had been pursued by an inspector with an appetite for absolute administrative correctness, I might have been reprimanded or dismissed.

But it was a project that offered no direct personal gain and, even if they were paid much less than they could have been, was enthusiastically supported by the labour line who knew the ultimate beneficiaries were themselves and their families.

In bush situations like Guari it is difficult to suggest an alternative to what was effectively self-help apart from flooding the area with cascades of development money, which in economic terms might never be justified.

It follows too I had accepted that the Christian missions, along with the Australian government, were each manifestations of western culture that had overwhelmed PNG and would continue to influence its development.

It does no good to pretend that its stone-based technology and scattered, perpetually warring, tribes could have lain undisturbed by world impetus for ever.

The real argument over Australia's presence should begin, not with whether it had a right to be there, but what might have happened if a potentially harsher Japanese or Indonesian administration had taken over the country before it became independent instead.

It was inevitable that one of these three powers would have done. That is a fact. Much as some may have disliked it Papua New Guinea and its people could not have remained in hiding forever.

A culture backed by superior technology would, as surely as night follows day, have eventually imposed itself on them. That it happened to be an unusually benign Australia, which crucially put more cash into PNG than it ever took out, is incidental.

Huge islands cannot be permanently blocked from world view by mists and cloud, or millions of people be endlessly concealed behind huge mountains. That is irrefutable and like many truths it is harsh.

It was also becoming obvious that investigating murder in post-Independence Guari could become even more difficult because sudden deaths might no longer be reported immediately, or even reported at all – which once again raised the possibility that a primary connection between Kiap-government and Kiap-governed, perhaps the most important link of all, was already beginning to weaken.

This disturbing thought was encouraged by contact with Port Moresby's Police Department which was struggling to suppress the ever increasing number of murders linked to Goilalas living in shanty town settlements which included a Kunimeipa stronghold near the Brown River.

It had passed on information about a multiple murder and the names of a couple of Kunimeipa suspects. These had been handed over to the station's interpreter and police with instructions to immediately let me know if they returned to their village.

I was told I had shaken hands with one of these men, while out on a routine patrol, only when I was about to leave the station and there was no chance of being able to set out to arrest him.

This was profoundly worrying, even ominous, because it pointed to either an internal conspiracy of silence, universal fear of reprisal, or widespread complacency at police and interpreter level, which the next Kiap at Guari might also be unable to overcome.

I was aware of just one sudden death in the villages surrounding the station over 1974-75. The man's body had been found, unmarked except for marginal bruising on the neck and jaw, in a boulder strewn stream halfway between the station and Kamulai. He was middle-aged, had lived on the station alone, was described as *long-long* (weak in the head) and his demise was presented by both police and people as a puzzling accident.

I could do nothing to disprove this even though I suspected he had been suffocated after his nostrils and throat had been blocked with soft linen cloth. The radio at Kamulai was used to call for a pathologist to conduct a post-mortem but this proved impossible and so there was nothing concrete to confront a possible suspect with.

Initial Kiap determination to descend on every sudden death like a ton of bricks was a critical element of successful post-contact control because it undermined simmering inter-clan hostilities and paved the way for the fear-free travel that was essential to the development of stronger local economies.

It was also fundamental to the extension of the successful pax-Australiana by an independent PNG's administration. However, this critically important link between government and governed was already dissipating at Goilala level and a depressing situation was not helped by there being no radio at Guari and pathologists in Port Moresby being either unwilling, or unable, to travel into the bush and undertake post-mortems either.

I thought the unfortunate man might have died because a prominent male on Guari station had wanted, for no other reason than to build a local reputation, to test his ability to successfully pursue covert murder through a trial run and thought someone who was harmless, and had no obvious family connections, was an ideal first victim. Only Kiaps who later worked with the Kunimeipa people will know if this speculation was correct.

#1 The Kiap at Laiagam was Ian Douglas and the "arsenal" in his office was an untidy line of around thirty decrepit shotguns that had been confiscated from village people because they were either unlicensed or unsafe. This had been made clear to the academic who appeared either not to have understood, or to have ignored, his explanation in her libertarian pursuit of the notion that fundamentally aggressive Kiaps and Kiap-style government no longer had a place in PNG's administration.

CHAPTER SEVENTEEN

The airstrip at Aulaipa

"Each time the machine tore down the clearing rice, flour, axes and goods of all descriptions came hurtling to the ground. The local people sat in awe and bewilderment, their eyes wide open at the sight. To them the aeroplane was a messenger from the heavens bringing food to spirits who had been stranded. Some old men actually told us by signs that they were ready to depart with us to our world above."

(Jim Taylor after an air drop of supplies for one of his 1933 Highland patrols.)

Cargo cults are an obvious symptom of cultural destabilisation. They are not peculiar to PNG. They have been recorded among the native people of North America, West Africa, and other locations as well. But they are common in the South Pacific and so, along with tales of buried treasure, mutiny, whale hunting, lost tribes, stone clubs, blackbirding, cannibalism, and piracy have wormed their way into its folklore too.

Insight into the turmoil they can create began in 1969 when I was hopping around Madang with a broken leg and introduced to a local girl who combined social attributes of wit, elegance, and charm with great personal appeal that was underlined by the contrast between her blinding smile, shining eyes, and smooth brown skin. Her English was good, her conversation bright, and her arm was wrapped around an escort – a stocky young Australian who was infatuated with her.

I met him many months later in entirely different circumstances when, over a series of evenings and a number of beers, he outlined a tragic story. He worked for a large offshore coconut plantation, spending much of his time in Madang, and the girl was from a tiny village on an island just off the coast, which over the years had become embedded in cult activity. One day she was told by her family that because she was beautiful she must seek out a suitable white man, seduce him, and persuade him to reveal the cargo secret.

The Australian had fallen easily into this trap and was soon invited back to her village. There he was made welcome and great efforts made to reassure him he was offending none of their codes. He was encouraged to swim and fish over the best coral reefs too.

He took the village's reaction at face value, relaxed among its people, and believed he was being made welcome because he loved the girl. Inevitably she began to interrogate him. Gently, and with patience, he assured her that there was no ritual exclusive to Europeans that delivered their great material wealth. However, her questioning became so insistent he began to feel uneasy.

One day the frustrations between them erupted. She fell on her knees before him, prayed aloud to him, called him God, and Jesus, clung to him, hit him, wept, and promised anything within her power to give as long as he revealed the cargo secret.

Because he loved her, and also because he had still to understand what she wanted from him, he tried to reason with her. But she interpreted this as a refusal to co-operate and with this unbridgeable chasm between them they parted – the white man perhaps suffering more than the black girl.

One of the most widely reported cult incidents took place in Halopa, also near Madang, in 1964 where a villager cut the throat of another in front of Archbishop Noser of Alexishafen after communion had been given in the village square. The victim met his end willingly and it is assumed he did so because he thought his blood being spilled just after the sacrament had become the blood of Christ opened the way to Halopa being blessed with cargo.

Anthropologists, and many others, maintain with clear justification that cults are a manifestation of local discontent over the colonial presence of white administrators. They share, despite their variety, the underlying principle that the presence of Europeans is a barrier to the material advancement of local people. Essentially villagers want European wealth and consumer goods but reject the restraints, and cultural impositions, that come with them.

Most cultists believe western goods, and first world expertise, are rooted in the world of gods and spirits. They would watch, as did Highlanders on the occasion of Jim Taylor's first patrols, huge quantities of provisions and other material arriving by parachute out of an otherwise empty sky. There appeared to be no obvious method of procuring it. They saw no money changing hands, no other exchange being made, while in most instances the goods were distributed among Europeans with only a trickle seeping down to the people themselves.

Because the intricate processes of industry and commerce were beyond comprehension, and faith in their own gods persisted, villagers would hark back to traditional fertility rites and earth magic in an attempt to secure cargo. Sometimes these rituals were mixed with Christian ceremony, even bureaucratic procedures, because it seemed that

251

everything inexplicable might be explained this way – and if the latest attempt did not work then another could be tried instead.

In 1975 the type of cultist expression Kiaps were most likely to stumble on were bizarre, covertly political, socialist co-operatives or village societies which yearned to acquire wealth through vaguely programmed income generation and tended to be steered by university graduates.

But in July 1973 the Kunimeipa people surrounding Guari had been the focus of an especially disturbing example of a more old fashioned type. A villager, Patrick Pezoi, was tried in the High Court for the murder of his fifteen month old son, David, and his pre-trial statement, which was taken by the Guari OIC, Noel Tererembo, is reproduced below.

"I am a Christian and my people are also Christians. I have read the New Testament in which I read about John the Baptist and other prophets. I was also concerned about some ways of bringing knowledge and wisdom to me and my people. I have thought about this for a long time and made up my mind that the only solution was to kill my own son. My original plan was to crucify the child but on the day I took him up the mountain I forgot to pick up my nails so instead I killed him with an axe.

This is how it happened, on Wednesday July 25th 1973 about 6 o'clock in the morning, my wife, my child and I left Tonamena and walked towards Guari. We walked for a mile and then she went to the garden. Before she went to the garden I told her I was going to Loloipa to give the child away to my uncle. She said that's alright you can take the child to your uncle. She then went to the garden and I took the child and went up a mountain called Bjore.

Just before I reached the top of the mountain I stopped. I dug the grave on the spot. After I have finished the grave I took the child and let him sit on my laps (sic). I was sitting then beside the grave facing Guari station.

I hit the child twice on the forehead with the sharp edge of an axe. These two blows on the head killed him but I cut other parts of the body to indicate the fashion of crucifixion. Then I took a small knife and cut the stomach open just below the centre of the chest down towards the left hip. I removed the heart and burned it. The purpose of this action is so that the smoke of the fire would reach heaven and God would be sorry about me and help me.

I put the body in the grave, by then it was dark. That night I slept with the body in the grave. I slept in the grave for another two nights. I was expecting his spirits to show me something new but since nothing happened I left the place on Saturday morning after covering the grave. I walked to the top of the mountain and followed the footpath down to Tonamena. In the village I cooked two bananas and ate them. After this I went to a small hamlet called Ciarig and slept there."

Patrick was judged unfit to plead and committed to a mental institute for life. But several angles to the case were puzzling so while I was at Guari I asked questions of my own.

David had been a particularly fine child whose size and robust development were constantly being remarked on by other villagers. Patrick had been a lay teacher with the mission at Kamulai and I suspect, because the explantion covering the absence of his wife is laboured, that when he set out to kill his son he was accompanied by her as well as others in his immediate family.

It is significant that David was murdered at a place that overlooked Guari's airstrip – the most obvious delivery platform for the bulk of incoming cargo #1 distributed within the Kunimeipa area. I think too the child's heart was removed but instead of being cooked was cut into pieces and offered in a similar style to Holy Communion.

It is also possible that other people knew that a fresh attempt to secure cargo was being staged and waited to see if Patrick was successful before news of his failure spread and eventually reached government ears.

David's death had a profound impact on conversation among Europeans and it was from this I learned how a group of Kunimeipa people reacted when they were introduced to Mission thinking. When they were told about heaven they immediately tried to get there by jumping. At first it was just the men – leaping like a squad of rugby players warming up at the start of a training session.

Later, after reflecting that they would like women to be in heaven too, they jumped with their wives. Later still they burdened themselves with food. One day a curious swallow flew low over the jumpers. Taking it to be a messenger from heaven they found scraps of paper and waved them enticingly hoping the bird would pluck them from their hands and return to heaven with their message.

One afternoon an unusually intense villager, Lucas Taia, crept into Guari's office and laid out a number of hard, bright objects which he claimed had been placed in his hand by Jesus himself. They included a small magnifying glass, a commemorative issue twenty cent piece, a medal and a regimental badge as well as a small metal shelf ornament. They were exactly the type of item a magpie might covet or steal.

He whispered that while he slept at night Christ came to him in his dreams and when he woke he found one in his hand. Later, when on patrol in Upper Kunimeipa, he took me into his home.

The main room was uncluttered and unusually neat with what can only be described as an altar dominating the furthest wall. Displayed among vases filled with grasses and flowers, and backed by colourful drapes of cloth, were the metal objects he had shown me.

A large, technicolour, mediaeval portrait of Christ was the centrepiece and on each side were pictures of a naked man, and a naked woman, which had been taken from a pornographic magazine. He told me they were Adam and Eve.

We sat in silence as I struggled, and failed, to interpret the symbolism that confronted me. Scattered around the hut were several other pornographic pictures which looked to be German. Lucas was watching carefully. He told me the room was a church and he slept there when he wanted to talk to God. The pictures represented the Garden of Eden.

I had briefly encountered cultism in the Highlands but compared with the religiosity that fuelled the Kunimeipa's distress it smacked more of confidence trickery or extortion. At Nondugl an old woman had attracted temporary attention when she claimed that if she was fed a special diet she could produce shillings from the palm of her hand. The cult did not survive a month because investment was greater than return.

Another straddling the Mount Hagen-Minj administrative border in 1972-73 generated more fuss. It was known as the Red Box Cult because a selection of wooden boxes was being hawked around villages by a man who claimed that they should be filled with stones which would eventually be converted into money.

Critical to this lottery style transformation was the accurate delivery of a sequence of incantations. Attempts by Kiaps to expose the fraud generated indignation because the purveyor claimed worried Europeans were sabotaging his efforts. However, when local people opened boxes in their own time, and they too found stones, they lost interest and the seller retreated.

In June 1975 I took a patrol into a valley in a remote section of the Waria region and so may have strayed into the Northern District. I made the effort because Bakaia had chuntered for months about a group of villagers who had established a new community at Aulaipa, well beyond normal government reach, and needed to be returned to the fold.

It was a strange journey because I was walking in the opposite direction to my Kiap inheritance. It had been my forerunners' job to contact new people and file their names in government record books. This time I was setting out to find villagers whose names were on census registers, but who had rejected Port Moresby government, and were hiding.

It was a tough walk from Guari and I knew we had moved into unfamiliar territory when, as was my habit, I asked the name of the river we had just forded and no one could tell me.

Next to the village was an "airstrip" and next to it was a "church" which had an intriguing room, not dissimilar to a large pigeon loft, tacked against the highest point of its gable end. This extension had an outside door, so high off the ground no human being could have used it without a ladder, but there was no connecting door between it and the large, presbytery-like chamber it was attached to.

The leader, Agi, was a grim old man. He said that when he and his fellow cultists met in the church their ancestors flew into the attic extension and talked to them through the wall. Their advice had been to build the airstrip, which when it was finished would attract cargo planes, and from then on the cultists would be self-sufficient.

A huge amount of energy had been invested in its construction. From virgin bush the people had cleared an area around 300 yards by 75 yards and made an effort to remove tree stumps and level the site too. Nevertheless it was equally obvious a plane would never land. The surface was so pitted with pot holes and stones it could not have been negotiated by a four-wheel drive road vehicle. It also tilted at a twenty five degree angle and the uphill gradient was similarly steep.

There was a thatched passenger lounge, and a booking office in which tickets were represented by lined paper taken from a school exercise book, but if the project was meant to attract in-coming planes in the same way a baited cage trap might entice a passing bird it was doomed to fail.

That evening Agi was resolute when I asked him to return to his government's embrace. He would not go. Nevertheless I stood in front of his community the following morning and invited them to point out its schools, its medical aid posts, its trade store, and roads connecting it with Guari and beyond.

They could not so I returned with perhaps thirty people, mainly in family groups, who had been persuaded to take up life a little nearer home. They burst into spontaneous song when we rounded a spur and they could once again see the Kunimeipa's valleys.

But behind me there was still around sixty. I didn't think they were all waiting for a plane that would never land. Some clearly preferred to live in isolation with Agi and might have been hoping I was the last interfering European they would see.

We had been gone about an hour when an RAAF Caribou, a transport plane, flew low across the valley. It had been chartered to take bridge building materials from Lae to Guari and I told the people so. Nevertheless it may have raised the hopes of those that had decided to stay behind. They may even have thought their project still had a future, and they could have caught it, if they had made their airstrip more enticing.

Discourse between Europeans and Papua New Guineans could be plagued with pitfalls created by ambiguities amplified by cultural misunderstanding and misinterpretation. I have since wondered whether

257

my advice to Kunimeipa villagers to concentrate on maintaining the road link between Guari's airstrip and the mission at Kamulai, and not between Guari and Tapini, might have reinforced the latent cultist ambition that swished and swirled within their thinking.

The pidgin word was *kago*. It covered all goods carried in from an outside source. Every form of transport carried *kago* and the English word cargo had been adopted by Europeans in PNG as an every-day, cover-all description of routine deliveries made by air or road too.

CHAPTER EIGHTEEN

A return to reality

"Sorry brother, sorry more,
In this country you Kiaps were the boss before.
We ourselves are now prepared and straight.
We too impatient and cannot wait.
We people of this place here.
Wish that you would clear.
O sorry brother, sorry friend.
We are burdened with much pain."

University of Papua New Guinea, Port Moresby, 1975

As my time in PNG closed out there were opportunities for indulgence and one of the targets was Mount Yule, the near vertical, volcanic plug, which frowned over Guari Station like a fortress. With me were Ian and Betty Douglas, and a crowd of Kunimeipas, many of them women, who wanted to stand on its summit too.

Mount Yule presents itself as a formidable obstacle but can be easily overcome if it is approached from the rear. © Ian Douglas.

On the second night out from Kamulai we camped above a typically ghostly stand of Koroka ready to move just ahead of first light so we would enjoy the peak before it was submerged in cloud which billowed up from the valleys beneath about three hours after sunrise.

This formidable mountain had been ambushed by taking an undemanding circular route before approaching the only real obstacle – the transfer from our adjacent slope to its castle-like crown.

The narrow fifty yard path was carried by a knife edge arête which sheered immediately, and precipitously, to previously unseen gorges hidden deep below. Betty recoiled and would not cross, Ian mounted it like a horse, sitting legs astride, hauling himself forward with his arms, I took a deep breath to stagger over without too much wobble, and the local people strolled over as if it was a motorway. #1

The peak was a plateau with only a gentle slope, the vegetation was Alpine, and when we stood on the high point almost all the mountains in the Owen Stanley Range, which dominated eastern PNG, lay before us. Yule Island was easily seen to the south and cloud formations on the northern side of the Waria section of these ranges suggested they were hiding its coast. We thought we could see Mount Wilhelm in the distant west.

The Kunimeipas lit a small fire then heaped on damp grass to make a dense, vertical column of blue smoke. "We are here" it declared. The immediate response, from a dozen or so hamlets strung along the nearest valleys far below, was the building of similar smoke signals which said "We see you too".

We stayed until thick cloud puffing its way up the cliff face could no longer be ignored. Other Europeans, missionaries from France and Switzerland, and Kiaps from Australia, had stood there too but I was the first from the UK.

The last afternoon as OIC Guari was spent at Kamulai cutting firewood for the cook house before sitting down for a farewell meal. As the sun began to set I took a walk and sat down at the tip of a ridge. There was a beautiful skyscape within which boiling clouds, alternating brilliant grey and pure white, burst, erupted, spiralled and spun against the unyielding stone profile of the Kunimeipa ranges.

The valley's many hamlets were almost obscured, swallows swooped low over the grass covered point, and a squat insect with a blue carapace clambered earnestly through hair on my leg.

A man my own age jogged into view, carrying an awkward pile of branches on his shoulder. He threw it down with a grunt of relief and sat beside me, pulling a half smoked cheroot from behind his ear. The scent of smouldering bush tobacco took me back to Bundi where I had struggled to understand how something so acrid could possibly be enjoyed.

We exchanged some pleasant sentences before he re-loaded his firewood, counter-balanced its weight with an axe, and trotted off. A shaft of light probed like a torch on the far side of the valley at Suassi then the sun dropped behind western mountains and the day was over. A frog burped and swallows swung even lower. I waited until night had fallen, picked myself up, dusted my backside, and made my way back.

The PNG flag flying at Guari Patrol Post in June 1975. The station has since been abandoned. © Ian Douglas.

A week later I hitched up the Highlands Highway from Lae. I was helped to Goroka by a European but declined his offer of a lift the following morning and took my chance with locally owned vehicles instead. A battered Landcruiser carrying sacks of coffee parchment pulled up, I climbed onto them and settled back to enjoy the journey.

Michael Nuglai swept past, sitting in the back of a speeding police vehicle. He was wearing a sergeant's stripes. We waved. I thought that was that but he had other ideas because the *kopikar* (coffee car) slowed to an unexpected stop and he was running beside it waving a ten dollar note. I shook my head but he was insistent and giving up on Pidgin ordered me in English to "Take it! It's a gift!". We only had time to shake hands because he had to hurry off to yet another inter-tribal fight.

White owned copra (coconut), rubber, and occasional cocoa plantations fringed much of PNG's coast. Livestock farms and market gardens had sprouted in urban hinterland and after 1950 coffee, and some tea, plantations were established in the principal valleys of the Eastern and Western Highlands. Among these only the Wahgi, especially land lying between Minj and Banz, could claim to be a settler's paradise.

It may have been a poor cousin to Kenya's White Highlands, or Simla in India, which acquired almost mythical status at the height of Europe's colonial boom; nevertheless, its wide, cool valley had become home over the past twenty five years to many entrepreneurs. Those with tea interests had mainly moved in from India while Australians, who had arrived filled with zeal and thought they had settled for life, preferred coffee.

Surrounding them were two comfortable hotels, a nine-hole golf course, a cricket pitch, tennis court, social clubs at both Minj and Banz, two airstrips, good Post Offices and a social calendar that included an annual race meeting. There were few more pleasant locations. In contrast with much of PNG there were no mosquitoes, no leeches and few snakes, and because the climate was eternally spring-like no unpleasant heat rash either.

It was still – despite obvious signs of decline because some roofs at one of the hotels had been destroyed during an arson attack since I had left just two years earlier – being promoted as a tourist centre, describing itself as the country's equivalent of Shangri-La. It was not an exaggeration. Even in international scenic and climatic terms it was a most agreeable place.

I stayed with planter friends – a married couple whose adult children were either studying in Australia or job training in PNG. Paula and I had enjoyed their hospitality many times and thought their home, with its large veranda, cascading shrubs and panoramic outlook was ideal.

But their mood had changed. They were certain that the plans they had nursed as young people were about to be overtaken. The plantation they had built from nothing would not be managed by one of their sons. They would not retire to linger at mid-morning coffee on the veranda. They would not be visiting cheerful neighbours for early evening drinks or yet again arrive in evening dress anticipating a long night of enjoyment at the annual Minj Ball.

My hostess was especially bitter. Over dinner she revealed fears that selling the plantation might be difficult; transfer, perhaps to a co-operative of local people, or the Wahgi Council, might not be orderly; and that their lifetime's work was no longer the attractive asset it had been.

There were no histrionics. No diatribes. Just terse acceptance that within the lifetime of their children the Wahgi Valley had seen tumultuous change and their hopes of settling there permanently, which the Australian government had encouraged them to nurse when they'd arrived in the aftermath of the Second World War, were unlikely to be fulfilled. She was pessimistic about comfortable advancement for Wahgi villagers too. "It's moving too far too fast. They'll be out of their depth," she said.

My last exchange with PNG's village people was at Hagen Show – a biennial gathering dominated by noisy dancing displays staged by hundreds of people assembled from dozens of regional clans and tribes.

I was drawn to a group from the furthest fringe of Western Papua. Contact with them may have been delayed until the late 1960s and in traditional terms they were the real deal. The genital covering for the men was a penis-gourd. It was long, curved, thin, and held in place by a thong attached to its tip which was tied around the wearer's mid-riff. It fitted snugly over their penis but left their testicles exposed, and wobbled like a giant erection when they walked.

They had attracted the attention of a group of teenage boys, all wearing shorts and shirts, from villages near the showground. The mocking from these *mankis* (youths), who were surely repeating the *tok-ples* equivalent of "those stupid kanakas are too ignorant to hide their naked knackers", was fierce, unrelenting and unrestrained, and each of these men was, of course, carrying an axe.

They were being shepherded by a harassed Kiap who was doing his best to prevent the taunting descending into outright provocation, but not being helped by the most excited of his charges sporadically peeling off from the safety of the group to take a tour of the showground trailing a jeering mob.

He was worried one of his group might eventually feel affronted, even be slapped or kicked, and let fly with his axe in retaliation, so along with a handful of other Kiaps I worked that afternoon as unofficial guide and protector for his periodic strays. It was not an easy job and there were occasions when the jeering became cruel.

Later in the day when there was less excitement we had time to talk about his work. His response was curious. Before coming to Hagen he had been tracking mysterious parcels of meat that were moving between these people's villages.

Pork was commonly carried in perfectly wrapped, extremely neat, oblong packages in which paper was substituted by banana leaves, and string with thin cords of vine, but on this occasion there were suspicions the flesh might be human.

It had been seven years since I arrived in PNG after taking on board many references to old-fashioned cannibalism in books and this was the first time, just days before leaving, I had picked up a whisper. #2

Colourful dancing displays also attracted regular bus loads of tourists who concentrated on the village communities living either side of the Highlands Highway or exploration of the equally extraordinary spectacles offered by the people of the Sepik River and tribal groups scattered along PNG's northern coasts.

The reaction of these high paying visitors could be bizarre. Even though they travelled in mini-buses on PNG's main highways, some Japanese men arrived in jungle survival gear, right down to miniature bush knives tucked into sheaths tied just below their knees, and often carried butterfly nets. There was one occasion when the butterflies won and the party charged off in pursuit of a fluttering intruder, leaving the dancers marooned.

And then there was the elderly American who confided he was "blowed" if he could tell the difference between traditionally dressed men and women. He had arrived at a regular stop near Kabalku, which lay between Nondugl and Banz, where a group of Wi Kupa's people were happy to dress themselves in paint and feathers to stage a "wedding" each Thursday morning in exchange for a regular payment of around thirty dollars.

That morning the bus was early so instead of keeping the visitors waiting they were invited to step back stage to watch the dancers getting ready. Behind each hut was a battery of mirrors in front of which men and women were assembling headdresses and putting on face paint.

Both sexes were bare chested and if seen from the side their entire body was uncovered except for the wide bark belt which held up the *bilums, pul-puls* or *tankets* which covered them front and rear.

There were many reasons I was returning to the UK – including being a political dinosaur whose time had passed and so obliged to leave the stage and become extinct. I was part of the feebly wagging tail that had once been a powerful political dog.

The European style of colonialism, the cultural and capitalist phenomenon which began in the fourteenth century when hopeful trading ships from Lisbon, Cadiz, Amsterdam and then London began to find harbours in sub-Saharan Africa, the Americas, Australia, South East Asia and China, ended when PNG, part of an enormous island, which, because of its hostile coast and formidable interior, had resisted organised occupation, exploration and penetration until the late 1800s, became independent.

Even in the 1930s, when a handful of Australian Kiaps armed only with rifles made first contact with, began to subdue, and then advance, a million perpetually fighting people living in previously unknown Highland valleys, colonial administration was beginning to wane at world level – and formal links with Canberra were extinguished on September 16th 1975 when PNG set out to manage her own affairs.

From then on Kiaps – men who patrolled sparsely populated bush, trailing lines of carriers, arresting murderers, building roads, conducting elections and spreading government propaganda – could no longer be white. Perhaps the greatest political crime hoisted by liberal academics and political strategists in the second half of the 20th century was an expatriate whiteman being able to put an indigenous blackman in jail.

I left voluntarily, to join Paula and our children in the comfort of my own people, in my own *ples*, because the only thing that might have persuaded me to stay was no longer a card on the table.

Many Europeans throughout the phenomenon broadly described as colonialism moved to a distant country for a temporary period, became excited by it, embraced it and its people, fell in love with it, married it, and lived in it till death did them part.

PNG was in those terms only a short term affair. Men like myself who might have engaged with her permanently were not able to. Young and educated Papua New Guineans were impatient for independence and could not wait for us to go.

We treated her nicely but each took from the other what they could and then parted relatively easily because the temporariness of the connection kept it thinner than it would otherwise have been. There was no long term gain in continuing to relate with a country with which we might be able to briefly extend a heady romance but in the end would jilt us.

Some white Kiaps lingered after Independence but for many others it had the finality of a funeral. The relationship was dead and it was best to go. I left six weeks before the big day. By way of a bonus I had breached the qualifying period for a superannuation cheque and Ian Douglas had helped me to persuade the Chief Minister's Department it should offer a termination payment too.

I returned to my wife and family, which now included Matt who had arrived in June, regretting they could not have stayed with me in a less polarised PNG. My last five months at Guari had been no more than a final fling with myself under genuine bachelor status savouring a little of what might have been if I had come to that gripping island twenty five, even fifteen years earlier.

Arrival in Britain on August 8th 1975 was a return to reality in more ways than one. We had three children, no home, and until money gathered in PNG was transferred, no assets either.

To solve the problem I worked as woodman for Lord Allendale on Bywell Estates in West Northumberland, following in the footsteps of at least one great-grandfather and one of my grandfather's brothers, so we lived, rent-free, in a tied cottage.

I especially remember cutting back the hedge around St Peter's Church at Bywell while occasionally wandering off to watch a kingfisher on the far bank of the nearby Tyne, putting up field fences on tenanted farms in the 'Shire, and flitching logs at the saw mill below Dukesfield too.

After the last payments had dribbled in we discovered we had accumulated almost £14,000 in PNG including a £4,700 termination payment, £1,900 in superannuation, and a heap of savings. Livestock traded at Minj had netted £1,200 and Paula had scraped together over £3,000 in dozens of dribs and drabs including re-writing the Wahgi's census records, being a Presiding Officer in the 1972 elections, managing Tapini's Post Office, and many spells behind trade store counters.

We purchased, and modernised, a cottage with almost two acres, moving there in January 1977, only to discover no one wanted to employ a thirty year old college dropout whose CV was entirely focussed on a distant country and who only recently had worked as a lowly estate woodman too.

We also found school and college friends were enjoying a huge head start and already advancing successful careers. In contrast we were forced to discover that growing potatoes, even collecting, then selling, spagnhum moss taken from hidden hollows deep in local pine woods, were handy ways of supplementing a worryingly thin income.

After a dispiriting six month spell on the dole, and thirty months in the circulation department of the *Chronicle and Journal* in Newcastle, I began a late career in agricultural journalism at the *Hexham Courant* in January 1980.

We met no one from a PNG village until 1990 when a multi-location troupe of dancers were among the cultural attractions at the National Garden Festival staged at nearby Gateshead.

Almost immediately we saw a man in the crowd whose beard, skin colour, and hooked nose marked him as a native of Mount Hagen. I told him so in Pidgin, his jaw sagged, he grabbed me in a way that signalled his profound astonishment at bumping into someone familiar with his distant home, and to the delight of my family gave me a bearlike hug. We asked the tour manager if we could come back the following afternoon and take him and three others back to our house in nearby Riding Mill.

They were enthusiastic when they were shown the PNG flag, the first to be flown in the Mid-Wahgi in 1972, which was draped on the wall above Daniel's bed and even more pleased when they discovered he had been born in Hagen too.

An ornamental conifer was pounced on and stripped because they thought its branches would be better dancing decoration than traditional tankets. Paula found some seedlings which were put in pots with advice they should be planted at around 8,000 feet in a *ples kol* when they returned home. Then they were taken through neat fields and regimented pine woods, Riding Mill's tame equivalent of the bush, where they were stung by nettles, and wet their feet crossing streams.

The *dinau* (return payment) was an invitation to a dinner and disco at their hotel, the Marriott, which stood on Dunston Staithes. I ate with them, danced with them, and was amused when traditional *bilas* began to appear and a mischievous group from the Sepik River pushed bones through their noses before they took the floor.

The local lads on the disco team were open mouthed and more than ready when, as the evening came to the end, I asked if they would join me in singing the Tyneside anthem, "Blaydon Races". It was to be our puny counter-thrust to PNG's overwhelming cultural challenge.

Its choice was especially appropriate because Blaydon was only a couple of miles upstream and the string of landmarks that feature in the second verse, Armstrong's Factory, the Robin Adair, and the Railway Bridge, were lined up on the opposite bank of the river too.

I raised my voice and called everyone to order. What else could I say except, as every Kiap in PNG had when calling for silence at a village meeting, *"Harim yupela"* – which might be translated as "Attention please".

The group response – there were men and women from Goroka, the Trobriand Islands, and the Chimbu too – was immediate and amused. Elbows nudged ribs as the message *"Kiap stanap na em i laik toktok nau. Sarap yupela. Harim nau. Em Kiap ia. Sarap"* (The Kiap's about to address us. Please be quiet. Listen please. He's a Kiap. Be quiet) susurrated through the room.

I explained that the song we were about to sing was about *"ples iet"*, this very location, and had been sung by our *tumbunas*. Then we stood in front of them and delivered Blaydon Races at full throttle. Mouths wide open. Neck muscles strained. We didn't just sing it. We bawled. We were Geordies. We were proud people too. This was our culture. The Tyne was our river.

#1 Papua New Guineans are universally entertained by two European traits. Immediate lameness after the removal of footwear and our general inability to walk without wobbling over narrow log bridges – or any other obstacle demanding surefooted negotiation in a straight line.

#2 The Kiaps I was working with quickly pointed out I had been stationed in the wrong area. They also said that the bulk of the pre-contact cannibalism that dominated the high altitude, protein starved, and most remote sections of Papua's Western District had been suppressed remarkably easily.

CHAPTER NINETEEN

Looking back

No one, especially villagers whose first global contact began in the 1930s, can say, "Stop the world I want to get off", even though there will have been many occasions when they, as well as every human in history, would have liked to slow the clock, hoping they might be able to live, even for a moment, in calmer, more predictable, social and economic waters.

Northumberland 2017

Apart from comments on the chance meeting with the dancing troupes at Gateshead Garden Festival in 1990, I have tried not to corrupt, undermine, or confuse observations on pre-independence PNG by introducing new knowledge acquired beyond the date line that was so firmly drawn in August 1975 when I climbed into a plane at Port Moresby and flew away.

This account was written, with the help of Patrol Reports and other office papers, between February-May 1977 when I was an unemployed thirty year old and my memory was fresh.

But after a gap of more than forty years, additional perspective feels the need to push its way through.

The contrast between the colour, drama, occasional near chaos, and almost perpetual anticipation that something new and wonderful would bounce up to confront me, that dominated my years on that exciting island and the ordered, pastel, mainly gentle, and occasionally antique, life I have since lived in Northumberland could hardly have been greater.

The United Kingdom has become even more crowded since 1975 and I am certain, because I have had to travel there often enough, I could never have lived and worked in London or any other British city.

I have survived because I became an agricultural journalist – it helped me smell hay, cattle, and the wide outdoors even when I was working at my desk – and also because, as a result of doing my writing at home, I was able to sit down at most meals with my family, which, after Jessica was born in 1979, had expanded to four children, instead of being jostled endlessly, to and from work each day, in a crowded commuter train.

In career advancement terms the decision to sit tight and stay rural was costly but being able to avoid near permanent claustrophobic frustration in a congested, increasingly regimented, UK also hung on the anarchic release generated by being able to ride a progression of huge, strong, jumping horses through open Northumbrian countryside including the Cheviot Hills, both sides of the Tyne Valley, the 'Shire, and long sections of the Roman Wall lying west of Hexham.

The last of these 700-800 kilo heavyweights – on a soaking wet day, covered with mud, in full tack, it would have been interesting to have recorded how close our combined weight stood to a tonne – was a surefooted, cantankerous chestnut called Grumpy.

Each of us appreciated the Common Ridings, staged across the Scottish

Borders each summer. These are as exciting as you wish to make them because to put wind in our ears we had only to hitch up with a group of riders as adventurous as ourselves.

I was also aware I was taking part in a celebration of Scottish horse raiding tradition that in the 16th and 17th centuries would have mixed, each on opposing sides carrying spears and firebrands, ancestors of men like myself from the English side of the Border with those of many of the Scots riding beside me as we thrashed out over boggy ground, and leaped open ditches.

Grumpy rides out in the hills above Hawick in the summer of 2013. His breastplate, an essential item of equipment for rough riding, prevents the saddle from slipping while careering around on steep hills. © ILF Imaging.

In my desk drawer there are lapel badges earned after completing two of the most difficult journeys. One from Hawick to Mosspaul certifies me as a "Moss Rider". In Northumberland we would have said "Reiver".

The other covers a rideout from Jedburgh to commemorate a skirmish at Redeswire in 1575 when truce negotiations called by Sir John Forster of Bamburgh with Scotland's reiving representatives disintegrated into a fight in which many men were killed and Forster himself was held hostage – an incident that carries echoes of what might have happened during the failed compensation ceremony between the Oganas and the Berubugas at Minj in 1973.

I do not claim to be a descendant of Sir John. He had a position at the wealthy end of the clan. My people were woodcutters despatched from Bamburgh to Dotland Park in the 'Shire towards the end of the 16th Century to help the Priors of Hexham Abbey expand their labour line at a hunting lodge outpost. #1

Nor did the Scots always win. Fabled North Tyne warrior Barty Milburn is credited in 1570 with riding down a Borderer who had stolen some of his stock and decapitating the man so neatly his head sprang from his shoulders and "rolled along the heather like an onion". And on another occasion Northumbrian Reivers were so outraged that the sheep they had driven off were corrupted with a pestilential skin infection that they rode back and murdered the original owners.

There are similarities between these now distant internecine hostilities between Border English and Border Scots and the constant inter-clan friction, and resulting death, which plagued much of Papua New Guinea in 1975 and continues to trouble its government, and many of its people, today.

So will there be a time when Highland clans like the Kambilikas and Tangilkas are able to stage similarly harmless annual ceremonies to celebrate group steadfastness during long buried cultural hostilities, and will Goilala people learn to manage their day to day affairs without trying to conclude their most difficult problems with a shotgun or an axe?

PNG's long term challenge continues to be social fragmentation – a problem underlined by it being marvellously, almost unfathomably, unique. Not only is its topography unrelentingly hostile but its people and their cultures are overwhelmingly diverse too.

Its 800 languages – back in 1975 these were shared between just three million people – continue to underline the existence of a multiplicity of cultures so complex, so mutually exclusive, that the search for a basket of national common denominators, a unifying assembly of shared concepts, is still difficult and must be frustrating.

It is not fanciful to think that throughout PNG's extended pre-history it must have become home to so many incoming waves of ethnically diverse people, a hovering Skywatcher could be forgiven for thinking the Gods must have enjoyed taking a pan and brush, sweeping up representatives from every brown skinned community within reach – then shaking the contents randomly over the most extreme, sea bound, compilation of mountain, swamp and river on our planet.

The result of this diversity is that PNG – which is much bigger in square mile terms than the United Kingdom and the Republic of Ireland combined – can legitimately claim to be the most socially exotic, and most culturally disparate, country (island) on earth.

How then, in these testing circumstances, can the apparent impermeability of Papua New Guineans to blanket political agreement, the ingrained, near exclusive, loyalty of its multiplicity of peoples to those with whom they share a birth community, while ignoring the welfare of others who even now may only be living along an adjacent spur, be overcome?

The only sensible answer is time. The country did not get off to a quick start and its accommodation of global economic pressure and technological innovation, which now include mobile phones, every feature of the internet, and home owned AK47 rifles, is already impressive, alarming and immense.

In 1850 stone tools were endemic throughout the island. Even in 1932 the only axes in the Bismark Highlands and the Wahgi Valley were stone crafted, while in 1963, and sometimes beyond, Kiaps were handing out iron axe heads to the Biamis as well as other tribal groups in Western Papua and at the same time noting this critical technological advance had, at a stroke, slashed their wood cutting, house building, and garden construction workload by something like eighty per cent.

Europeans should not feel superior. In the Iron Age, long after stone implements had been abandoned, Britain was a cruel place. Roman, Saxon, Viking and then Norman invaders hacked down local resistance – the latter reducing the North of England to wasteland so it could be controlled without the need for regular, and expensive, military visits.

As for indifference towards human beings living beyond a group's immediate sphere of reckoning, Sir Walter Scott, the 19th century Scottish novelist, makes clear that Norman barons journeying in winter would warm their feet within the steaming pit of a Saxon peasant's freshly slit belly if they ever felt the need and were so inclined.

European tradition can be slow to change too. Echoes of the Norman Conquest and its feudal system still linger in Northumberland where its wealthy Duke, a straight line descendant of a Norman invader who helped subdue the Saxons immediately after 1066, continues to live in his castle stronghold where a handful of his oldest retainers might still be seen touching their cap.

The establishment of reliable infrastructure, both economic and physical, and the problems created by inter-clan violence still dominate PNG's development. All of these are familiar to Kiaps – although the days, which were already beginning to fade towards the end of the 1960s, when they were able to call tribal fights to a halt by standing between combatants, waving their arms, and commanding the warriors to go back to their villages, and do something useful like building a road, or planting coffee, are long gone.

The internet confirms there is a bridge at once-isolated Binaru that can carry commercial traffic from coastal Madang and Lae through Bundi and then into the Chimbu before connecting with the main Highlands Highway.

Local and corporately owned coffee and tea plantations have replaced expatriate private enterprise in the Wahgi Valley, but inter-tribal fighting throughout the Highlands, backed on occasions by homemade shotguns and the threat of automatic rifles, can be disruptive and fierce.

Mekeos and Roros continue to organise their lives to their liking and have benefited, by virtue of being able to resist a return to pre-contact tribal argument, from a dramatic improvement in their road links with Port Moresby and the addition of dry rice cultivation to their betel nut enterprise.

The murder rate at Tapini has soared, and it is obvious that a pre-Independence administrative high tide mark was established at Guari where the Patrol Post has long stood derelict and, more latterly, the Catholic Mission at Kamulai, where a priest was murdered with a shotgun, has been abandoned as well.

The internet also underlines that Kiaps are, after years of routine post-colonial denigration, beginning to enjoy a good press. They still have their academic critics, and continue to be blamed by others for introducing cultural confusion, but older people who lived mainly in newly contacted

Highland areas that were unlocked in the 1950s and 1960s have stepped forward to say they appreciate the stability, and the development, that followed their arrival and, to the astonishment of some, many of their educated children have said they do too.

The bulk of the kudos has to go to individuals active from the 1950s who, armed with remarkable stamina and little else beyond abundant ethnic confidence underlined by their strange white skin and new technologies as simple as a .303 rifle or a bag of steel axe heads, almost immediately subdued unknown millennia of ingrained hostility and violence.

In doing so they opened the way for the Papua New Guineans they pushed and cajoled into taking their place within the world economy to join the rest of humanity in being pinned, and pained, by the relentless acceleration in global cultural evolution that was the dominant feature of the 20th Century – and which continues to pick up speed today.

No criticism of Kiaps, or PNG's people, is implied because no one, especially villagers whose first global contact began in the 1930s, can say, "Stop the world I want to get off", even though there will have been occasions when they as well as every human in history, including individual Kiaps, would have liked to have slowed the clock, hoping they might be able to sail, even for a moment, in calmer, more predictable, social and economic waters.

#1 Family lore records these woodmen camped at notoriously windblown Yarridge on the south side of Hexham before descending into what would have been almost unbroken oak forest and crossing the Dipton Burn to emerge at an equally exposed hill still nicknamed, almost despairingly, as "Dowly" Dotland, where they built their homes.

A storybook sixteenth century Border Reiver rides out.

People

Ch 1

John Forster: First Forster known to have been buried at Whitley Chapel.

Willie Jameson: Lease holder at Ladycross Quarry, Slaley.

Tsengelap clan: Influential group of people living on north side of Wahgi Valley.

Kauga Kua: Chimbu born Kiap stationed at Minj.

Jim Crace: Editor of *Birmingham Sun* and prize-winning novelist.

Gordon Burn: Features contributor to *Birmingham Sun* and award winning author.

Ian Fazey: Education Correspondent on *Birmingham Post*.

Big Jim Ford: Gangerman for Taylor Woodrow in Birmingham.

Voluntary Sercice Overseas: UK government sponsored organisation adept at placing volunteers in locations where their skills could assist the development of local people.

Annie Forster: My Great Aunt and surrogate Grandmother.

Mori: Reliably cheerful labourer at Bundi Mission's sawmill.

Ch 2

Marcus Dam: Labourer at Bundi's saw mill.

Kari: Diminutive labourer at Bundi's saw mill.

Nicholas Kebma: *Boss-boi* at Bundi sawmill.

Max David: Lay missionary developing new cattle station at Brahmin.

Otto Dirumbi: Leading labourer at Bundi Sawmill.

Yabanai: Prominent among labourers at Bundi sawmill.

Ch 3

Fabian Kamtai: *Kuk-boi* at Bundi sawmill.

Ch 4

Paula: Paula Green who became Paula Forster, my wife.

Frank Cotton: Kiap stationed at Simbai Patrol Post.

Kaspar Gene: Labourer at Bundi sawmill.

Kelly: Gangerman for McAlpine in Birmingham.

Graham Forster: One of my two brothers.

Father Jiezke: Elderly priest at Bundi Mission.

Mr Clezy: Orthapeadic surgeon at Madang Hospital.

Ch 5

Neil Mockett: Kiap stationed at Minj.

Yuak Dju: Luluai representing Kambi people of Minj Sub-district.

Nopnop Tol: Important man among people living on south side of Wahgi Valley in Minj Sub-District.

Jim Taylor: Pioneering Kiap who entered Highlands of PNG in 1933.

Ian Douglas: Assistant District Commissioner at Minj.

Betty Douglas: Wife of Ian Douglas.

Ch 6

Michael Somare: First Chief Minister of Papua New Guinea.

Tangilka: Clan living at Tomba on south side of Wahgi Valley.

Kambilika: Clan living at Danal on south side of Wahgi Valley.

Brian Corrigan: Kiap based at Minj in 1953.

Marie Reay: Anthropologist studying people living near Minj in Wahgi Valley.

Mont: First victim of clan struggle between Tangilka and Kambilika.

Kos: Tangilka clan killer of Mont.

Sergeant-Major Siwi: Veteran of Royal Papua New Guinea Constabulary (RPNGC) stationed at Minj.

Swiss Missionaries: Staff attending mission stations built by Swiss Mission church.

Kaibelt Dorum: Frontline Kegerinkabam fighter.

Councillor Muga: Leader of Tangilka clan.

Councillor Koilmal: Front man for Kambilika clan.

Ch 7

Kaibelt Diria: Member of the House of Assembly (MHA) for Mid-Wahgi constituency.

Tom Ellis: Historically influential District Commissioner in Western Highlands.

Abba Kip: Pivotal member of Tsengelap clan.

Dick Theile: Australian planter based near Banz in Wahgi Valley.

Komunka: Sub-clan living near Nondugl in Wahgi Valley.

Ogana: Dominant clan in Nondugl area.

Richard Theile: Son of Dick Theile.

Kaibelt Op: Fight leader of Komunka clan.

Tippuary: Minj based constable in RPNGC.

Mapa Dei: Driver working from Minj Sub-District office.

Daniel Forster: Our first child.

John Kamp: Australian educated man from Mount Hagen.

Goroka Mud Men: Totemic dancing group from Eastern Highlands who wore huge head masks made from grey mud.

Ch 8

Kaiyer Auwin: Fight leader of Omgarl clan.

Omgarl: Clan living in Milep area.

Nigel Van Ruth: Assistant District Commissioner at Minj.

Ch 9

Kapuli: Interpreter at Minj Sub-District office.

Danga: Clan based at Bolimba on north side of Wahgi River.

Ch 10

Peter: Southern Highlander who was *kuk-boi* for Forster family at Minj.

Konumbuga: Dominant clan in villages surrounding Minj.

Meg Taylor: Daughter of Jim and influential political figure in her own right.

Kisu: Important clan at Kudjip on south side of Wahgi River.

Talu Bol: Nondugl based Vice President of Wahgi Local Government Council.

Berebuga: Large clan from Tombil on south side of Wahgi River.

Pugmal Wisik: Leader of Berubuga clan.

Konjiga: Clan based in villages surrounding Banz.

Ch 11

Mekeo: The dominant group in villages surrounding Bereina Sub-District Office.

Roro. Important group of clansmen occupying coastal villages in Bereina Sub-District.

Erico Aufe: Legendary Mekeo escapee.

Nicholas Ain'au Okua: Mekeo villager who absconded from Bereina Corrective Institution.

Wani: RPNGC Constable stationed at Bereina.

James ToWalaun: RPNGC Constable stationed at Bereina.

Ch 12

Bruce Hides: Planter living near Kobuna in Bereina Sub-District.

Dulcie Hides: Wife of Bruce.

Ruth Forster: Our first daughter.

Dr John Guise: Deputy Chief Minister of Papua New Guinea.

Josephine Abaijah: Regional MHA for Central District.

Anton Gawi: Sub-Inspector in charge of Bereina's Police Detachment.

Lofty (Peter Barton-Eckett): Kiap stationed at Bereina.

Department of Civil Aviation: Authority which controlled airstrip safety standards throughout PNG.

Ch 13

Tauade: People living in villages surrounding Tapini Sub-District Office.

Jeff Van Oosterwijck: Temporary ADC stationed at Tapini.

Sergeant Gabume: Senior sergeant of the Tapini Police Detachment.

Michael Nuglai: Constable stationed at Tapini.

Jack Hides: Brother of Bruce Hides and early explorer of Papuan Highlands.

Fuyege: People living in villages surrounding Woitape Patrol Post.

Kunimeipa: People living in villages surrounding Guari Patrol Post.

Kukukuku: Notoriously combative hill tribe in Morobe District.

Peter Ivoro: Tauade convicted of murders in Port Moresby.

Karto Kartogi: Tauade convicted of murders in Port Moresby.

Roy Edwards: Kiap who patrolled Goilala region immediately after end of Second World War.

Father Abel and Father Morant. Gelignite blasting, road making, Catholic priests based at Kamulai Mission.

Tumai Mumu: Tauade leader from Tatupit Village.

Robin Hood: Legendary English resistance fighter in period after Norman Conquest.

Oulaine Papaite: Female victim of gang execution at Tapini.

Opu Anuma: Charged with Oulaine's murder.

Maia Papaite: Brother of Oulaine.

Tuta: Important witness to events preceding Oulaine's murder.

Katai Anuma: Opu's sister.

Bill Graham: Kiap working at Tapini in 1969.

Tau Inam: Tauade villager murdered in 1969.

Kaga Lava: President of Tapini Local Government Council.

Kepara Lamoro: Witness to events surrounding Oulaine's murder.

Tatai Kila: Charged with Oulaine's murder.

Aia Paimere: Charged with Oulaine's murder.

Meto Wanuwe: Charged with Oulaine's murder.

Norman Silk: Farmed Spring House at Slaley.

Stuart Silk: Son of Norman Silk.

Ch 14

Apua: RPNGC Constable posted to Tapini.

Panai Koai: Murder victim at Kariarita village, Tapini.

Amuna Ipoi: Convicted of Panai's murder.

Ke'ere: Panai's wife.

Aito: Panai's daughter.

Mavi: Old man living at Kariarita.

Kaita Kamo: Convicted murderer and new leader at Kariarita.

Gitai Ino: Victim of revenge murder at Erume.

Alama Kaita: Convicted of Gitai's murder.

Bakaia: Senior Constable stationed at Tapini.

Mana Ivoro: Kariarita villager charged with murder of Gitai.

Kaga Lava: President of Tapini Local Government Council.

Judge Lalor: Justice of PNG's Supreme Court.

Ch 15

Louis Mona: MHA for Goilala constituency.

Class Six: Gang of thieves based at Kabalku, Minj Sub-District.

Rosemary Green: Paula's sister.

Ex-Sergeant Toro: Holder of the Queen's Police Medal.

Ch 16

Peto: Thief on run from police at Port Moresby.

Suiz: Influential villager living near Guari Patrol Post.

David Suiz: Son of Suiz.

Father John Momis: Leader of breakway movement on Bourgainville.

Father Ignatius Kilage: First Chimbu to become Roman Catholic priest.

Ch 17

Adolf Noser: Bishop of Madang Catholic Diocese.

Patrick Pezoi: Kunimeipa cargo cultist.

David: Son of Patrick Pezoi.

Noel Tererembo: Kiap in charge of Guari Patrol Post in 1973.

Lucas Taia: Kunimeipa cargo cultist:

Agi: Kunimeipa cargo cultist.

Ch 18

Wi Kupa: Councillor at Kabalku and a charming individual too.

Lord Allendale: Large landowner in Northumberland.

Matt Forster: Our third child.

Ch 19

Jessica Forster: Fourth child of Forster family.

Sir John Forster: Warden of Northumberland's Middle Marches in late 1500s.

Barty Milburn: Renowned reiver in late 16th century Northumberland.

Biami: People occupying villages surrounding Nomad Patrol Post in Western District.

Sir Walter Scott: Nineteenth century writer of romantic novels focussed on Jacobite rebellion of 1745.

Duke of Northumberland: Large landowner

Places

Ch 1

Hexhamshire: Amalgam of four parishes lying south of Hexham – West Northumberland's principal town.

Whitley Chapel: Important hamlet in southern section of Hexhamshire.

Slaley: Biggest settlement in Slaley Parish which lies five miles south of Hexham.

Houtley: Farm in Low Quarter of Hexhamshire.

Smelting Syke: Smallholding in Middle Quarter of Hexhamshire.

Queen Elizabeth Grammar School: Large school in Hexham.

Birmingham College of Commerce: Forerunner of Birmingham City University.

Wahgi Valley: Important river valley and centre of settlement in Highlands of Papua New Guinea.

White House: Dairy farm in Slaley Parish.

Birmingham: England's second largest city.

Healey Mill: Farm straddling Marchburn on boundary between Slaley and Healey parishes.

Port Moresby: Capital of Papua New Guinea (PNG).

Alexishafen: Administrative headquarters of Divine Word Mission in PNG.

Madang: Coastal town and administrative centre for Madang District in northern PNG.

Bundi: Mission Station and Government Patrol Post in Madang District.

Brahmin: SVD Mission cattle station in Madang District.

Newcastle: Newcastle-on-Tyne: principal city of North East England.

Ch 2

Ramu: Main river of Madang District.

Binaru: Site of sawmill run by SVD Mission at Bundi.

Queensland: An Australian state that lies immediately south of PNG.

Hawaii: Iconic mid-Pacific island that is part of the United States.

Vanuatu : Scattered group of islands, formerly New Hebrides, lying east of PNG.

Stonehenge: World Heritage site on Salisbury Plain in England which features an imposing circle of Neolithic stones.

Rabaul: Administrative centre of New Britain District in PNG.

Mount Hagen: Administrative centre of PNG's Western Highlands District.

Ch 4

Simbai: Mountain Patrol Post in Madang District.

Gembogl: Patrol Post at head of Chimbu River, Chimbu District in PNG.

Emigari: Large village near Bundi Patrol Post.

Edgbaston: Residential suburb of Birmingham, UK.

Ch 5

Minj: Location of Sub District Office for Mid-Wahgi administrative area in PNG's Western Highlands.

Karimui: Patrol Post at southern extremity of Chimbu District.

Bol: Area of land earmarked for re-settlement by Komanka people of East Kambia Census Division, Minj-Sub-distrct.

Ch 6

Dong: Area of land beside Wahgi River whose ownership was disputed by Kambilika and Tangilka clans.

Tomba: Principal village of Tanglika clan, Minj Sub-District.

Danal: Principal village of Kambilika clan, Minj Sub-District.

Goilala: Mountainous Sub-District in PNG's Central District.

Ch 7

Wahgi-Sepik Divide: Formidable series of mountain ranges lying between Wahgi and Sepik rivers.

Nondugl: Principal settlement in north east section of Wahgi Sub-District.

Kumbala: Abandoned tea plantation near Nondugl.

Bonong: Abandoned land purchase near Nondugl.

Banz: Principal town on north aside of Wahgi river, Minj Sub-District.

Munumul: Main settlement of Ogana clan near Nondugl.

Bourgainville: Large island off north coast of PNG which became centre of a struggle for partition from PNG.

Kudjip: Headquarters of the Nazarene Mission on southern side of Wahgi river, Minj Sub-District.

Healey, Minsteracres and Blanchland: Small villages near Slaley in South West Northumberland.

Chapter 8

Milep: Village near Nondugl in Wahgi Valley.

Laiagam: Site of sub-District Office at western extremity of Western Highlands District.

Molka: Settlement immediately north of Banz in Wahgi Valley.

Chapter 9

Bolimba: Main settlement of Danga clan between Banz and Nondugl.

Chapter 10

Tombil: Main settlement of Berubuga clan on south side of Wahgi River.

Chapter 11

Bereina: Location of Sub-District Office in PNG's Central District.

Angabunga Ferry: Important crossing over Angabunga River, Kairuku Sub-District.

Kuni: Location of villages lying northwest of Bereina.

Inika: Isolated village in Bereina Sub-District.

Kobuna: Catholic Mission Station, Bereina Sub-District.

Chapter 12

Yule Island: Original off-shore site of Kairuku Sub-District headquarters now located at Bereina.

Waima: Coastal village near Bereina.

Veifa'a (Beipa): Important Catholic Mission Station near Bereina.

Tapini: Location of administrative headquarters for Goilala Sub-District in Central District.

Chapter 13

Aibala: River flowing below Tapini Station.

Pilitu: Land area occupied by village people living south-west of Tapini.

Tatupit: Village immediately above Tapini Station.

Edmondbyers Moor: Remote location south west of Newcastle, England.

Spring House: Farm lying immediately to north of Slaley Forest, Northumberland.

Black House crossroads: Location lying one mile south of Hexham in Northumberland.

Ou Ou Creek: Plantation lying between Bereina and Port Moresby.

Chapter 14

Pomutu: Remote village in mountains behind Tapini.

Kariarita: Large village in mountains behind Tapini.

Erume: Area of land north west of Tapini.

Waria Valley: Mountain location in PNG's Northern District.

Guari: Patrol Post for Kunimeipa section of Tapini Sub-District.

Chapter 15

Goroka: Administrative headquarters for PNG's Eastern Highlands.

Kabalku: Village on original Highlands Highway near Kerowil, Minj Sub-District.

Skyline Drive: Section of original Highlands Highway near Kabalku.

Lae: Largest coastal town in Morobe District of PNG.

Wau: Large, Morobe District, town in Owen Stanley Ranges.

Owen Stanley Range: Spine of mountains between Morobe and Central Districts.

Chapter 16

Mount Yule: Dominant mountain of Kunimeipa area.

Mosman: Suburb of North Sydney.

Kamulai: Headquarters of Catholic Mission in Kunimeipa.

Konedobu: Location of administrative offices for Chief Minister's Department in Port Moresby.

Waigani: Location of University of Papua New Guinea in Port Moresby.

Chapter 17

Halopa: Village between Alexishafen and Madang.

Aulaipa: Remote village in Kunimeipa.

Chapter 18

Bywell: Village by River Tyne in West Northumberland.

Dukesfield: Location on Slaley side of Devils Water, South West Northumberland.

Newcastle: City on northern banks of River Tyne.

Gateshead: Large town on southern banks of River Tyne.

Riding Mill: Comfortable residential village on south bank of River Tyne near Hexham.

Dunston Staithes: Land on southern banks of River Tyne lying west of Gateshead.

Blaydon: Town on southern banks of River Tyne.

Trobriand Islands: Archipelago off coast of Northern District, PNG.

Chapter 19

Roman Wall: Administrative barrier built by Roman Empire lying between settlements in England and Scotland.

Hawick: Horse mad town in Scotland's Cheviot Hills.

Jedburgh: Prosperous market town in Scotland's Cheviot Hills.

Redeswire: Border point between England and Scotland on A68 trunk road now known as Carter Bar.

Bamburgh: Coastal castle headquarters of Forster family in 16th Century Northumberland.

Dotland Park: Farm in Middle Quarter of Hexhamshire.

North Tyne: Location description covering land either aside of North Tyne river in Northumberland.